MUSIC HALL AND MODERNITY

MUSIC HALL &
MODERNITY

The Late-Victorian Discovery of Popular Culture

Barry J. Faulk

OHIO UNIVERSITY PRESS   ATHENS

Ohio University Press, Athens, Ohio 45701
© 2004 by Barry J. Faulk

Ohio University Press books are printed on acid-free paper ⊗ ™

First paperback edition 2014

HARDCOVER   12 11 10 09 08 07 06 05 04   5 4 3 2 1
PAPERBACK   22 21 20 19 18 17 16 15 14   5 4 3 2 1

Library of Congress Cataloging-in-Publication Data

Faulk, Barry J.
    Music hall and modernity : the late-Victorian discovery of popular
culture / Barry J. Faulk.
            p. cm.
    Includes bibliographical references and index.
    ISBN 0-8214-1585-9 (cloth : alk. paper)
    1. English literature—19th century—History and criticism. 2. Music-
halls (Variety-theaters, cabarets, etc.) in literature. 3. Music-halls
(Variety-theaters, cabarets, etc.)—England—London—History—19th
century. 4. English literature—England—London—History and criticism. 5. Performing arts—England—London—History—19th century.
6. Popular culture—England—London—History—19th century.
7. London (England)—Intellectual life—19th century. 8. London
(England)—In literature. 9. Performing arts in literature. 10. Popular
culture in literature. I. Title.
PR468.M86F38 2004
820.9'357—dc22

                                                        2004008199

To Moscovia and Richard

Contents

Illustrations

Acknowledgments

It is a great pleasure to acknowledge those who supported me in the process of writing this book, and who made it possible for me to complete it. I am indebted to Patrick Scott for introducing me to the study of Victorian popular culture, and to James Hipp and Marc Demarest for their support and friendship. This project began in earnest at the University of Illinois at Urbana-Champaign, where I was fortunate enough to have world-class mentors: Amanda Anderson, Michael Bérubé, Peter Garrett, and Dale Kramer. At that time, cultural studies had emerged as a force to be reckoned with in the American academy. This book is tied to that moment: it owes a great deal to the work of the visiting scholars I was fortunate enough to witness during my time at Illinois. I am indebted to Peter Garrett, Lawrence Grossberg, Cary Nelson, and Paula Treichler for promoting cultural studies research at the University of Illinois through the Unit for Criticism and Interpretive Theory. I was also lucky in having generous, brilliant, and caring peers: these are too numerous to mention, but the members of my dissertation writing group—Stacy Alaimo, Rick Canning, Brady Harrison, Lauren Onkey—deserve special mention for all they taught me. Robert Steltman generously shared his expertise in popular culture with me. Michael Thurston furnished me with a model of the engaged scholar: I learned a lot from him, and still do. I encountered David Chinitz's work on T. S. Eliot and popular culture at this point in my career; I am grateful that he remains a careful, insightful reader of my work. And although great cultural studies scholarship was happening all around me, I'm not certain that I would ever have linked it to Victorian studies if Amy Farmer hadn't encouraged me to make that connection. Thanks, Amy.

I am grateful for the institutional support provided by Florida State University during the writing of this book, especially for the boon of a research semester, provided by our dean, Donald J. Foss. The English Department at Florida State has made me feel welcome since I arrived, and I am deeply indebted for all that our department chair, Hunt Hawkins, has done to assist and support my scholarship. The book owes much to intellectual exchanges with my colleagues in the English Department, such as R. M. Berry, Helen Burke, Martin Foys, Robin Goodman, James O'Rourke, W. T. Lhamon, and Daniel J. Vitkus, to name but a few. Their acumen is matched only by their generosity. I am also grateful to those who read portions of the book in manuscript form, especially to Mark Garrett Cooper and Leigh Edwards. I owe Mark special thanks for years of collegial support, and for generously sharing his intellectual expertise. I can take the credit only for my mistakes.

Finally, I owe a great deal to the patience, guidance, and support of my editor, David Sanders, who was willing to take a chance on the project when I was seeking a publisher. My anonymous readers all provided essential advice and made the book, I hope, worth reading.

Introduction

THE POPULAR NOT THE PUBLIC

> There is no simon-pure thing
> —*Countee Cullen*

This book studies the many literary and journalistic representations of Britain's first indigenous and fully capitalized mass culture form, the music hall.[1] The London music hall reached its commercial zenith roughly between 1880 and 1919. A miscellaneous revue of art and amusements, a night of music hall could feature song, dance, comic routine, acrobats, and animal acts. As the music hall grew from roots in local, raucous pub sing-alongs into a large-scale capitalized venture, it welcomed more styles of entertainment, as well as a large paying segment of the nation itself.[2] The London music hall provides the central focus of my book, since the many descriptions of these halls by the London intelligentsia serve as the core texts for this study.[3] My work addresses the discourse produced by the metropolitan intelligentsia at the moment when the music hall reached its commercial peak.

I argue that this discourse provides a pioneering example of a now familiar story about the inevitable loss of cultural possibilities. Late-Victorian literary intellectuals like Max Beerbohm and Elizabeth Robins Pennell framed a narrative of cultural rise and decline using their experience of the music hall. As they understood it, culture forms emerge with an appealing vigor, vitality, and charisma. Popular entertainment stands in some honest, responsive, and authentic relation to its patrons. Inevitably, the bloom leaves the rose; entertainment becomes commercialized, co-opted, appropriated, and vitiated. Popular, working-class, or otherwise marginal expressive forms gain momentum, marshal force, and become transformed utterly in the process. Sharp edges are sanded down; tart humor and song are run through the propriety mill. Energy gets channeled and the improper made acceptable by salaried tastemakers. The commercial success of the form spells its predetermined failure as genuine vernacular expression.

So the argument goes, in the accounts of the music hall provided by the London intelligentsia. These critics had a point. The most successful arts remain those which circulate with the greatest ease, and which require the least elaboration or translation for the public. The details that give savor and piquancy to an art form can become lost in the effort to draw larger crowds. Expressive modes that bond small, intimate audiences lose their puissance; they get harnessed to the profit drive, the infamous bottom line. Crowds march in, and local knowledge is lost in the accompanying shuffle. Like all cultural forms in the marketplace, the music hall was enlisted by larger social forces, and its initial significance was refined and redefined.

Nevertheless, I demonstrate that the inevitable mediation and abstraction that accompany the commercial success of formerly marginal cultural forms still permit opportunity for constructive social change. I provide close analysis of several kinds of music-hall accounts, including readings of public media controversies involving London music hall. I look to contemporary cultural studies, particularly the creative commentary of the Birmingham School, for a new way to tell the story of the music hall. The work of Raymond Williams, Stuart Hall, and many others counsels us to face the fact that art and culture are produced under impure conditions, and to profligate effect.[4] Cultural messages get scrambled in the transmission;

they face resistance, appropriation, and acclaim. Performance forms meet and miss their intended targets, lose and find new constituencies, over and over. Stuart Hall reminds us that popular culture in particular exists as process, not essence, in a series of negotiations between different, class-specific perspectives. The popular is a manifest contingency or construct, existing in discursive and therefore shifting relation to any social group.[5] Similarly, Paul Gilroy details the rhetorical pitfalls that intellectuals with honorable motives can fall prey to in the search for reassuring traces of identity and authenticity in music and its accompanying rituals. Treating the complex forms of musical production as natural, spontaneous eruptions, as an opposite to craft, amounts to intellectual bad faith.[6] The search for the authentic within a performing art inevitably produces essentialist claims that overlook modes of production. Ironically, the very move that seems to validate "the popular" can place it beyond the reach of all but the most expert critics.[7]

Just such a move animates the powerful, elegiac narrative that emerged in the late-Victorian age through the writing of such key figures as Max Beerbohm, Elizabeth Robins Pennell, and Arthur Symons on the music hall. These writers expressed and often maintained their fondness for the variety theater in its "purest," most genuine—that is, most authentically proletarian—form. Through their accounts, these cultural professionals endeavored to conventionalize a distinction that was largely semantic between "mass culture," tainted by its association with commerce, and untainted vernacular culture. Their testimonials on music hall endeavored to parse out authentic expression from more contaminated forms. The result was a selective reading of class identity that repetition consolidated and reified. Observers located and often celebrated the "vulgarity" of the halls, further suggesting that vulgar expression was the natural outcome of the bracingly bad taste of "the people."

The testimony of Beerbohm, Pennell, and others proved highly influential among readers of their class. Indeed, precisely because their representations of music hall were so persuasive, it still requires some doing to demystify their colorful accounts. These writers expended considerable labor to solidify a link between the London music hall and the English working class; they often generalized about the character of that class based on the form and content of music-hall performance and the enthusiastic response these entertainers drew from large crowds. Literary intellectuals endeavored to define what could count as English by virtue of their inside knowledge of the people's entertainment. In the process of telling the story of the music hall's rise and fall, they authorized professional critics like themselves to distinguish the authentically English from its commercial degradation.

In so doing, Symons and company participated in a broad-based and often contentious dialogue about the nature and significance of cultural expertise. The peak years of music hall coincided with a time when distinctions between amateurs and experts began to make a considerable difference.[8] The ambition to be recognized as an authority gained a new impetus in the late nineteenth century, with the growth and consolidation of the formal professions: not only law and medicine, but social work and civil service. Contemporaneous music-hall criticism allowed literary intellectuals to write themselves into the new class of managers analyzed in essential accounts by social historians Harold Perkin and Burton Bledstein.[9]

There was some evidence for the critic's complaint that the commercial music hall had become cleansed and capitalized. The 1880s saw the spread of the music hall from shady neighborhood spots into affluent London suburbs, an increase in entertainments that targeted family audiences, and the rise of managers who sought to make the form respectable.[10] Yet the educated middle-class observers who first leveled this complaint against the music hall had an interest in promoting just this kind of story. I contend that the narrative of vernacular decline facilitated—even licensed—a new kind of professional critic. These critics credentialed themselves by dint of their capacity to read the deep meanings of the entertainment in terms of significant issues such as national history, urban administration, and national hygiene. The culture critic who produced this weighty commentary assumed a place in a division of labor that increasingly privileged the trained and credentialed specialist.

Professionalism constituted a hallmark of British modernity. "Modernity," of course, is now a blanket term, if not a cottage industry, in scholarship; it gathers together many discrete elements of social change. In *A Farewell to an Idea*, T. J. Clark's recent endeavor to define modernity for an imagined posterity, the term encompasses the secularization process, a collective embrace of contingency and risk in social life, the new information society, and, important for this study, what Clark describes as "the de-skilling of everyday life (deference to experts and technicians in more and more of the microstructure of the self); available, invasive, haunting expertise."[11]

My study focuses on Clark's last descriptive cluster. For my purposes, "modernity" designates a crucial transformation in the development and middle-class reception of London music hall in the late-Victorian era, and nothing less than a structural change in discourse on the halls. I employ the concept of modernity, a decisive break from an earlier social order organized according to tradition or collective wisdom, to explain the differences between social explorer Henry Mayhew's account of the penny gaff and the pronouncements of late-Victorian intellectuals on the music hall. The gap that separates these accounts is remarkable; it constitutes a major shift in consciousness and discursive protocol. Increasingly, middle-class observation of the halls no longer simply condemned the form as too vulgar, but worked more subtly to appropriate it to another construction, the popular.

I demonstrate that the late-Victorian discourse on the popular served several purposes. First, such rhetoric fostered a notion of culture that bolstered another powerful fabrication, the nation, which in turn created a climate of opinion congenial to the growth of the centralized state. Second, the popular was invoked to legitimate both music hall and the savvy views of the critical professional. The discourse of the late-Victorian music hall can be labeled "modern," since it reflects the transition to a world of administered opinion, in which relations between the popular and individual subjects are increasingly mediated.

The popular remains a ruling concept of modernity, crucial enough for the purposes of social hegemony that it must be managed, organized, and often neutralized. It was important, for example, for late-Victorian observers of music hall to construct a version of the popular that hailed the people as citizens of the nation, and not as, say, disruptive idlers, social delinquents, or working class. Detailing the construction of the late-Victorian "popular" music hall does not require that we rehearse the old debate over whose culture is legitimate and whose illegitimate, which culture form is more or less subversive. In the case of the late-Victorian halls, it is more pertinent, relevant, and above all more interesting to study the various effects of this "popular" discourse.

The zenith of commercial music hall coincides with the rise of the modern professional, as well as the production of a crisis narrative that cultural specialists applied to this entertainment, and by extension to English popular culture. I claim that these seemingly discrete phenomena existed within a complex set of relations. The power and responsibility of intellectuals and the social effects of their discourse have always been on the agenda of cultural studies research. However, with the exception of Stuart Hall and Bill Schwarz's essay "State and Society," relatively little cultural studies work has linked cultural production and discourse with the protocols of the key ruling group of capitalist culture since the 1880s: with the professional middle class, the bureaucrat, and the managerial intellectual. Even Hall and Schwarz's essay grants less time to the practices of professional intellectuals than to the deployment of cultural value in redefining the proper aims of state power, or the role of state apparatus in constituting hegemony and maintaining social control. The result has been a persistent gap in cultural studies scholars' addressing the status quo they desire to change: capitalist culture and its attendant structures, its modes of consumption, its forms of identity making, its construction of social reality. The gap has diminished the range and descriptive power of the "culture" that cultural studies desires to analyze and transform. My focus on the discursive production of the popular in late-Victorian professional rhetoric, on exchanges between would-be opinion makers and their public, and on the rise of the managerial subject and consciousness intends to redress this imbalance in cultural studies work so far.

My emphasis on the necessary relationship between the commercialization of "popular" forms and the success of professional critics distinguishes *Music Hall and Modernity* from the ample scholarship that inquires into the origins and practice of music hall, its demographics, and discernible shifts in its performance styles.[12] I provide an anatomy of Victorian professional culture by analyzing a new rhetoric of the popular that emerges with the commercial prominence of English music-hall entertainment at the end of the century.[13] Contemporary middle-class accounts of music hall often made class lines separating mass audiences more visible. Perspectives on the aesthetic quality of music-hall performance often reinforced the trained prejudices about art and the people held by social elites. Accordingly, the rhetoric of the popular often reinforced the cultural protocols of an upper-middle class. Thus the endeavor to signify the popular helped consolidate the group identity of a professional cadre, authorized by their unique and often exclusive knowledge of art and culture.

Various experts, then, spoke for music hall in the late-Victorian media, thereby raising and settling broader issues of social and cultural hegemony. If this process could be described simply as the middle-class appropriation of subaltern forms, it would not warrant in-depth analysis. However, as I argue, the assimilation of the music hall into professional discourse set some key terms of expert discourse, such as authority and expertise, into play. Representations of the popular often bore internal contradictions; the attempt to forge consensus could foreground the fabricated character of claims to "real" authority. While I am aware of the class biases of professional culture, I recognize the appeal of professional discourse, then and now, to anyone wishing to escape from the excesses of possessive individualism or the determination of all social outcomes by market forces. It is my wish to defend some aspects of expert culture without providing a mere apology for professional hegemony.

From Mayhew to Modernity

For middle-class cognoscenti, the success of music hall amounted to a paradox. The popularity of the entertainment seemed to offer the reassuring suggestion that there remained something healthy and robust about the English national character, a notion that apparently required more evidentiary basis at the end of the nineteenth century. The continued prominence of the halls constituted a heritage that these savants did not wish to entrust to the people themselves. Rather, the popular was to be protected through the recognition and care of a new, savvy connoisseur. There were trade-offs in this cultural exchange. The popular found a frame and was thereby saved from being relegated to the margins of the culture; however, the rhetoric assumed in defenses of the popular was often exclusive.

There were substantial differences between the music hall of 1850 and the fin-de-siècle hall. Managers of late-Victorian suburban halls worked to present entertainment palatable to audiences accustomed to West End standards of respectability; this often entailed extricating bawdry from song and jokes rooted in popular traditions. Music-hall managers also endeavored to untangle the halls from their links with the criminal element, which meant keeping a watchful eye on the disreputable crowds attracted to the promenade of the hall. Crucially, the character of middle-class commentary on the music hall also changed over the span of the century. Mid-Victorian urban investigator Henry Mayhew represents the halls as an underworld where London youth find instruction in unlawful, illicit behavior; he is accordingly alarmed by his "discovery." In contrast, late-Victorian music-hall observers increasingly sought to pass as insiders within the popular culture they interpreted for their middle-class readership. Paradoxically, participating in the popular allowed these writers to stand outside the very public they spoke for.

In retrospect, the most significant and seemingly the most influential of the many chronicles of the music hall that proliferated in little magazines, newspapers, and journals of the 1890s was produced by the noted art critic Elizabeth Robins Pennell. In "The Pedigree of the Music-Hall," she formalized a mode of perception and relation to the popular broadly characteristic of the criticism I describe. "For centuries," Pennell writes, "Englishmen have been shaping their variety entertainment into its present form, and now, like a child with the toy it has been crying for, they are doing their best to destroy it. Nowadays proprietors and managers, working men patrons and artistes protest that the variety show is a great moral force, an educational factor and a safeguard against intemperance."[14] None of these apologetic points, Pennell concludes, seem particularly relevant. The music hall stands as a quintessentially English entertainment with a history, and the popular is treated as if it were a distinct character or personality, existing in relative autonomy with regard to other social practices.

Yet who exactly recognizes these salient facts about the popular? Pennell suggests that the authentic music hall is intuited not by the public at large, but rather by an insightful, far-seeing, and select few. "Evidently," she concludes, "[the music hall's] days are numbered. When too late, when it is no longer to be studied at first hand, the scholar will learn its value." This is no mere gesture toward a wiser posterity, enlightened enough to appreciate the aesthetic and social value of an entertainment form that had many contemporary detractors. Her invocation of an uncomprehending public constitutes rhetoric with an interpellative purpose, aimed at an educated readership. Pennell's lament for a benighted public that is incapable of assuming a proper, critical vantage point toward the music hall in effect separates this public from an authentic connection to the popular. The essay interprets the entertainment as reflecting the larger verities of national character while simultaneously insisting that music hall's many patrons failed to perceive this continuity between entertainment and Englishness. To grasp this pedigree requires the vantage point of a sympathetic historian. Pennell's rhetoric has the effect of establishing those in the know as the most trusted caretakers of cultural forms. "The Pedigree of the Music-Hall" draws a clear line between the popular essence and the public, then, to formulate lines of professional power and identity. Interpretive rights over music hall are thus expropriated from the public, and instead the status and authority of a critical elite are confirmed.

The urge to speak as cultural arbiter structures many of the chronicles of music hall that circulated in middle-class journals in the closing decade of the nineteenth century and beyond. It is necessary to sustain the analogy between cultural professionals and other experts, since it foregrounds the class matrix from which both groups derive. One can usefully bring Magali Sarfatti Larson's criticism of professionalism, as "an attempt to translate one order of scarce resources—scarce knowledge and skills—into another—social and economic reward," to bear on Pennell's music hall commentary.[15] Larson's skepticism toward professionalism highlights the gap between the service ideal of cultural professionals and the self-interested or self-serving consequences of their rhetorical work. Most music-hall accounts were covert skirmishes in a war to win legitimacy for the vision of proper culture maintained by aspiring culture critics.[16] Pennell's effort to speak for the music hall offers a template for the various interventions of Arthur Symons, Max Beerbohm, and T. S. Eliot. Her rhetoric serves to delineate and clarify the popular as well as illuminate her superior place in a critical hierarchy.

The possessive stance Pennell adopts toward the popular is by no means unique to her or to late-Victorian cultural elites. Henry Mayhew's midcentury account of subaltern Victorian culture provides a telling point of comparison. His chronicle of the Penny Gaff, included in the extensive survey *London Labour and the London Poor* (1851–52), arguably marks the beginning of the managerial strategy I am describing. The great social investigator records his unsettling visit to this ancestor of the music hall, the Smithfield Penny Gaff (the name reflects the price of admission to illegitimate theater), in the following terms:

> It is impossible to contemplate the ignorance and immorality of so numerous a class as that of the costermongers, without wishing to discover the cause of their degradation. Let any one curious on this point visit one of these penny shows, and he will wonder that *any* trace of virtue and honesty should remain among the people. Here the stage, instead of being the means for illustrating a moral precept, is turned into a platform to teach the cruelest debauchery. The audience is usually composed of children so young, that these dens become the school-rooms where the guiding morals of a life are picked up, and so precocious are the little things, that the girl of nine will, from constant attendance at

such places, have learnt to understand the filthiest sayings, and laugh at them as loudly as the grown-up lads around her.[17]

It is not the ability of music hall to amuse or arouse but its public instruction in sexual misconduct that both startles and transfixes Mayhew. He creates the impression that the gaff instructs its audience before the spectacle begins. Apparently, merely standing in line can get steamy in this Smithfield assembly.

> The visitors, with a few exceptions, were all boys and girls, whose ages seemed to vary from eight to twenty years. Some of the girls—though their figures showed them to be mere children—were dressed in showy cotton-velvet polkas, and wore dowdy feathers in their crushed bonnets. They stood laughing and joking with the lads, in an unconcerned, impudent manner that was almost appalling. Some of them, when tired of waiting, chose their partners, and commenced dancing grotesquely, to the admiration of the lookers-on, who expressed their approbation in obscene terms, that, far from disgusting the poor little women, were received as compliments, and acknowledged with smiles and coarse repartees.

Obviously the assembly exceeds bourgeois standards of decorum, even if the entertainment that unfolds before the crowd seems relatively tame. However, Mayhew's alarm suggests that something more than sexual frankness is at stake here; prudishness does not entirely explain his anxious response. Rather, the gaff seems alarming precisely because, in Mayhew's view, it is not mere unreason or anarchy: it represents a discernible structure, a pedagogic enterprise rivaling that of the urban investigator. It is not only that the gaff audience learns about sex, but that, more broadly, they leave the gaff believing they are generally in the know.

Mayhew himself models one form of discursive power, based on authoritative observation. Yet his tale of the gaff presents a competing knowledge base, produced from within the subculture he scrutinizes. On one hand, there is the sociologist/observer's knowledge of culture; on the other, the gaff stands as its own instructional site, circulating local knowledge with awesome efficiency and frightening (to outsiders) self-sufficiency. The exchange between Mayhew and his informants is limned with plural anxieties, just beneath the edgy surface of the text. The outsider produces his knowledge of lumpen youth in competition with the news-gathering agency of the penny gaff. One passes on the knowledge and tradition of the poor, outside state auspices; the other produces knowledge sanctioned by a central authority, about but not for the subjects he chronicles.

Now, it has been argued that Mayhew, far from being the anxious subculture interloper, secretly delights in the subterranean culture he digs up in the street.[18] I have no problem with this claim, provided we allow that Mayhew might be anxious about what he sees, much as he savors it. This particular encounter with coster culture, after all, is enough to spur Mayhew, a detached, nonstatist observer, to a shrill call for state suppression of the gaffs, a charge anticipated by far less temperate urban observers such as James Grant.[19] When it comes to authority, the social explorer seems in this case to lag behind the gaff's young patrons. After all, Mayhew's writing is still performed under the aegis of commercial journalism, before the rise and consolidation of a disciplinary sociology capable of elevating his account and making it the basis of state action. In stark contrast with a fledgling popular journalism that always gets the message out too late, the penny gaff appears to have deep, tentacular roots within the metropolitan center; it provides its audience with real news.

The young hipster poaches on the resources of the mother tongue in the presence of the well-meaning, and alarmed, social recorder. Mayhew's account insinuates that the young are taught by the gaff to communicate with each other confidently, brashly, and in an argot that catches the ears of curious outsiders but that also keeps them at arm's length. An exchange Mayhew overhears in the ticket line confirms his suspicion that prematurely wizened, flash youth have mastered a stretch of urban space. "To discover the kind of entertainment, a lad near me and my companion was asked, 'if there was any flash dancing.' With a knowing wink the boy answered, 'Lots! Show their legs and all, prime!'" (38). The boy shows neither fear nor alarm when faced by outsiders; in fact, the boy's speech proves more disconcerting than his demeanor. "Quips, backtalk, and sneers are weapons," Wayne Koestenbaum reminds us, "that conquer severely limited terrains."[20] This remark captures the cadence of this exchange between outsider and cool young insider; it also prepares us for the casual, stylized insubordination to follow. The young man requests a "yennep" for "tib of occabot" and brandishes a cool remove that one easily imagines Mayhew finding more disheartening in terms of practicing his vocation than the boy's excitement to enter the peep show. It is not merely that the patrons are innocent of modesty—they suggest the presence of a set of standards entirely foreign to Mayhew's Liberal code of conduct. The gaff presents the social investigator with a subordinate but clearly intelligible culture active on the margins of the dominant order.

The shrillness of Mayhew's call for order may be proportional to his alarm at the prospect of fully restoring calm to the wilds of London. The social explorer lags behind knowing boys and girls, confident in their urbanity, achieved outside state auspices. Mayhew's exploration of the gaff clearly anticipates Peter Bailey's suggestion that music hall was a broadcast medium circulating subtle ways of knowing.[21] Music-hall regulars, as early as the penny gaff and as late as the middle-class camp devotees, consistently prided themselves on knowing more about the city than did novices. Music-hall habitués, then, might well feel that they alone had the real scoop on modernity; that is, they had an authentic experience of vernacular culture unsullied by bourgeois convention. Their accounts, circulated orally and in print, helped fabricate the notion of music-hall authenticity. It appears that the London halls provided the kinds of experience or awareness that fostered such confidence. In contrast, Mayhew's media outlets, the newspaper and social survey, seem less capable of moving and persuading a core middle-class readership.

It seems that variety insiders also gained a lesson in sex and the city. As Mayhew's account insinuates, sexuality was a major preoccupation of the form, as with most forms of modern culture. It is difficult to generalize about music hall, since it tended to be as various an entertainment as the heterogeneous ethnic, gendered, and classed groups hailed by the form. A single night of performance might include highly sentimental, sometimes abrasive song; punning humor; broad-humored sketches; and novelty acts. Music-hall dance in suburban halls of the late-Victorian era itself included wildly disparate practices: the skirt dance, the notorious high-stepping of Lottie Collins (the celebrated "ta-ra-ra-boom-de-yay"), and the spectacular, opulent, high art productions staged by choristers at the upscale Alhambra and Empire music halls. Until Diaghilev's ballet company toured England—another music-hall event—upscale suburban houses remained in fact the primary providers for continental dance. Music-hall entertainment also included the staging of tableaux vivants, another conceptual hybrid. These tableaux recreated high art moments (often imitating celebrated statuary) but added a perceptible salaciousness that reminded viewers of the standard, vernacular peep show.

Yet music-hall entertainment was more than a direct address to the libido. Educated, cultured observers such as the poet Arthur Symons were able to bring the language of formal aesthetics to bear on the music hall, in part because of the increasingly rich lyrical content of music-hall song. Keith Wilson provides a fascinating analysis of the lyrical content of popular music-hall tunes from the 1880s and 1890s, arguing that a surprising number of songs revolve around the sheer bewildering and exhilarating fact of London itself.[22] In Wilson's account, these lyrics constitute an elaborate song cycle, a self-aware commentary on the apparently endless significance of the five or six miles bordering on Charing Cross Road. In the Haymarket area, off Shaftesbury Avenue and Tottenham Court Road, rich and poor lived, if not worked, in proximity. Some music-hall songs broadcast and codified the ways that working-class or coster audiences negotiated diverse city spaces; other songs downplayed hard-earned local knowledge of the town and instead extolled London for impressive but abstract qualities of the city, its size and scale. Wilson concludes that music-hall song represented the city as the ultimate space of liberty for all, though details as to what constituted liberty were a bit sketchy: apparently, it was enough merely to live in what seemed to be the capital city of the world, no matter who you were or what your station.[23]

Wilson's essay also underscores the contradictory nature of urban knowingness. Precisely because it underscores the people's acumen, Mayhew's account of the penny gaff is more complicated and resonant than the moral panic that often accompanied the emergence of vernacular culture throughout the nineteenth century. As styled by these youngsters, the popular bears a family resemblance to the sophisticated, savvy commentary Elizabeth Pennell produced to capture the essence of the popular. Both discourses suggest a mode of participation with an elite or exclusive aspect. In both instances, the popular takes shape as insiders draw lines that separate them from outsiders.

The Victorians delighted in drawing and redrawing the lines that set off cultural insiders from outsiders; half the fun, and all the stakes, rested on figuring out which side of that all-important line you found yourself on, or might persuade others that you resided on.[24] The Victorian popular appears both to have been experienced and articulated as possession. Still, likely the most significant difference between the two modes of participation resides in the greater access of trained, credentialed intellectuals like Pennell to media that permit one to broadcast, rationalize, and thereby universalize their impressions. Both Pennell and Mayhew's insouciant gaff patrons speak and act on the notion that they have some scoop that others have missed. The acquisitive ethos that marks winning behavior in the marketplace serves as a natural analogue to this possessive stance toward the popular. Despite the shared nature of music-hall experience, market culture shaped the forms assumed by the Victorian popular: this means that the Victorians knew the popular as something they possessed over and against potential competitors.

Still, Pennell is not Mayhew, in part because her more family-oriented, middlebrow music hall is not Mayhew's. Another crucial difference separates the two spectators. The music-hall experience that Pennell inherits has a substantial discursive component, manifest in an increasingly sophisticated journalistic criticism of the halls. She crystallizes the rhetorical stratagems of the cultural specialist, but largely because she is surrounded by middle-class observers who base their authority as reporters on their familiarity with popular culture. Ironically, these middle-class chroniclers seem to model themselves less on Mayhew, who admits to his profound alienation from the penny gaff, than on the cunning, working-class gaff fans he describes.

The largely interactive account of music-hall performance and culture composed by actor and theater critic Percy Fitzgerald also bears the premium late Victorians placed on being, or posing, as if in the know. While Fitzgerald's encomium cum ethnography of the London halls, *Music-Hall Land* (1890), offers some pointed criticisms of the lower-middle-class audience for music hall, and at one point expresses distaste for what he describes as the "monotony" of music-hall culture, his criticism of the entertainment remains gentle. Throughout his account, Fitzgerald seems willing to deny his distance from the form and its public, and thus sacrifice his critical authority, in order to promote the image of his own prodigious familiarity with the popular.[25]

Music-Hall Land bears the ambitious subtitle "An Account of the Natives, Male and Female, Pastimes, Songs, Antics and General Oddities of That Strange Country" (see figure 1), and the complex range of the title serves to document a conflicted moment in expert protocols regarding the popular. His handbook on the halls describes the entertainment, promoting it to an imagined community of middle-class male readers also capable of both participating in the popular and seeing around it. One can imagine that for some readers *Music-Hall Land* served to substitute discourse for the music-hall experience.

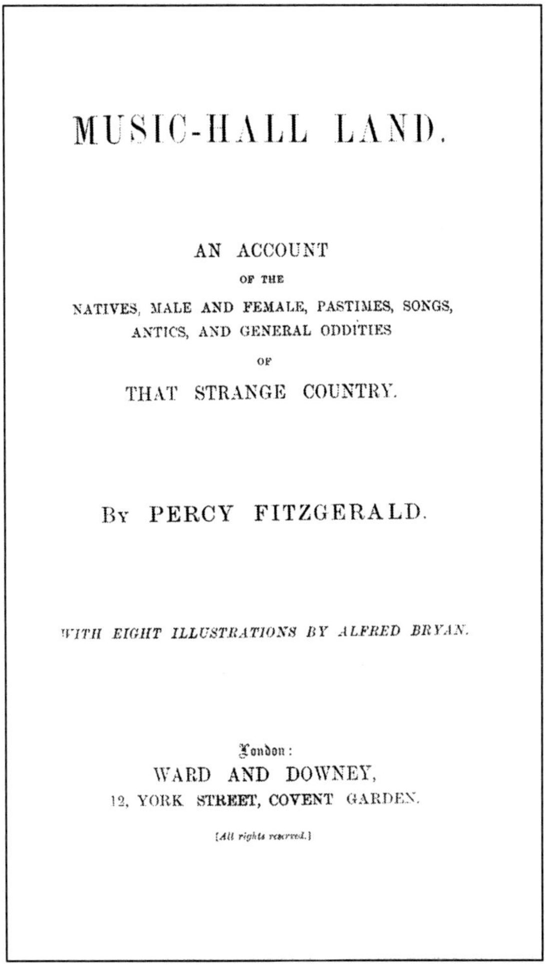

Figure 1. Making music-hall experts. Title page of Percy Fitzgerald, *Music-Hall Land* (London: Ward and Downey, 1890).

The text bears witness to how the democratizing of culture transformed relations between middle-class critics and their public. Perhaps Fitzgerald's general purpose in providing this guidebook to the halls was to qualify the attraction unsophisticated audiences felt for music-hall performers, and thereby elevate the "rude, rough character of the audience."[26] There are passages in *Music-Hall Land* that address social-climbing, lower-middle-class patrons, who foolishly believe they might rise above their station merely by blending into large, mixed-class crowds. Would-be swells are singled out for special reproof in this regard. "To have a box, at, say, the Pavilion or Empire, and to enter in due state, arrayed in dress-suit, a pink handkerchief, protruding from the waist-coat is indeed high ton. Some of these beings are strangers to town; others hang loose upon society; others, again are persons in houses of business and offices, hurrying on the downward course, but the sight is always significant, even tragic. It is the Idle Apprentice over again" (8). Fitzgerald's ambiguous reaction to music hall's lower-middle-class audience extends to the illustrations of celebrity music-hall performers that augment his prose account. The suggestion of the larger-than-life appeal of these performers is reinforced by the many images of performers in the text that accent their outsized body shapes. The volume, height, depth, and excess of music-hall performance find a visual analogue in the caricatures with immense faces and prominent features that stare out from the pages of Fitzgerald's book. These comics and singers with large eyes set in massive heads appear to exist in some heightened space far from quotidian life and its more normal shapes and perspectives. At the same time, these caricatures exact a subtle revenge against the performers, since it is difficult to imagine that these enormous presences move comfortably outside of the footlights. It is even a task to imagine most of these figures in motion, with the exception of the Sisters Wriggles, a dancing team caught in midstep who have pride of place on the book's title page (see figure 2). The pictured dancers occupy their ground with confidence and poise; they move on stage, but are rendered as if permanently situated—or trapped—on the other side of the footlights. The many performers whose pictures adorn Fitzgerald's text seem doomed to remain on the periphery of an imaginary London, as local color or an exotic species.

However, the text lingers on performance styles, snatches of lyrics from music-hall songs, and, importantly, various characterizations of music-hall audiences and their highly emotional participation in the stage performance. Typically, Fitzgerald describes Jenny's Hill's performance of Little Gyp, as "a regular drama, . . . followed with breathless attention from beginning to end" (87). The many images of audience and performer interaction amount to idealized representations of social cohesion. Fitzgerald provides these ideal communities as an attractive frame for his "rough" audience, but these images also provide evidence of his desire to be read as both critic and participant in the crowd. It appears that once the conceit of an autonomous "music hall land," the nation within the nation, gets formulated, no one,

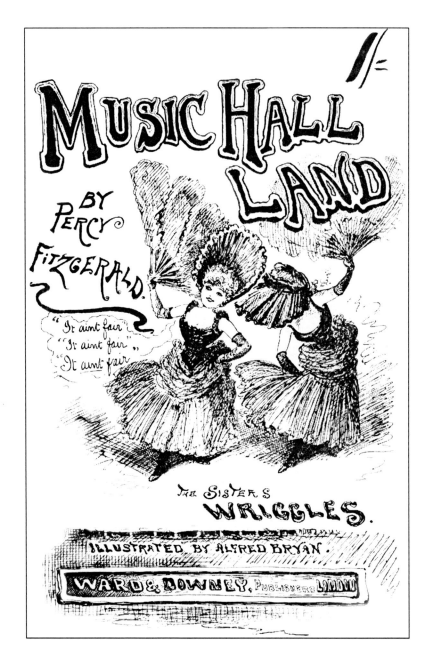

Figure 2. "The Sisters Wriggles." Illustration by Alfred Bryan. Cover of Percy Fitzgerald, *Music-Hall Land* (London: Ward and Downey, 1890).

not even the author, desires to be outside the charmed circle of knowing-ness the text conjures. Fitzgerald's account provides a critical perspective while avoiding dogmatic aesthetic judgments.

Fitzgerald never quite arrives at the conclusion that the identity of the people, or the nation, requires the mediating force of a skilled performer for its healthy articulation: this argument would have to wait until T. S. Eliot's 1923 eulogy for singer Marie Lloyd, in which the poet suggests the popular is doomed to decay with Lloyd's death, and the loss of her unique skills in expressing the national popular.[27] As an account by a middle-class observer of the music hall, Fitzgerald's book reflects myths about and prejudices to-ward its lower-class audience, and likely idealizes the coherence that per-formers stamped on various audiences. However, the guidebook also draws self-conscious attention to itself as a construction: a mediation between the music-hall public and middle-class readership. Fitzgerald takes great pains to situate himself, finally, on the inside of that culture, rather than accept the role of mere onlooker like Mayhew. The music-hall guide blurs the bound-ary separating participation from observation, alienation from communion with the crowd. Maintaining such boundaries would augment the writer's distance from the audience, and Fitzgerald the music-hall interpreter seems unwilling to turn down the role of knowing participant, since it would weaken his credibility as a professional observer.

Music hall became a social site that allowed for the articulation of vari-ous kinds of knowing attitudes and stances, and a means of negotiating what it meant to belong to knowing elites. The topic of music hall, this pub-lic discourse on the popular, gave some coherence to group identity. Yet the effort to represent the popular to the public resulted in semantic complica-tions. Walter Frith's attempt to explain the meaning of music hall in *Corn-hill* magazine offers a striking instance of such category blurring. In "The Music-Hall" (1887), Frith turns his grim verdict regarding the "hopeless vul-garity" of music-hall entertainment into an argument for the higher wis-dom of the public. He is puzzled initially by the success of the halls: why would lower-middle-class and working-class people patronize representa-tions that in Frith's estimate mock the values they live by? The love of the people for their own entertainment serves as proof of the national superi-ority of English character and occasions some frank xenophobia.

The Turk, the Persian, and the Hindoo, all these races without a history, or a literature really worthy of the name, would in all probability stab, poison, or bowstring the best of our character artistes, our funny comics. . . . Unhappy, then, the nation that has no appreciation of hopeless vulgarity! Woe to the country that has no love for senseless laughter! The day when England echoes no longer with an utterly foolish and inexplicably popular comic chant will be the day when the knell of her decadence will most surely have struck.[28]

We may wonder how the popular, here characterized as "hopeless" and "senseless," can nonetheless signify the elevated status of the English over the rude folk of lesser nations.

Surprisingly, the wisdom of the public rests on what Frith regards to be the public judgment that the popular is best viewed with full detachment.

> [at the music hall] there is no reflection there of love, of honour, or reverence, or obedience, nor, to speak the brutal truth, of any very cheerful or honest merriment. But to the really thoughtful these very deficiencies are a happy and a worthy sign. . . . For let it be remembered that these audiences, mainly composed of honest tradesmen, of men and women whose lives are full of order, duty, labour, self-denial, are not laughing with the artistes, but at them.[29]

The people maintain, in Frith's startling reversal, a final distance from the performance they witness, and remain spectators rather than participants in the entertainments that they nevertheless patronize. For Frith, the popular is not the place where public identity is clarified and articulated: rather, the public's defining characteristic is its collective detachment from the music-hall spectacle. The music hall testifies to the public's innate capacity to safely aestheticize spectacle: it is the people's critical distance, their special sight lines, their disinterested observation (they "are not laughing with the artistes, but at them") to which the popularity of music hall bears witness.

Frith's assertion that the public constitutes its identity in reaction against popular performance rather than through it leads to the inevitable but surprising conclusion that the public and the cultured observer remain practically impossible to distinguish from one another. The verdict of the "really thoughtful" observer regarding the meaning of music hall merely replicates the distance that Frith asserts marks the response of the English public to the popular. In its principled remove from what it nonetheless patronizes, the public largely resembles the isolated culture critic as spectator. Unlike

Fitzgerald, Frith does not wish to present himself as advocate or aficionado of the form. By asserting that the public shares his virtuous distance and unprejudiced remove from the entertainment, Frith blurs the lines separating public survey from expert observation. Yet the common ground Frith and Fitzgerald share is significant. They seem to agree that some distance is a prerequisite for critique: they merely disagree about whether a member of the crowd can have this distance. If the crowd can perform these cognitive tasks, then it constitutes a version of the public; if not, the crowd enters the degraded category of the mass.

By the close of the Victorian era, the music hall had become a site for the public articulation of professional conduct and culture. The discourse on the halls in middle-class venues often created and reinforced group cohesion among the middle class, even as it promoted the illusion of familiarity of this class with other class fractions. The public discourse on music hall served as a forum in which intragroup identity, as well as the perception of cross-class knowledge, could be figured. It is not surprising that discourses of cultural solidarity prove highly unstable, and efforts to draw firm lines between cognoscenti and various others have unpredictable consequences.

A new kind of critic emerged, eager to do more than dismiss the popular on the grounds of its low cultural cache. On the contrary, this new critic insisted on the importance of the entertainment she or he analyzed, while at the same time making the crucial distinction that other, less capable viewers who missed the connection between the music hall and issues of national health and hygiene—representative expert concerns—saw the entertainment incorrectly. In the process, the particular, local ways of knowing promoted by music-hall entertainment were often misread and misconstrued, and the form compacted and diluted for middle-class consumption.

Still, if a transformed music hall drew others besides its old core constituency, the dominant culture, too, changed and grew enough to accommodate the entertainment. Social elites have the power to appropriate subaltern forms, but seldom without doing some damage to the critical prejudices held by those in power. This book attempts to provide a model of music-hall criticism that neither celebrates the authenticity of the popular sensibility that it somehow discovers, nor romantically overestimates the autonomy of critical observers from lived categories of capitalist experience, such as expertise, administration, and professionalism.[30] I demonstrate how articulating the Victorian popular provoked competition over the various meanings conveyed by English culture. Yet this competition was not of the sort that

can be won decisively—it produced an intrinsic conflict between the admiring fan and the would-be expert.

Music Hall and Modernity demonstrates how such pioneering cultural critics
as Arthur Symons and Elizabeth Robins Pennell used the music hall to secure
and promote their professional identity as guardians of taste and national
welfare who were, at the same time, devotees of the spontaneous culture of
"the people." Examining late-Victorian controversies over philanthropy and
moral reform, and fiction from Walter Besant, Hall Caine, and Henry Nevinson, as well as performance criticism from William Archer and Max Beerbohm, I argue that discourse on music-hall entertainment helped consolidate
the tastes and identity of an emergent professional class. In such writing, we
see the first flowering of the now-pervasive paradox in which celebrations of
popular culture as authentic confirm the need for professionals to discover,
interpret, and defend what makes it so.

By moving from literary representations to media controversies, I do
more than merely suggest the diversity of opinions regarding art and expertise current in late-Victorian London. I assert a broader claim, rooted in the
historical evidence I uncover: namely, that these various actors were involved
in a common struggle to be recognized as cultural specialists. Then as now,
debates over aesthetic taste and social decorum had sometimes profound
repercussions for how gender conventions were lived; then as now, debates
concerning the character and regulation of aesthetic forms mobilized a host
of interested parties competing for the right to represent the popular. Mimicking the moral and aesthetic criteria of high art, professional discourse
arguably demolished the vernacular practice it set out to celebrate and preserve. At the same time, writing about the halls negotiated issues of class, respect, and empowerment. Once it had been established that one could be a
music-hall "expert," it turned out that a diverse crowd could seize and utilize
this rhetorical authority. By emphasizing a communal interest shared by Victorian elites and popular audiences in their desire to be recognized as experts,
I wish to reclaim professionalism from its conventional reading as the sub-
servience of a middle-class segment to a capital-owning elite.[31]

Music Hall and Modernity attends to the declarations of self-declared
experts and cultural managers, whether reformers, models, civil servants,
aficionados, or literary intellectuals. Their accounts suggest that managing
the popular did not entail the evasion of hard questions, such as the relations
between cultural capital and the resources for social capital. Although my

study details some of the inequities of late-Victorian professional culture, I also relate what I take as its egalitarian effects. This is as it should be: for in the face of a possible end of art, or its full marginalization, the cultural appropriation of the popular by authorities and experts becomes a risky but necessary alternative to a world without art.

I

Music Hall

The success of the penny gaff, the precursor to variety entertainment, stirred a moral panic in otherwise seasoned mid-Victorian social explorer Henry Mayhew. The prodigal creativity of working-class audiences elicited his alarm and apprehension. Less than a century later, cultured observers appeared certain that music hall acculturated its audiences. Moreover, they found that the form offered a reliable index of national vitality and values, and the most authentic expressive form of native Englishness. Star performers received acclaim by critics as the true curators of their culture, as representatives of English character. Whereas Mayhew proclaims that music hall endangers the moral fiber of the English laborer, T. S. Eliot argues that the death of

Marie Lloyd, "the greatest music hall artist of her time in England," constitutes a decisive crisis for both the working classes and England itself.[1] Eliot's
1923 pronouncement proved durable. In 1940, George Orwell praised comedians like Little Tich and Max Miller as caretakers for English culture, observing that they expressed "something which is valuable in our civilisation
which might drop out of it in certain circumstances."[2] Similarly, when John
Osborne needs a metaphor for the nation in his 1958 play *The Entertainer,*
he finds it in the music hall, and embodies his sense of national decline in
the failing career of an artiste gone to seed.

What exactly caused this sea change in attitudes? How did a decidedly low-
brow practice come to be invested with "deeper" meanings, let alone come to
gain the status of national treasure? To produce this shift in critical reception,
I argue, professional intellectuals reworked potent metaphors of cultural vitality and decay. The earliest generation of middle-class observers of music
hall treated the art form as an alien, threatening "other." Professional culture
criticism of the 1880s and 1890s, on the other hand, provided a structure for
the integration of the music hall into the canons of middle-class culture. In
fact, the new discourse of professional criticism reflects a novel bourgeois imperative to integrate the popular within its symbolic repertoire.

In contrast, literary professionals ranging from Max Beerbohm to Elizabeth Robins Pennell to T. S. Eliot formulated a well-nigh Manichean opposition between music-hall entertainment and what they cast as middle-class
conformist culture. In the process they produced a new genre, the music-
hall lament, in which what was most vital and most endangered about the
English people could be found in the music hall. Thanks to this genre, the
music hall retained its centrality as trope for England long after it ceased
to be a privileged entertainment form. The "lament" served as a perennial
rhetorical resource from the 1890s, through the generation of Eliot and Orwell, and extending to subculture observers such as Colin MacInnes in the
1950s, as well as 1960s British pop bands such as the Beatles and the Kinks.[3]
Even those who looked for Englishness in other forms appear to have been
compelled to offer an interpretation of the music hall in order to speak cred-
ibly for the English public.

The roster of culture producers who endeavored to speak positively on
behalf of music hall includes a host of major and minor figures in the arts:
Arthur Symons, George Moore, Joseph Pennell, Elizabeth Robins Pennell,
and Herbert Horne, in addition to Max Beerbohm, Selwyn Image, Rudyard
Kipling, Theodore Wratislaw, and painter Walter Sickert.[4] These figures were

hardly univocal in their shared music-hall lament. In the case of Symons, for instance, the music-hall account could spiral into complex, reflexive commentaries that suggested a new, self-conscious spectatorship. Max Beerbohm, on the other hand, felt free to send up Symons's claims to have discovered the deep meaning of the music hall.[5] Even so, Beerbohm himself insists that music hall needed perceptive critics to appreciate the aesthetic achievements of its star performers. What these observers shared was a commitment to a stylized experience of patronizing the halls, and an intimation that the form struck at the foundations of middle-class taste.

The music-hall lament bears the stamp of a class-specific ideology. The theatrical entrepreneurs, newspaper writers, theater reviewers, playwrights, and professors who developed the discourse were not only attracted to music hall, but also often directly involved in it as a commercial venture.[6] It was in their interest to develop an image of London music hall as an essential adversary to monolithic establishment conformity, forged by consumer capital, supervised by professional critics, and resolute in its hostility to reigning discourses of propriety while at the same time quintessentially English.

Yet music-hall criticism did more than authorize these upstart professionals. It also made explicit basic tensions in the rhetoric of cultural expertise. Should culture critics stake their status on fidelity to core values communicated by a stable canon that could be mastered through education and training, or should they claim a unique capacity to map the shifting territory of the popular? In the 1890s, among English intellectuals, disagreement over the status of music hall amounted to a methodological turf war; it was also a covert debate about the value and possibility of alternative culture practice in an increasingly commercial society.

Consider the notable 1890s argument between drama critic William Archer and the vocal defenders of music hall. Archer, a prestigious drama critic and advocate for the theatrical avant-garde, assumed that theater should have a pedagogic function for the educated public. In his many pieces for the *World* newspaper, he extolls theater over the halls at every opportunity. In doing so, Archer adopts the function conventionally assumed by intellectuals with respect to popular culture: sorting out good culture from bad, superior achievement from inferior work. Then and now, intellectuals declare what is worth recognizing, and what is best forgotten, in the overcrowded storehouse of cultural production.[7]

It no doubt seemed to Archer as if the hall's partisans were bent on rejecting the very standards that should have defined them as intellectuals.[8] He draws sharp distinctions between theater, with its rigorous and demanding pleasures, and the broad-based, large-gestured humor and song that constituted music-hall fare. Archer insinuates that music-hall partisans are too self-absorbed and self-interested to be trusted in their preferences. In his 1895 essay "Theatre and Music-Hall," he seeks to win his public to his more demanding, rational taste, and perhaps win back those writers (and readers) who share his training, his values, but, oddly enough, not his tastes. He hints that defenders of the halls mistook their "physical comfort and mental idleness" for a more genuinely intellectual enjoyment.[9] Archer could rely on class-bound tradition to distinguish theater culture from music-hall crudeness. The acolytes of music hall worked to invert those valuations, to blur lines between the cultured and the vulgar, and to challenge the customary relations between critical attention and "cruder" forms of apprehension.[10]

The music-hall lament was forged in large part by Archer's intellectual competition. Self-proclaimed aficionados of the music hall made their partisanship of the form public in the same media venues that published Archer and his ilk: prestigious, liberal newspapers and periodicals read by the salaried and college educated. Nonetheless, these popular culture partisans founded their rhetorical authority on different grounds than taste arbiters like Archer. They did not parade their class status, innate sense of cultural authority, or college educations. Instead, this unconventional faction stressed an organic relation or kinship to popular taste, a special ability to assess public needs. They created a discourse that connected a distinctly "popular" culture to nation and history.

To sketch this debate, then, is to show how the music-hall aficionado effected a change in the critical lexicon of the educated class, and made possible a new homology between national vitality and vernacular identity. Music hall mattered among this critical elite precisely because its vulgarity seemed to offer an escape from an established system of critical, cultural, and economic values that, by the 1890s, left little room for new critical work. In praising the form, the music-hall cognoscenti necessarily reified it. The value of music hall, they insisted, resides in its essence as folk culture. Certain that they knew the popular character better than the people themselves, they made of "the people's culture" an object every bit as static and ahistorical as the tradition that Archer embraced.

Like a later generation of "hip" cognoscenti, music-hall aficionados took pleasure in being populist insiders. They prided themselves on their "advanced knowledge of the illegitimate," in Andrew Ross's phrase.[11] Yet, as

William Archer knew quite well, these adepts were also movers, shakers, and, importantly, managers in the field of cultural production. Rather than a battle of elites versus populists, the tensions in music-hall criticism are better regarded as structural contradictions within managerial ideology.[12] Music-hall acolytes observed the same professional protocols as competing intellectuals. The freedom that music-hall devotees had in mocking authority presupposed the prior elaboration of a dominant discourse of taste, produced by morally serious, responsible, and judicious critics, like William Archer himself, for its full intelligibility.

Music-hall partisans thought in terms of the perpetual struggle between two clearly defined and unequal antagonists, capitalism at its most venal and the authentic expression of the folk. In order for the vernacular to have a fighting chance, it had to be made visible and shed its lingering parochialism. This entailed a paradox. The forces that made the halls popular made them susceptible to commercial appropriation, and therefore dilution. Music-hall advocates based their critical authority on their ability to evaluate, and "rescue," formerly illegitimate cultural expression; but they also believed that this expression faced inevitable doom from larger forces of commodification.

While the contradictory and often flamboyant celebration of the music hall did not in the end supplant Archer's sober and respectable critical practice, the cult of the halls had a lasting impact on English cultural criticism. Especially significant was their tendency to associate national health with the resistant capacity of popular culture. It was a seductive discourse, based on inside knowledge, but it was also a reductive one, with the students of popular culture often claiming to know more than their instructors. In defending the people, the music-hall cultist often occluded the complexities of music-hall audiences. The myth of the inherently subversive popular, a compressed image of complex vernacular practice, was passed off as a timeless truth of national character. Once abstracted, the general debate over the resistant potential of cultural forms, and the challenges posed and faced by popular culture, flows into a larger discourse on the abiding patterns of Englishness.

As Krishan Kumar observes, the end of the nineteenth century found English intellectuals in different fields working on a common project to "define more closely what was meant by Englishness—and with unmistakable intent, to celebrate it."[13] Historian, poet, novelist, literary critic, and folklorist elaborated Englishness as a secular essence discernible in shared cultural practices. In various intellectual discourses ranging from education reform, to linguistics, to the sociology of rural culture, Englishness was

derived from the study of different local practices and linked to different do-
ings of "the people." However, if the cognoscenti imagined a place for the
people within their construction of English character, inclusion was offered
on quite specific conditions. As Philip Dodd suggests, late-Victorian intellectuals offered an "invitation to the working class to take its place in the national culture," but the "acknowledgment" was tied to terms that "fixed" the
"identity and nature" of the people.[14] Nonetheless, these arguments did not
simply bolster the authority of would-be music-hall experts. When music-
hall partisans articulated claims of national vitality to the London variety
stage, they inevitably raised broad questions concerning the work of institutions and collectives within the nation-state. Music hall came to signify
the possibility that an expressive practice outside the leveling impulses of
capitalism, urbanism, and modernism could exist and would be desirable.
This amounts to an early instance of an oppositional, modernist criticism,
despite its late-Victorian trappings.

Making a Subculture

While a critic of the form, Archer nonetheless assumed that music hall remained a unique reflection of English character, a "mirror" for demotic
tastes (as the title of Max Beerbohm's careful consideration of the music-
hall populism, "Demos' Mirror," would have it). The music-hall partisan
found the essence of the entertainment in formal aspects of the fare: in the
celebrated call and response between singers and audience, and the insistent
vérité collapse of the fourth wall in comic sketches and songs. These stylistic elements served to convince the halls' more dedicated defenders that the
very essence of the English people was reflected in its variety entertainment.

At moments, Archer himself seemed persuaded by the argument that
music hall not only originated in popular ritual, but also still served as a
unique, not a stylized, expression of the proletariat. He was accordingly
tempted to take music hall as a true transcription of the vernacular voice.
Archer read social commentator, art critic, and music-hall defender Elizabeth Robins Pennell and quoted approvingly her history of music hall and
her claim that variety theater constituted an art form whose essential character was outside history. Like many of the cultists he decried, Archer relied
on historicist arguments to support his points about the character of contemporary variety theater.[15] Pennell's argument that music hall constituted
a peerless populist form and existed in counterpoint to mundane commer-

cial culture gave even Archer, who wished to accord theater that status, some pause.[16]

In Pennell's influential 1893 account, the defense of music hall develops through an account of the lineage of the form. She locates the essence of music hall in the popular desire for variety. "Variety" itself, broadly understood, constitutes the recognized essence, not only of popular entertainment, but also of popular desire. Pennell's essay then provides a full inventory of the many different embodiments, but single essence, of popular variety, from medieval times to the present day.

Once Pennell alights on her central analogy, she proceeds boldly, with willful anachronism. The link between the people and variety entertainment blurs the distinction between the two terms while maintaining the character of both as essential truths. "Before the first Miracle play had been invented," she proclaims, "the people of England had clamored for the variety entertainment, and been given it. There was not a castle throughout the land that had not its own special London Pavilion or Alhambra in miniature" (575). "The Pedigree of the Music-Hall" abounds in clever analogies: "Then as now, the audience were free to go and come; likely enough, free to keep their hats or helmets, if they chose; to join in the chorus, to throw things at the performer who failed to please. . . . No, already in feudal days, the idea of 'turns' had been developed: the minstrel gave place to the acrobat, the acrobat to the dancer, the dancer to clever dog."[17] The current charm, or at least the contemporary success, of music hall, she insists, resides precisely in its fidelity to a national essence. The value of the halls rests on their genetic resemblance to rustic comedy like miracle plays and mummers drama.

To convince, Pennell's essay demands that its readers assume a similarly unchanging essence of the English people: "Acrobats and jugglers, bears and dogs, by the same feats and the same tricks—you can see them in illuminated MSS. And old woodcuts held Saxon and Norman spell-bound, as they hold the Cockney today. Not one number of the programme could be cited which has not its medieval counterpart. More of the past lives in the music hall than in any other institution."[18] Pennell justifies music hall as "heritage culture"; at the same time, the many corresponding faces of variety require from the reader a faith in a static, unchanging, popular character that is also English character.

Pennell's survey of variety itself expresses an English tradition of thought concerning culture, beginning in Burke and Coleridge, extending through Matthew Arnold and Carlyle, and reaching forward to modernists like

T. S. Eliot. These thinkers, as Terry Eagleton observes, tend to "naturalize culture."[19] Pennell follows suit: for all her effort to set cultural forms within a historical context, she shrinks from rupture and discontinuity in the historical record. Like those of her predecessors, Pennell's essay works on history, ordering its crooked ways, avoiding difference, and constructing, as Eagleton puts it, in a "seamless evolutionary continuum."[20] The music hall emerges as a collective form, endowed, in Eagleton's words, with "all the stolid inevitability of a boulder." Pennell sanctifies the desire of the English people to escape "monotony"; stylized folk expression becomes a representative national form.

Thus locating the pedigree of the people, Pennell comes perilously close to claiming that the people's culture is fully determined by the past. In fact, the English folk share qualities otherwise associated with various cultural and biological primitives abroad (she is hardly unique among leading Victorians in holding fast to this homology). Both the tribesman and the native Englishman are believed to possess an essence that sets them outside of history. Similarly, Pennell's music-hall apologetic has the paradoxical effect of announcing the vitality of an art form while at the same moment proclaiming it's nothing new.

The music-hall criticism of Max Beerbohm, wit, caricaturist, and aesthete, takes up many of the themes sounded by music-hall partisans like Pennell. As a critical observer, he was fascinated by the communal circuitry evidenced by the interplay between performer and audience at the halls. Like Pennell, Beerbohm forges links in his essays between music hall and the character of the English people, especially its working class. Beerbohm also echoes Pennell's reductive analogies between the music hall and English character. In "Demos' Mirror" (1903), Beerbohm evinces a cockeyed confidence that music hall reflects—or produces—traits of the national character.[21] "Indeed," the critic avows, "there is not one peculiarity of our race, good or bad, that is not well illustrated in the Music Halls."[22]

Unlike Pennell, Beerbohm provides a theory behind music-hall evolution: "The entertainments in Music Halls have grown, feature for feature, from the public's taste. They are things which the public itself has created from its own pleasure; they know no laws of being but those which the public gives them." The fidelity with which the music hall reflects popular essence suggests that its development obeys a popular logic that transcends its character as commercial enterprise. Beerbohm heralds the music hall both as mirror and coproducer of folk essence, and its various performers emerge as publicists for the singular truth of national character.

However, by 1899, with the publication of "The Blight on Music Hall," Beerbohm began to question the harmonious relation he supposed between the people and the people's entertainment. In his most elaborate, programmatic piece on music hall, "The Older and Better Music Hall" (1903), he worries over the growing incongruence between music hall's origins and its current state. Characteristically, the solution to the contradiction that he proffers exalts the trained, informed evaluator capable of making the necessary distinctions between good and bad music hall. Like "Demos' Mirror," written in the same year, the essay attempts to make sense of a perceived change in the content of music-hall performance.[23]

The essay articulates Beerbohm's dissatisfaction with the current state of the commercial music hall: as these halls draw more entertainers and audiences outside the working class, so they seem to him necessarily less authentic. Yet, importantly, "The Older and Better Music Hall" declares Beerbohm's personal allegiance to, and seeming possession of, the "older and better music hall" over against the "clever," progressive (according to middle-class standards), and more commercial variety theater. Against a shallow, "stripling reader," who attends music hall and applauds finer conditions, slicker entertainment, "clever poodles, clever conjurers, clever acrobats, clever cinematographs, clever singers and clever elephants," he pits his own stance as a reactionary, "passionate" for what once was. Why is the older music hall—of less than a decade before—"better" than its newer variants? The conclusion follows from Beerbohm's premise that the first music halls moved in lockstep with real working-class sentiment. Music hall loses its credibility once it hails other audiences besides the working class; it wins new patrons at the cost of losing its critical cachet as the authentic popular. "This is one of the advantages of the old music hall over the new," Beerbohm insists; "it does reflect, in however grotesque a way, the characters of the class to which it consciously appeals." Unlike the "stripling reader"—the youthful music-hall partisan, whom the critic assumes to have been taken in by ersatz culture—Beerbohm remains in touch with the "good old days," when "an unbroken succession of singers" performed "in accord to certain traditional conventions."[24] In contrast, Beerbohm's erring readers extol music hall for the wrong reason: for being a merely "clever" approximation of authenticity.

Beerbohm's distinction between an inauthentic "clever" and a valuable, essential "vulgar" does not explicitly appeal to learning or critical convention for authority. The critic's definition of folk culture, however, reprises familiar terms—"barbarous," "stupid," "outside history," all serve as binary foils to "clever" variety.[25] The resulting image of a barbarous and stupid England that was nonetheless truly English underscores the desirability of class difference. When Beerbohm suggests that the turn away from the older, better music hall means the acceptance of homogenized culture over genuinely free expression he equates popular freedom with ruling-class domination.

Partly as a result of his assumptions, the struggle he posits between authentic expression and commodified entertainment remains a battle the latter has won in advance. Recalling his younger days, Beerbohm presents his memory of the old halls as nothing less than principled nonconformity; nostalgia becomes elevated into an existential imperative. The critic's youth is associated with a time when nonconformity was still a possibility, when the critical observer might maintain a position one step ahead of the crowd, yet in lockstep with the people. Music hall, too, was "young," that is, unassimilated. Both the spectator and the culture remember a time of lost, critical potency.

The "older" music hall was "better" but always already vanishing, and this disappearance is proffered as the inevitable fate of adversarial culture in a commercial society. "The Older and Better Music Hall" advances the notion that the lag time between genuine artistic expression and the dilution of this expression was quickening. This all-encompassing logic of appropriation necessarily includes the music hall's cultivated acolytes, since their recognition speeds on the canonization of dissident forms; the authorized music hall must always signify the twilight of the form as a viable, expressive medium.

In an attempt to dodge his own conclusions regarding the inescapability of middle-class cultural appropriation, Beerbohm engages in subtle play with the key notion used to frame his music-hall observations. The essay leaps from a realist expression of the inevitability of history to a modernist fantasy of a past recaptured. The aficionado becomes uncharacteristically hopeful, even cheeky, about his ability to do the impossible, and claim a lost past that he alone recognizes. At the essay's close, Beerbohm reassures his readers with his personal discovery of an oasis of cultural purity that remains in the midst of more luxurious, fully commercialized palaces of "variety" (the critic's own scare quotes, to mark the form's inauthenticity). Paradise, a haven for the cognoscenti, remains on nightly exhibit: "Can we anywhere recapture the olden pleasures? Indeed, yes. I have found a place. Nothing could seem more brand-new than the front of this Metropolitan Music Hall; but enter, and you will be transported deliciously into the past."[26]

"The Older and Better Music Hall" concludes then with a fetish figure, in the form of music-hall singer Harry Freeman. Freeman becomes the object of Beerbohm's impossible desires: to recapture a vital moment in a popular form, the health of the imagined community that the critic addresses, and indeed, the writer's own vitality. The singer allows the critic to imagine an escape from mere commerce located, paradoxically, in the heart of the metropolis. Freeman provides the critical spectator with a means of representing his loss and simultaneously denies it. "We tremble lest [Freeman] has truckled to changing fashion. Not he! . . . A thousand memories sweep back to us from that beaming face under the grey bowler hat. That face radiates the whole golden past, and yet, oddly enough seems not a day older than last we looked on it."[27] Freeman's "face" embodies all the contradictions that have accumulated in the course of the essay. Beerbohm's observations are, after all, fueled by a loss that has not in fact occurred. "But, certainly, the Metropolitan is a great discovery. Let us go to it often, magically renewing there our youth. And in those dreary other halls let us nevermore set foot." A vital cultural form clings to life, along with its most authentic practitioners and most trustworthy witness, despite having been lost.

Despite Beerbohm's subtleties, the differences between his cultivated stance of music-hall appreciation and Pennell's more academic historicizing are less significant than their common ground. Both must exit history in order to extol the halls. In Pennell's account, nothing can change the national character, or the popular desire for variety, outlined in her panoptic survey. Since historical change cannot kill an essence, one would assume that nothing could stop the populist advance embodied in "authentic" variety. Importantly, however, Pennell also anticipates Beerbohm's own doubts as to the durability of popular culture. The music hall that Pennell describes, magically transforming and renewing itself in lockstep with the English people, still develops only so far. She contends that the entertainment is now poised on the brink of disaster through its very success, a triumph that has brought in a mass of experts and entrepreneurs, who serve only to rob the form of its essential working-class qualities.

Music hall developed alongside the English people, the story goes, changing with them along with the mode of production. Yet management and capitalism cannot coexist with a fully popular form; one must give way, and with the onrush of scrutiny, Pennell hints, the hall will inevitably face a total assimilation. Unable or unwilling to imagine the persistence of popular culture within the dominant culture, she conjures up the form's imminent demise.

Her account spills over into a pell-mell rush, with the critic calling down plagues on both sides of the cultural divide; she expresses her distrust of the people's ability to maintain their own culture and distaste for what a league of competing authorities—managers, artists, legislators—have done to variety. "For centuries," Pennell laments, "Englishmen have been shaping their variety entertainment into its present form, and now, like a child with the toy it has been crying for, they are doing their best to destroy it."[28] She takes aim at the forces of moral reform that have pressured the halls to clean up their act; she also points fingers at the various entrepreneurs who streamline the entertainment and transform it into a suitably bourgeois venture. Indeed, her closing peroration excuses no one: "patrons" and "managers" are alike to blame. It also argues an impossibility: that the essence of Englishness can pass away while still attracting the people themselves as paying patrons. Try as they may, the people can't quite see the music hall for what Pennell believes it is. "When too late," Pennell warns, "when it is no longer studied at first hand, the scholar will learn its value."

The death knell sounds for music hall at the height of its commercial success. Tabulating deep structural continuities between the popular now and then, Pennell passes on to readers a vague but expansive sense of lost certainties. Her argument for music hall as diminishing cultural resource, praised by the discerning critic just as it disappears, leaves readers with a striking example of the ultimate vulnerability of culture forms. It is an argument meant to make her reading audience nervous, and thus serves as a brief for a managerial elite that might, at least rhetorically, finesse the crisis that this very elite identifies as such.

William Archer versus the Aficionado

The defenders of the halls sought new rhetorical figures to express their relation to music hall and, by extension, to the popular. John Stokes notes that the era's most ardent and self-conscious music-hall devotee, Arthur Symons, used the word "amateur" to encapsulate his unique mix of engaged and critical appraisal of the entertainment.[29] In his first full commentary, however, Symons alights on the more apt, because more ambiguous, term of "aficionado." The primary use of the term "amateur" was, and is, to denote a binary opposite to the professional. It is harder to separate the categories of passion and expertise conveyed by the word aficionado, which makes it a more appropriate signifier for the complex, syncretic stance that Symons adopted toward the music hall.

As Symons describes it in "A Spanish Music-Hall" (1891), the aficionado moves in a critical middle ground, moved by passion but also taking a critical distance. He is something more than the novice and something less than the specialist. The aficionado thus stakes out ground in unstable territory. Symons sought to persuade his readers that his cultural reports were more invested and therefore more legitimate than competing accounts. This, of course, conflicts with a main tenet of the prevailing aesthetic discourse, that disinterested views and orderly appraisal are necessary preconditions for evaluation.

Despite this tension between involvement and disinterest, the aficionado meets several of the criteria of professional criticism. First, the figure defines fields of interest or specialty. By staking out a territory that a portion of Symons's middle-class audience might not be inclined to map out themselves, the aficionado provides services to the public. Like the professional, the aficionado is open to criticism by other experts. The aficionado seeks the ratification of intellectuals in his class who might not share his tastes. Finally, like the expert, this music-hall partisan seems to exist above mundane concerns and petty wrangling, yet still competes and struggles for his achieved truth with a singular passion that appears aggrandizing.

Aficionados may assume a democratic approach toward matters of taste. Nonetheless, they deploy their rhetoric to convince members of their own class rather than the general public. The internal nature of this taste dispute is evident in a piece of public correspondence in which Symons sets another music-hall critic straight. "As an *aficionado* of the music halls," he writes in a letter to the *Star* newspaper, "allow me to express my feelings of pleasure at 'Spectator's' second visit to the Pavilion, and his admirable eulogy of Miss Jenny Hill."[30] Symons then insists that the *Star*'s critic has made some fundamental errors of naming and recognition. "But may I also be allowed to protest, in the most convinced way, against his rash assumption that 'nothing is so much like one music hall as another music hall—that the difference between the Pavilion and the Trocadero, between the Tivoli and the Royal, is doubtless only that 'twixt Tweedledum and Tweedledee.'" Symons adds: "To a discriminating amateur, each music hall has its cachet, as definitely each music-hall artist worthy of the name; one could no more mistake the programme of the Royal for that of the Tivoli than one could mistake Miss

Marie Lloyd for Miss Katie Lawrence." Here Symons's rhetoric defines a speaker in relation to a specific field of study with flair and a confidence that underscores his authority. The correspondence draws a circle around the speaker that distinguishes the writer from many others, including the *Star's* critic. If we accept Symons's conclusion, we must also grant his premises: namely that the best critical observers defeat their competition by means of their greater accuracy, expertise, and achieved perspective. This contest can have only one winner. On this point, the aficionado plays by the rules of a traditional criticism that saves its greatest scorn for those with other critical axioms. Just so, Symons's letter to the *Star* challenges claims made by the *Star's* theater critic, A. B. Walkely, that music halls were too uniformly vulgar to differentiate and therefore analyze.[31]

The contrast between Symons's critical practice and Pierre Bourdieu's late-twentieth-century critique of the popular expert is worth remarking. "The dominant in the artistic and intellectual fields," Bourdieu reminds us, "have always practiced that form of radical chic which consists in rehabilitating socially inferior cultures or the minor genres of legitimate culture. . . . To denounce hierarchy does not get us anywhere. What must be changed are the conditions that make this hierarchy exist, both in reality and in minds."[32] Bourdieu's charge presumes that social and economic structures of injustice can find a remedy without a prior symbolic resolution. In contrast, Symons's partisan defense of music hall, a statement of his own expertise, presumes that criticism modifies social practice. He proceeds as if expert attention transforms the objects and practices it scrutinizes, bringing them within the field of legitimation. It seems at least plausible to pit the charmed circle of legitimating energies that the aficionado draws around performers, the critic, and a culture form against Bourdieu's extreme pessimism as to the outcome of self-interested intellectual labor. Symons's legitimating claims may not undo hierarchy, by Bourdieu's too-exacting standards, but they clearly do more than simply leave an established hierarchy intact.

Further, in the hands of its most deliberate practitioners, music-hall fandom could draw mischievous attention to the arbitrary nature of the evaluative game.[33] As passionate experts, members of the music-hall cult produced unsettling imitations of professional criticism that appeared to "signify" on the professional ideal.[34] The expert rhetoric of music-hall cognoscenti might be said to parody the rules of the critical game through punctilious observance. However, another consequence of this rhetoric is the blurring of lines between cultural mavericks and the establishment, since they both use the same idiom.

The aficionado's ability to mime the idioms of the cultural conservative incited the fury of competing literati. William Archer found the music hall distasteful, but he never got quite as exercised over working-class vulgarity as he was by the sight of persons with proper training sharing common tastes. It was bad enough that such renegades expressed a liking for music hall, but far worse for the stolid rationalist was their insistence that they possessed more authority to describe it, and better "taste," than those who were not "in the know."

Archer takes careful aim at the music-hall champions in "Theatre and Music-Hall" (1895). Here the critic surveys the field of middle-class taste. He pretends that the would-be aficionados of music hall represent the consensus of expert opinion and have in fact convinced the rest of London's theatergoing audience of the superiority of the halls over the theater. In other words, he casts himself as the renegade in an effort to satirize the aficionados' rhetoric and turn it against them. To counter their "dominant" preference, he charges it with being covertly elitist. If, as Symons and company assert, differences in taste shouldn't be managed, then why, Archer asks, do music-hall experts insist on the significance of their own preference for the halls over conventional theater? He thereby implies the excessive self-regard of these quasi-specialists.

> I merely wish to inquire why, in a world where tastes proverbially differ, this preference [for music hall] should pass for the mark of a highly enlightened, and truly modern soul, while the contrary preference stigmatises any one who confesses to it as a person quite beyond the pale of culture. Don't tell me, dear reader, that you are not aware of this fact. Your ignorance merely shows that you are a besotted playgoer, without even the grace to be conscious of the abject inferiority of your tastes. . . . Is it possible you don't know that the theatre is dead, quite dead, this many a year, and stinketh in the nostrils of the truly refined and aesthetic; while art, real high-toned, all-alive up-to-date Art, has taken up its abode in the Syndicate halls?

Casting himself as the firebrand, Archer audaciously exposes the "real" music hall as "the art of elaborate ugliness, blatant vulgarity, alcoholic humour and rancid sentiment."[35] Although the works of Archer and Symons differ in content they share a rhetorical form. In each, a wry and savvy authority strives to win the hearts and minds of the cultured bourgeois by attempting to place himself on the side of a majority as opposed to a self-regarding elite.

The aficionado, in Archer's estimation, acts against the public good in the name of an unprincipled devotion to poor culture. Archer turns the music-hall devotee's predilection for the entertainment into irrational, and proud, affectation. To distinguish himself from this self-serving aesthete, Archer presents himself as the humble, more civic-minded, and ultimately more capable critic. Archer's critic, unlike the aficionado, is not carried away by fashion, and therefore exercises trustworthy judgment. The "truly refined" youths of Archer's account emerge as overqualified, oversophisticated, and prodigal about money, reputation, and status, hell-bent on squandering their hard-earned cultural capital. "The music-hall critic is now quite as indispensable to any self-respecting paper as the musical or dramatic critic, and is indeed a vastly superior person," he sneers, while "the average dramatic critic is of very common journalistic clay, and is apt to live a humdrum suburban and domestic life. Your typical music-hall chronicler is a young blood more or less fresh from the University, who probably has chambers in Piccadilly."[36] The implication that music-hall chroniclers are simply immature versions of men like himself gives Archer some confidence that the rift between the groups can be healed: "The curious thing is that the educated fanatics of the variety-show admit ... when you catch them singly [that] they have a hearty contempt for the greater part of the music hall entertainment; indeed, they resort to the variety shows for the very purpose of luxuriating in that emotion. It is precisely the vulgarity and the inanity of the 'comedians' and 'serio-comics' ... that attracts them to these halls of dazzling light."[37] "Theatre and Music-Hall" closes with a utopian resolution: that the defenders of the vulgar can be made to see the light, and be convinced that their links with popular taste are rooted in snobbery.

For all its polemic, "Theatre and Music-Hall" brandishes an olive branch to those culture workers who have strayed from the path and who refuse to respond to popular forms in a manner befitting their class status. The argument, after all, is productive for Archer—it allows him to set himself off from the traditional snob and confirm his own criticism as professional. Importantly, he cedes to music-hall advocates the authority to define the style of debate. Archer describes his own theater partisanship as a kindred "fanaticism," adding, "I am far from contending that we theatre-lovers are absolutely right and the fanatics of the variety-show absolutely wrong. . . . All I suggest is, that they might live and let live, recognizing that it is not a love of 'art,' in any rational sense of the term, but simply a love of physical comfort and mental idleness, that draws them to the music hall."[38] Archer looks forward to a time when unruly experts recall the salient difference between intellectual distance and the undemanding pleasures that hold suspect sway in popular entertainment, a distinction they have forgotten in practice. The assumption is that this wayward class fraction would then resume the proper roles of experts within the managerial class and tutelary intellectuals. A mass public remains, desiring to be won over and receive the necessary training to achieve Archer's own critical clarity.

Indeed, we can see just how far music-hall advocates made Archer bend at the time by looking at his return to the subject nearly two decades later, in 1916, reviewing a history of the music hall by H. G. Hibbert. By this time, the aficionados are in retreat, and the judicious critic monopolizes the field. No longer needing to keep the peace, Archer is more bilious in his assessment of the music-hall partisan: "There was a craze in the nineties, among a certain aesthetic set, for exalting the music hall at the expense of the theatre. It was too shallow and factitious to impose on a man of Mr. Hibbert's shrewdness."[39] Archer finds the craze a "poetic" affectation, "an invasion of the music hall by young poets, who wrote of it in foolish rhapsody."

Where Archer once insinuated that music-hall partisans were distinguished primarily by their assumed superiority to those who failed to share their taste, he now refuses to concede that their taste is anything more than an intellectual fad.[40] The defenders of the music hall deluded themselves that they "discovered genius in red-nosed buffoons whose art consisted in sheer effrontery, and in wearing threadbare clothes five sizes too large for them. . . . Nothing is so incomprehensible to the outside observer as this cult of squalid ugliness." The error of the music-hall defenders was in following the bad taste demonstrated by the well-meaning but deluded English public: "[M]any people, who in ordinary life are decent and intelligent enough, seem to take a perverted pride in accepting with apparent relish any sort of nauseous trash that is put before them in the guise of entertainment." Even high-ranking military officers are not immune from infection. Archer finds it especially pathetic that those "who have been living on the brink of death for months have nothing better to do with their scant time of respite than to haunt amusement houses," a phenomenon that "make[s] it seem very doubtful whether England is worth fighting for." It is difficult to read irony into such hyperbole. The military officer with bad taste recalls the fear prompted by the aficionado that expert training does not ensure a more informed and capable public. The officer qua aficionado serves as an alarming reminder of the breach between class status and personal taste. Here, Archer stands in a long line of Victorian sages who refuse to acknowledge that the failure of their cultural pedagogy suggests the limitations of their own educational program. The tutelary intellectual requires a perpetually unlearned public, without whom the project of taste tutorials makes no sense. Rather than acknowledge this, the intellectual projects the failure back out onto the public, whose inability to be taught underscores their meager inner resources. Although Archer retreats from the rhetoric of "live and let live" in regard to taste, he remains indebted to the music-hall aficionado for linking music-hall appreciation with national health and state administration—both distinctly professional realms.

As in the 1890s, the music hall in Archer's review essay provides the key pretext to reiterate the need for a class of authorized evaluators, who respond to the influx of bad entertainment by stepping up their own efforts to legislate taste. He even wishes to give this class fraction of artistic professionals full state sanction. Those with credentials must aid those who lack the time, capital, or capacity to exercise judgment in matters of taste: "I have sometimes wondered whether it might not be possible to adopt in England a modified form of [the American Drama League]. That is, a body which undertakes to supply its members with guidance in the direction of intelligent playgoing. . . . As things stand at present, the ordinary man . . . is wholly without guidance in the selection of a theatre to go to, and can do nothing but follow the crowd."[41] Archer expresses a typical professional desire, for the "ordinary man" to become a client class for a disinterested assembly with the proper credentials and training. The committee members will be distinguished by their expert disinterest and therefore will be above "advanced aestheticism, Puritanism, or critical party spirit of any sort," responsive solely to "common intelligence and decency of feeling." With the music-hall partisan gone, Archer sees an opportunity for the ascendancy of a group of cultural managers who can assess intellectual wares based on their professional standards. "[A] great end would be achieved," he observes, "if some guidance could be supplied to the hundreds of thousands of entertainment seekers, both in London and in the provinces, who flock to imbecile and deleterious shows in total ignorance of what they are going to see, and without anyone to tell them that the relaxation of moral and intellectual fibre involved in the encouragement of such entertainments is a serious national evil." The choice Archer puts forth is clear, and resembles in this one key respect the point advocated by the aficionado: place the evaluation of art in expert hands, where it will be properly handled, or accept an inevitable decline in cultural standards.

Archer responded to the challenge music-hall acolytes posed to traditional modes of intellectual decorum. However, much of his ire seems motivated by professional jealousy and competition. For most of the 1890s and beyond, it looked as if these "educated fanatics" of music hall might win the battle for the hearts and minds of the managerial class and make "popular culture" the privileged object of critical evaluation. Archer's many indictments of music hall attest to his faith that art could not survive in a commercial culture absent a full consensus among trained literary specialists as to what constitutes art. Yet while Archer found it possible to attack the music-hall devotee as disruptive, he proved less capable of resisting the concepts of nation and "the people" transmitted by the music-hall lament. Indeed, his criticism of the 1910s reveals that the argument about the music-hall lament in which he earlier participated had wholly revised the terms according to which intellectuals could speak to and for a national public.

Proof of the success of the aficionado in transforming the protocols of professional cultural criticism is also manifest in the persistent treatment of music hall as a prominent mode to figure the temperature of the people and of the nation itself. The new consensus places the music hall at the heart of national discourse, whether or not the professional culture critic speaks from a Conservative or a Radical position.

The most striking paradox of the music-hall lament, its simultaneous aspect as statement of national pride and narrative of cultural decline, was also its most durable feature. G. H. Mair's 1913 essay "The Music-Hall," written for the Liberal periodical the *English Review*, follows Pennell's trope of the worthy but disappearing music hall point by point. Mair provides a sophisticated native informant account of the entertainment. He singles out the contemporary music hall as a unique return to early English folkways. Mair's music hall fulfills the desire for a "pure" and purely native kind of entertainment: "The music hall is our one pure-blooded native amusement. It has a pedigree that is clear and undoubted, through the tavern, that great agent of social continuity, back to Elizabethan days—to the days when the theatre did really represent and embody the soul of the nation."[42] In one respect, Mair's insistence on continuity between various forms and types of the popular introduces a bracing relativism to cultural analysis, assimilating the unique figure of Shakespeare, a fountainhead of legitimate culture, into

the broad, inclusive stream of the popular. For Mair, both Renaissance theater audiences and contemporary patrons of music hall share an interest in
acting skill for its own sake, a skill "lost beyond recovery" in the contemporary theater. Both sets of patrons, he asserts, "loved the virtuoso; mere skill
attracted [them]." In Mair's account, Shakespeare emerges as a shrewd diag-
nostician, capable of ascertaining and providing for public taste, rather than
as an ingenious wordsmith.

> The broadsword combat between Macbeth and Macduff, the rapier
> duels in a dozen plays, the wrestling between Charles and Orlando, were
> real tests of skill enjoyed by audiences for their own sake and outside
> their setting. The bear in the Winter's Tale, that made its meal off the old
> gentleman, was doubtless brought from one of the pits of the Bankside;
> and we know with what effect, in the Two Gentleman of Verona, Shake-
> speare could use the performing dog.

This analysis provides bold contextualizing of Shakespeare, but it also
sets limits on the range permitted to current popular expression. Although
both Mair and Pennell invoke a Shakespeare who creates an art that responds to popular taste, neither suggests that contemporary representatives
of respectable culture have an obligation to popular feelings or expression.
The synthesis of cultural elements these critics read back into the Bard has
no contemporary analogue—no current dominant culture figure is praised
for a strategic dialogue with popular aesthetics. The present merely repeats
an earlier historical moment; Mair and Pennell foreclose the possibility
that dynamic interplay between official and popular culture will continue
into the future. A pedigree grants the popular a measure of legitimacy but
without calling for a change in contemporary aesthetic forms. The result
situates the people's playwright, Shakespeare, in relation to popular history
but above contemporary relevance to the masses. For both G. H. Mair and
Pennell, cultural history leaves out the struggle of human subjects with necessity.

Nevertheless, there is something productive about these histories. The
music-hall interpreter offers readers a new basis on which to ground the history of the halls: the stable foundation of national culture. The links forged
between nation and variety theater did not pass away with the high noon of
Victorian aestheticism. Nor did the rhetoric of the music-hall devotee, a
contradictory lament about the timeless persistence and extreme fragility of

English culture, fully disappear. Pennell, Beerbohm, and Mair testify to the felt need of critics to imagine culture forms that set true partisans of the people above other official versions of national culture. They used their immense rhetorical skills to produce a capacious language of loss that could include an entertainment that did not signify English history at midcentury. They express in various modes the fear that capitalizing vernacular culture nullifies its counterhegemonic value. A community of mourning is addressed, imagined, and created in these essays, mobilized as a psychic defense to compensate for the loss of vital music hall, or—it amounts to the same—essential Englishness.

A National Subculture

The lament sounds again in T. S. Eliot's elegy to the most celebrated music-hall singer of the age, Marie Lloyd, upon her death in 1922. While the essay stands at a remove from the turn-of-the-century figure, it compresses in its brief pages the arguments and metaphors circulated in the work of an earlier generation of music-hall devotees. Eliot's intellectual debts to the late Victorians are now frequently acknowledged in scholarship on the poet. For example, while Eliot may censure Symons in *The Sacred Wood* (1920), his first major publication of critical essays, he read him closely and with respect as a young man.[43] The Marie Lloyd essay has come to stand as a locus classicus of modernist response to "popular art"; however, I believe it may be more accurately described as a document of professional culture that draws on the rhetorical arsenal of the late-Victorian aficionado. Like Pennell and Beerbohm, Eliot conveys a heightened sense of temporal crisis and marshals powerful essentialisms of English character.

Eliot avoids the terms "aficionado" and "amateur." Nonetheless, he appropriates the stance perfected by the preceding generation of music-hall partisans. Both rely on metaphor rather than propositions to establish their premises. They elaborate a dense texture of associations, presuming that repeating links will establish that disparate subjects or concepts—music-hall performers, audiences, England—in fact share an essence. And indeed, Eliot must have found the music-hall lament attractive for stylistic reasons as well as its content. As Colleen Lamos argues, Eliot's critical essays proceed "not by logical syllogism" but "through the repetitive and accretive heightening of the same point until the aggregate force of his assertion makes it seem self-evident."[44] The music-hall lament also made its emotive appeal through reiteration and persuaded through the accumulation of associative links.

Marie Lloyd, the singer, initially stands with the working class, but "Marie Lloyd," the poet's construct, comes to stand in *for* the working class. By means of the shift from metonymy to metaphor, Eliot proceeds to his audacious conclusion: the death of the singer is proleptic for the death of the class to whom she stands in essential relation. The extreme nature of Eliot's claims constitutes a difference in degree but not in kind between his essay and the chronicles of an earlier generation.

"Marie Lloyd" eventually received pride of place in Eliot's prestigious *Selected Essays* (1932). The inaugural form of the piece appeared in the poet's "London Letter" column for the *Dial*. In this brief letter, we see, as David Chinitz suggests, "Eliot's feelings before his cautious pen had the opportunity to tone them down."[45] The crisis of Lloyd's death is figured in stark relief, and the poet expresses barely muted anxiety. Lloyd's death is not simply "an important event" (the description enshrined in the final version of "Marie Lloyd," found in Eliot's *Selected Essays*), but "the most important event which I have had to chronicle in these pages."[46] Eliot elaborates: "You will see that the death of Marie Lloyd has had a depressing effect, and that I am quite incapable of taking any interest in literary events in England in the last two months, if any have taken place." (The publication of *The Waste Land* is among the recent cultural events laid low by the loss of Lloyd.) Despite a more "cautious pen," a sense of imminent peril still permeates the version of "Marie Lloyd" in the *Selected Essays*. Indeed, Eliot might be said to have escalated the sense of temporal crisis expressed in the "London Letter."

The poet emphasizes that Lloyd's death affects more than a single mourner and means much more than a setback for music-hall audiences; it constitutes a full-blown, national crisis. The essay proceeds to a chilling, inexorable climax, a glimpse of the inevitable extinction of working-class culture. "The lower class exists, but perhaps it will not exist for long. In the music-hall comedians they find the expression and dignity of their own lives; and this is not found in the most elaborate and expensive revue."[47] The music-hall-goer will turn to cinema, meaning that "he will also have lost some of his interest in life"; the change will accelerate the death by boredom that the poet suggests will be the fate made common by middle-class cultural hegemony.[48] Characteristic of the music-hall lament, the passage insists on the essential difference between Lloyd's genuine expression and the commercial "revue," or the cinema. More to the point, the close of the elegy completes the transfer implied by Eliot's links among the working class, Lloyd, and the music hall. The loss of the part stands for nothing less than the death of the whole, for the end of working-class essence.

To grasp the nature of the crisis as Eliot presents it, we must first unpack the professional/client metaphor that structures his argument. Lloyd's songs do not simply entertain her audience but perform a necessary service. Eliot assumes that the singer does for her audience, or clients, what they are unable to do for themselves. In some ineffable manner, she renders the people's virtues and vices visible. What the people have lost in Lloyd—an objectification of their communal values—is something they are not believed capable of performing themselves.

This is what makes the loss so devastating, as Eliot goes on explain: "My chief point is that I consider her superiority over other performers to be in a way a moral superiority; it was her understanding of the people and sympathy with them, and the people's recognition of the fact that she embodies the virtues which they genuinely most respected in private life, that raised her to the position she occupied at her death. And her death is itself a significant moment in English history."[49] The relation here is posited as a "moral insight"; Eliot speaks of romantic virtues like "sympathy" and "understanding."[50] Yet the account of Lloyd's rise makes better sense when conceptualized as a relation between a skilled professional and an untutored populace. She has relatively scarce and necessary skills they are assumed to lack.

The emphasis Eliot sets on the nature of Lloyd's authority reminds us that Eliot's music hall broadcast a clear message about the English laborer. Vital and earnest, he had limited capacity for self-governance. Like Pennell and Beerbohm, the poet believed that music hall somehow secreted working-class culture full-blown and enshrined the timeless, quotidian truths embodied in "real," proletarian life. Unlike Pennell and Beerbohm, Eliot stresses the ability of the performer to objectify this inarticulate mass disposition. Thus, a deep respect and admiration for—even envy of—Lloyd's achievement and virtues can coexist with a willful ignorance of the poverty, deprivation, and exclusion that mark the working-class private life, which Eliot admires for its moral strength and vitality.

The admiration of the poet for Lloyd blocks off alternative accounts of the meaning of her performance. For Eliot assumes that Lloyd's emotive ability, not her style but her "sympathy," stands as the salient factor behind her success. "It was through this sympathy," he writes, "that she controlled her lower class audience." Eliot remembers her for representing essential

English working-class femininity: losing and loving, facing down the extremes of human existence with a grin. Lloyd's exemplary nature resides in the emotional hinterland where, it is assumed, her kind always live. Above all, Eliot forecloses the possibility that a performer who lifts working-class expression to an art might herself occupy a critical relation to her own culture as conscious, elaborate, and constructed as the persona that dominates Eliot's own poetry. Eliot, one might say, borrows Lloyd's expertise and then disavows it.

In fact, there seems little doubt that the singer's success stemmed from her ability to represent and clarify certain aspects of her complex identity as a working-class woman, and that, accordingly, both audience and performer must have appreciated this role-playing in ways that Eliot couldn't. Lloyd began a career in a fiercely competitive profession that became fully capitalized within the span of her career. Her celebrity, moreover, in large part set her apart from her class and coworkers. To imagine Lloyd as working-class emblem requires our assent to the rather incredible notion that she was wholly determined by her origin—or, similarly, that only the "genuine" exemplar of a class can succeed with the home crowd.[51] The salient point is that Eliot's working class unceasingly seeks to find professional help: public folk who can represent their private lives.

Like the works of the previous generation of music-hall partisans, Eliot's essay closes with a paradox: the music hall is a present absence in the contemporary London scene. The music hall that Eliot imagines is also threatened by the implosion of the class-segregated culture that permitted working-class expression a degree of autonomy by virtue of its distance from regnant, middle-class standards. "The middle classes . . . are morally dependent upon the aristocracy . . . the aristocracy are subordinating the middle-class, which is gradually absorbing and destroying them. The lower class still exists; perhaps it will not exist for long."[52] Eliot's most expansive claim about the end of class hierarchy is an implied assertion of the need for cultural professionals to take up the function that Lloyd performed. If Lloyd is truly irreplaceable, the working class will no longer be able to fulfill its most basic needs, for the poet assumes lumpen virtue cannot sustain itself without adequate representation. Eliot imagines Lloyd to have served as a wedge separating working-class expression from middle-class absorption. Without her, the bourgeois forces of cultural cooptation will wholly absorb, without digesting, a source of cultural nourishment.

That the working class was able to admire Lloyd sustains Eliot's populist confidence, but it also marks the decisive limits of his populism. For the relation between expert and client in Eliot's essay is not reciprocal, nor are the exchanges made between the masterful, forceful Lloyd and the audience she provides for contracted on equal terms. Eliot's assertions concerning the significance of the singer's death aid and sustain the most dangerous dynamic of professional culture: the belief that professionals require and produce a servile client class.

"Marie Lloyd" calls forth a new community in consolation for the loss of music hall and its organic intellectual. The essay figures a pop apocalypse, but the end of the world is immediately followed by the reign of the saints: in this case, a community of partisans, based on backward glances and nostalgic recall. Eliot's elegy takes account of the end of nation, containing, or reterritorializing, a potentially incapacitating fear. There is little of Eliot's routine urbanity in the prognostications that close the essay: "With the decay of the music hall, . . . the lower classes will tend to drop into the same state of protoplasm as the bourgeoisie."[53] Yet "Marie Lloyd" seems to participate in the ritual behavior modeled by the singer Eliot mourns, and shares her flair for performance. It might be said to enact a small-scale substitution for the cultural disease it describes. The first substitution performed through the essay's rhetoric is the replacement of "the working class" with "Marie Lloyd"; the second transference is the exchange of "Marie Lloyd" for the category of "the nation." If the old order as represented by Lloyd stands on the verge of meltdown, then a new, imagined community stands to emerge, organized around shared totems of national identity and spoken for by the poet himself.

"Marie Lloyd" invokes class difference, even as it enlists readers to redefine their sense of belonging to something larger than class: a common, "lost" heritage in English working-class traditions. The elegy suggests that national aspirations and hopes depend on the ability of cultured persons to apprehend the crisis of culture manifest by the loss of the music hall. The poet's lament provides a unifying fiction. "Marie Lloyd" begins by imagining a bereaved crowd marked by their working-class status, but broadens to include all those who mourn the loss to the nation manifest by the loss of the singer. Like any fantasy of community, the poet's elegy centers on powerful, and largely exclusive, images of labor and purpose, requiring some hardy essentialisms to maintain coherence and rhetorical appeal. Even with music hall and the working class diagnosed as terminal, the form is nevertheless situated in the pageant of a specifically native history.

Most of all, the ties between Eliot's memorial and the music-hall lament are seen in the poet's firm lean toward the past. There is no future tense, and consequently no predictive value, in the intellectual construction of music hall as the salient English popular. Famously for Eliot, the end of music hall is easily confused with the last of England, though, as we've seen, the same apocalyptic rhetoric is evident in earlier readings of the halls. Faced with Lloyd's loss, Eliot abdicates the need for further, collaborative response to the form in favor of a supple and commanding rhetoric. Nation requites these losses with the image of an imagined community of mourners, more luminous because more exclusive. The admission of cultural decline is finally reclaimed as minor-key pleasure.

The music-hall lament was an expression of lost hopes and diminished expectations; it stands at a distance from the imperial hubris or expansionist bravado scholars of nationalism usually analyze and critique. However, the character of the lament both shaped and was shaped by the discourse of English nationalism; the lament expressed a fascination for things "typical," yet weather-beaten, autumnal, and receding. The music-hall lament is an expressive means of extracting pleasure from the recognition of how very English a particular bit of England was, reminding readers why this difference still matters (to the writer), and how it might be savored despite its decline. Similarly, what might first appear as a provincial instance of culture comes to signify the stuff of national tradition. Once exalted, the halls are set securely within the national trust, where they can, in the realm of imagination and memory, be preserved and displayed as a forever "green and pleasant land."

The critical practice of music-hall devotee Arthur Symons steered clear of the powerful, resonant, but limiting metaphors of authenticity and the compact images of nationhood projected by most fin-de-siècle partisans of the form. Symons relates accounts of the halls without searching for an authentic expression of the entertainment; he rarely takes up the music-hall lament. He finds in, or imposes on, the halls deep meanings, yet his interpretations tend to be provisional, open to revision, in part because Symons insisted on the accountability of the observer to other patrons and observers. He imagined his music-hall accounts as a form of collaborative effort.

Symons returned again and again to the problem of authority and expertise raised by music-hall performance. He situated his writing on the halls as a passionate amateur's attempt to provide a theory of the entertainment, which meant for Symons a deliberate, thorough discourse on the conditions and context that provoked his own passionate responses to the form. Symons's theoretical approach to music hall seemed presumptuous and risible to his contemporaries; however, his reflective method seems to have released him from some essentialist attitudes that beleaguered most music-hall interpreters. As modeled by Symons, the music-hall theorist is less eager to hide or repress the experience of cultural difference in music hall and more skeptical toward the lament's master categories of the nation and the people. Arthur Symons's music-hall chronicles explore the possibility that cross-class and cross-gender contact can occur without subjects losing their complex humanity in the process. My next chapter examines Symons's own escape from the rhetoric of lament elaborated both by his peers and by a subsequent generation of literary intellectuals. I argue that he gains this freedom, not because of his antiprofessionalism, but by articulating an alternative version of the professional.

2

Camp Expertise

ARTHUR SYMONS, MUSIC HALL, AND THE
DEFENSE OF THEORY

By the close of the nineteenth century, English music hall or "variety," an entertainment form that incorporated comic acts, animal tricks, dramatic sketches, and dance, attracted middle-class patronage, thereby losing its exclusive character as working-class entertainment. Variety halls such as the upscale Alhambra and the Empire now claimed the attention, not to mention lucre, of mass audiences. This chapter argues that the music hall provided a new testing ground on which enterprising intellectuals could flex their evaluative muscle. Perhaps more than any other late-Victorian man of letters, poet and critic Arthur Symons frequented the music hall with an eye toward representing it, a service that he regularly performed for newspapers such as the *Star* or more elite cultural journals such as the *Fortnightly Review.*

Crucial to my purposes, Symons theorized his relation to music-hall entertainment. It seemed that variety's mass appeal prompted some intellectuals to revise their previous understanding of aesthetic value. Symons took up this challenge. His accounts of the form exceed a mere description or review of music-hall performance: they evidence a reflexive awareness of the taste-making process and challenge traditional notions of cultural hierarchy.

The 1892 travelogue "A Spanish Music-Hall" stands as Symons's first extensive theoretical statement on the halls. Here Symons alights on the figure of the aficionado, or eager amateur, as shorthand for his role with respect to the entertainment. In his words: "I am *aficionado,* as a Spaniard would say, of music halls."[1] The claim has room to resonate before Symons substantiates it with an evidentiary list of different halls that he both patronizes and studies. The self-designation seems to suggest that Symons understands his devotion to the music hall as genteel, an amateur enthusiasm distinct from the work of the specialist whose emergence was redefining labor practice in the fields of law, medicine, and civic administration at this time.[2]

In point of fact, Symons's authority appears to stem from his having a special field of his choosing largely to himself: the aficionado has no clear collaborators as he moves among London's music halls, records the proceedings, and makes crucial distinctions. Aficionados seem distinguished by their isolated labor, a singularity that could also be seen to complicate their claims to authority, for these savants speak for what most cultured observers define as esoteric passions.

Symons further marginalizes his admiration for music hall by defining it as mere amusement: "And then it is so *amusing*" (my emphasis), he continues, "to contrast the Pavilion with the Trocadero, to compare the Eldorado with La Scala; to distinguish just the difference, on the stage and off, which one is certain to find at Collins' and the Metropolitan, at La Cigale and the Divan Japanois." These may be exceptional claims, but they also underscore the fragile grounds on which the dandy bases his evaluative privilege. The aficionado addresses culture for cultured readers, but seems to speak from the margins.

Yet Arthur Symons achieves something more substantial than a fan letter in "A Spanish Music-Hall." Even if the passionate nature of his commitment to the music hall compromises his claims, the search for critical authority remains central to the essay in instructive ways. The essay strives not only to amuse and provoke, but, in good Kantian fashion, to persuade readers of the rational basis for his appreciation. "To study the individuality of a music hall," he writes, "as one studies a human individuality, that is by no means the least profitable, the least interesting of studies."[3] Symons does not merely announce a passion for the halls, but makes the more provocative claim to have discovered a node linking desire with knowledge.

That an apology for studying the halls can eventually move to Kant-like claims for what constitutes a proper, humanist study suggests the aficionado has ambitions that counter his or her initial rhetorical modesty. I contend that the music hall provoked Symons to a considered rhetoric that challenges our still regnant amateur/expert binary. Aficionados appear to reside on the margins, where they proudly announce their unique autonomy and individuality. Yet once they accept the duty of representing their passions, they assume a more functional role. They address the public in an attempt to serve it. Initially, Symons resists putting the aficionado in the same category as the expert, but he comes to use the figure to remake the expert in a fashion that troubles a strict opposition between amateurs and professionals.

Still, Symons's aficionado likely raises our suspicions, since his or her private pleasures suggest a version of the contemporary, modish, cultural professional. When Symons declares to readers of the prestigious *Fortnightly Review* that a popular culture they may disdain is in point of fact creative, complex, or significant, he indulges in the rhetoric of discovery that Pierre Bourdieu associates with the bad faith practice of the academic professional: "It is a form of dominant chic among intellectuals to say, 'Look at these cartoons,' or some other cultural item, 'do they not display great cultural creativity?' Such a person is saying, 'You don't see that, but I do, and I am the first to see it.' The perception may be valid, but there is an overestimation of the capacity of these new things to change the structure of the distribution of symbolic capital."[4] Bourdieu would most likely dismiss Symons's posturing along with the moves made by later "chic" intellectuals. Yet we can claim with some plausibility that Bourdieu in turn underestimates the complex affective component behind professional activity. For Bourdieu's culpable intellectual is something of a stock character acting in accord with a single, and singularly bad, motive. Bourdieu views the freedom to flout conventional taste as merely a signifier of prestige, in a profession that licenses transgression for members with good standing. A narrow form of self-interest is the only reason Bourdieu can offer to explain why intellectuals might celebrate a common culture.[5]

A discussion of Symons's particular expertise in popular culture also requires a discussion of camp, a sensibility that saturates his critical vocabulary. Symons appears to have learned from the music hall that convention making and rule breaking are closely allied. "Camp" is a handy term for this dialectical, topsy-turvy insight into the process of taste making. Symons brought a camp sensibility to music-hall performance that even his shrewdest readers appear to have missed or ignored.[6]

"A Spanish Music-Hall," his inaugural piece on the music-hall phenomenon, announces the rise of the music-hall expert: at the same time, it serves as a primer on camp pleasures. Music halls, he declares, "amuse me, and I am always grateful to any one or anything that amuses me." In this instance, the aficionado distinguishes between the drama, a "serious art," and the "art of the music hall," which is "admittedly frivolous—the consecration of the frivolous." It is "frivolous" and therefore culturally peripheral. Yet the oxymoron—"the consecration of the frivolous"—remains suggestive: it suggests that frivolity contains enough charisma to reorganize a life. An ethical point lies behind the distinction: given a choice, the aficionado sides with the frivolous, or vulnerable and marginalized. When Symons writes on the music hall, he emphasizes the "love of the unnatural: of artifice and exaggeration" that Susan Sontag defines as camp.[7] Frivolity may be "nothing," yet it has the power to liberate: "And I come for that exquisite sense of the frivolous, that air of Bohemian freedom, that relief from respectability which one gets here, and nowhere more surely than here." The passage hails a "nonsense" that frees us from the coercive demands of the mundane. "A Spanish Music-Hall" does more than proclaim its writer an aficionado and expert: it announces that music hall is an excuse to camp it up.

Camp, a mode of being-in-irony, remains a vital part of our current style repertoire. In a hundred years or more, it has assumed a variety of forms. We can find it in our contemporary modes of consumer hauteur; in self-conscious, assertive fandom; even in media self-understanding and self-promotion ("Nick at Nite's" hyperreal, self-mocking ads turn their programming of sitcom reruns into high concept). Camp also has a venerable tradition in queer fandom, and a generative role in queer identity. If Symons anticipates the cultural studies intellectual and his or her concern with the popular in essays like "A Spanish Music-Hall," he also clears the path for camp experts. His wry distance and appreciation of the social performances that surround the music-hall stage honor camp imperatives: "In a music-hall the audience is a part of the performance. . . . Here we have a tragic comedy in the box yonder, a farce in the third row of the stalls, a scene from a ballet in the promenade. The fascination of these private perform-ances is irresistible; and they are so constantly changing, so full of surprises, so mysterious and so clear."[8]

Since camp also names a sensibility, it is difficult to situate cleanly within a historical frame. However, Andrew Ross provides a useful link between camp and the Victorian intellectual. As Ross observes, Victorian aesthetes re-fused to assume the role of the traditional intellectual, who shored up ruling-class beliefs, and that of the organic intellectual, who represented the people. Instead, this unaligned intellectual promoted values—frivolity, leisure, hedo-nism—that a hegemonic middle class disdained as aristocratic, and therefore obsolete.[9]

Ross correctly suggests that Victorian camp had a desperate, reactionary quality; the camp critic sought to reanimate poses and stances originally de-rived from an aristocratic matrix. In revolt against middle-class standards, Symons often assumed a pose of aristocratic hauteur in matters of culture. Yet this pose of mastery was clearly problematic when applied to popular culture. Cultivating a formal appreciation of practices either neglected or derided in the dominant culture is no sure path to popular success. In Symons's case, we need to balance Ross's claims with Raymond Williams's insight that invoking the residual tokens of a culture can have a destabiliz-ing effect. As often as not, these signs of the past assume a counterhege-monic force: "[A]t certain points," Williams reminds us, "the dominant culture cannot allow too much residual experience and practice outside it-self, at least without risk."[10] It is reductive to read Symons's appreciations of the music hall as simply iterating his critical authority; his camp views more likely ironized the whole business of taste making.

There is another reason for the links between camp and aesthetic expert-ise in Symons's music-hall accounts. Historically, camp taste has smuggled cultural contraband across carefully patrolled borders, often in the plain view of arbiters of taste. Camp legitimizes the distasteful, or the socially ab-ject; it lightens prejudice toward the unconventional. As Mark Booth puts it, camp works "to [annex] and [civilize] areas of delight that have otherwise hardly been explored. It has beaten tracks through jungles of enjoyment and made them accessible."[11] Camp taste, the expert assertions of the aficionado: the idioms overlap because both lay claim to an unstable middle ground of cultural endeavor, beyond the traditional high/low culture binary.

Symons's music-hall accounts reveal his faith that aesthetic hierarchies can be challenged if rendered in the rational idiom of the professional critic. He seems keenly aware of the ability of critical endeavor to legitimate its objects of scrutiny. Symons understood that criticism enabled relations of power, but could also reform them, so that the careful representation of culture forms amounted to an elevation of the "frivolous" and enfranchisement for the marginalized.

The expert's sense of purpose and the search for pleasure: Symons's meditative pieces on popular amusements suggest that disparate cognitive styles met in music-hall appreciation. Indeed, the two music-hall accounts early and late in Symons's music-hall patronage that I focus on, "A Spanish Music-Hall" and the 1896 essay "At the Alhambra," elaborate on the tension between participation and observation that defines critical spectatorship for Symons. He sought to embrace different tastes and represent this charged encounter to his readers. The results are tense and contradictory, but I suspect he believed the messy results unavoidable. The critic has no choice but to enter the fray. Bourdieu's critique of intellectual chic is salutary, but his call for a "redistribution of cultural value" that will put an end to the strict class tracking sustained by aesthetic value systems requires a collective endeavor that includes even the professional intellectual whom Bourdieu suspects.[12]

"A Spanish Music-Hall" and "At the Alhambra" negotiate the tensions between the critic's private taste and public obligation. Both elaborate Symons's central insight into professional behavior: namely, that expert claims need not shut down egalitarian impulse. In "A Spanish Music-Hall," the search for an expert view of the form levels class and gender difference. Outside its preamble, "A Spanish Music-Hall" details how camp both transforms and disciplines the critic. The effort to represent music hall, to speak for himself and others, involves Symons in a dynamic model of expertise humanized by camp views. And in Symons's later essay, "At the Alhambra," camp too gets criticized and recast. The limits of camp, particularly the privilege it accords detachment, provoke Symons to a passionate defense of criticism and theory. He argues for the critic's right to move from experience toward more reflective, and reflexive, views.[13]

Arguing for the right to theorize amounts to an apology for the professional, since, as Bruce Robbins observes, what distinguishes professionals from amateurs is "the necessary possession of theory."[14] The conclusion of "At the Alhambra" suggests that such conceptual rigor is required of the responsible, critical intellectual seeking to both participate in and reflect on culture.[14]

Camp, Race, and Modernity

An immediate problem of context and interpretation posed by "A Spanish Music-Hall" is: why Spain? Put another way: why is the music-hall intellectual translated into Spanish, into the "aficionado"? A postcolonial reading of the essay might provide answers to these questions. First, the desire is ascribed to the dandy to discover something new and different and claim it for his own. The self-styled modern travels to Spain in order to locate primitives who unsettle his identity while in fact establishing it, and securing his credentials as a cultured observer. And, at least in part, Symons's text is amenable to these criticisms. The author in fact lingers on the ease and control of the singers and performers he locates in a small music hall; he wonders exactly how these folks manage to command the nightly attention of the collective gathered at the Alcazar, a Barcelonan music hall.

However, the postcolonial critique of Symons is likely to conclude that Symons in fact believes that the power of these performers resides solely in some putative exotic character, in their inability to rise above local circumstance or essence. And this conclusion is precisely where a hermeneutic of suspicion does Symons a profound disservice. For while "A Spanish Music-Hall" often cagily—campily—begins by asserting that meaning is rooted in the body, it also expands on an alternative explanation for the performances that Symons witnesses. The playful deferral of the final meaning of these performances seems pure camp esprit, blurring the traditional binarisms of nature and culture, mind and body, esteemed in the dominant culture.

"A Spanish Music-Hall" is infused with camp attitudes and laughter; the irony marking Symons's description of the Alcazar signals both his distance from and his extreme empathic proximity to what he surveys. The space of the Alcazar follows the tourist imperative—"the most characteristic place I could find" Symons avers—but the space is no sooner discovered than it is recast.[15] Its hybrid qualities suggest the space has already been inhabited, remodeled to fit camp specifications. Symons's account brings out the in-between, unsettling nature of a space that is neither a café nor a theater, and whose patrons are also its performers. The room, Symons observes, is "just like an ordinary café." The place fills, but "the audience [is] not a distinguished one"; none of the women, Symons notes, "wear hats," and "few of them [assume] an air of too extreme superiority to the waiters."[16] Musicians and performers gather in the café, pass through a stage door, and after their performance return to the crowd from which they have been only momentarily separated or distinguished. The Alcazar is undistinguished enough for the spectator to feel superior to the surroundings, yet the proximity of performer and observer is enough to insinuate and unsettle spectator hubris.

A sketch is performed with "a mise-en-scene of astonishing meagerness."[17] Symons informs us that the puppet show he witnesses is something that he's seen before and better; "the repertoire of these miniature theatres," he notes, "seems limited." He complains that "the songs I heard at the Alcazar Espanol at Barcelona were almost without exception the same that I had heard at the Montagnes Russes at Paris." The blasé account is double-voiced, suggestive of Symons's superiority to, as well as his intense involvement with, what he describes.

This is not to claim there is no evidence on the face of things for a reading of Symons as colonial tourist. He lingers on the "native" dance, which appears to provide the English spectator definitive proof in an uncertain space of his own aplomb, status, and essential remove. Viewing the "Baile Sevillanas," Symons demonstrates a pedant's knowledge of the distinctions between Orientalisms. "Spanish dances," he orates, "have a certain resemblance with the dances of the East."[18] Yet where "the exquisite rhythms of Japanese dancers are produced by the subtle gesture of hands . . . the delicate undulations of the body," the Arab dance, from which, he claims, the Spanish dance derives, "is a dance in which the body sets itself to its own rhythm."

> Spanish dancing, which no doubt derives its Eastern colour from the Moors, is almost equally a dance of the whole body, and its particular characteristic—the action of the hips—is due to a physical peculiarity of the Spaniards, whose spines have a special and unique curve of their own. The walk of Spanish women has a world-wide fame; One meets a Venus Callipyge at every corner; and it is to imitate what in them is real and beautiful that the women of other nations have introduced the hideous mimicry of the "bustle."[19]

The passage seems straightforward, "naturalist" in tone and "scientific." It also seems decidedly uncamp: at its core, there is an affirmation of the freedom of the natural exotic, used in turn to denigrate the fashion world of the European feminine.

And yet: the invocation of the Moors seems designed less to set the dance within a biological frame, or a normative history, than to recognize the dance for what we might call its avant-garde qualities. The "Moors" here, then, are less the "Egyptians" of racial science or Orientalism than the decidedly artificial, kitsch figures that populate Walter Scott fictions (for the generation of Scott's readers after Scott). The homage to the dance celebrated in the passage seems an early move in what would prove a long, elaborate history of camp investment in, and transvaluation of, all things Egyptian and African.[20] In other words, this is less Orientalism than a fantastic camp reorientation of Spain and the Orient. This is translation without tact, performed less to explain the dance than to valorize—or better, to liberate—facts and bodies from the mundane order. Symons's sympathy for Mediterranean culture grants him a distance from conventional Western dance and Englishness that allows him to recognize their relative lack of edge, or "cool."

Symons's account of the dance, therefore, is an homage, not a biology lesson. Still, if Symons "saved" the dance by virtue of his self-consciousness, his account would be of interest but unremarkable. The account might simply attest to the critic's acute and intelligent self-consciousness. What distinguishes the essay is Symons's suggestion that a similar critical remove animates others at the Alcazar and not only the English tourist. He pays fascinated attention to how the dancers utilize space, particularly to how they negotiate the space between the public arena and the performing stage. In Symons's account, the "Baile Sevillanas" is fiery and furiously physical; it evokes a natural, libidinal, heterosexual charge; it reflects the frenetic excess of a natural and uncontrolled sexuality. Yet Symons also insists that excess gives way to the undoubted control of the dancers over their performance and their nature.

If we took Symons's body talk seriously, there would be severe limits placed on the Alcazar's performers; for one thing, stepping out of character would be as impossible as shedding one's history, or one's skin. But in point of fact, the performance of the erotic seems just that: a performance these actors can leave behind. The dance and the song of Senorita Villaclara that follows close upon it are the most libidinously charged events Symons witnesses at the Alcazar. The dance follows a male sexual logic; it grows frenetic, and then climaxes. "The dance grew more exciting, with a sort of lascivious suggestiveness, a morbid, perverse charm, as the women writhed to and fro, now languishingly, now furiously, together and apart."[21] However, after "two encores," Symons adds, "the women went tranquilly back to the corner where they had been drinking with their friends." We are reminded of what

Symons took care to establish as the central fact of the Alcazar's perform-ance: the flimsy, arbitrary divide between the stage and the audience. That these women can change so quickly and seamlessly from frantic bodies to coffee drinkers in a mundane, civil society could be said to reinforce stereo-types about "everyday life" in Spain: this world, Symons might believe, is one in which high passion, fierce desire, and violent turmoil rule. Yet it ap-pears the return to passivity suggests quite the opposite: the performers placidly negotiate different spaces, in control of their performance, able to turn off and on their charisma. Their ability to signify their Spanishness and distance themselves from it, their very mobility, has a ready equivalent only in Symons's own leisurely gaze. The performers, too, are experts who prove their authority by setting it at risk.

The not-so-hidden link between the aficionado and the spectator is un-derscored in Symons's account of the singer. Here, camp provides a way of admitting one's distance and one's attraction, the desire to cross the gulf be-tween the watcher and watched. A "fair complexioned woman, with dark sleepy, wicked eyes, and black hair trailing over her forehead," Villaclara blurs the lines between a European look and something duskier. She per-forms the "Malagueña," a local song that Symons returned to and heard from other "native" voices in his later trip to Seville. Here it is pregnant with a threatening and opaque alterity. "It was a strange, piercing, Moorish chant, sung in a high falsetto voice, in long, acute, trembling phrases—a wail rather than a song—with pauses, as if to gain breath, between." Wail, not song, the "Malagueña" signifies as noise and is marked by a repetition that spells threat:

> A few words seemed to be repeated over and over again, with tremulous,
> inarticulate cries that wavered in time to a regularly beating rhythm.
> The sound was like nothing I have ever heard. It pierced the brain, it
> tortured one with a sort of a delicious spasm. The next song had more
> of a regular melody, though still in this extraordinary strained voice, and
> still with something of a lament in its monotony. I could not understand
> the words, but the woman's gestures left no doubt as to the character of
> the song. It was assertively indecent, but with that curious kind of inde-
> cency—an almost religious solemnity in performer and audience—
> which the Spaniards share with the Eastern races. Another song
> followed, given with the same serious and collected indecency, and re-
> ceived with the same serious and collected attention.[22]

Another exotic voice, a Russian tenor intoning the liturgy, would prompt Roland Barthes to speak of voices that "bear along directly the symbolic, over the intelligible, the expressive," "the materiality of the body speaking its mother tongue."[23] Symons, too, seems to express here what Roland Barthes characterizes as "the impossible account of an individual thrill that I constantly experience in listening to music."[24] It is impossible because the voice signifies a conflicted project: the truth of the singer's body, which belongs to the realm of representation, and, at the same time, a body that somehow exceeds the mediation of the sign. For Symons, the "Malagueña" declares the primacy of the body over ideal notation and idealized truths, including the truths of his own system of representation. For Barthes, and Symons, too, the grain of the voice signifies the real and sidesteps the symbolic. The noise attests to a camp truth, even truism: meaning and significance begin and end with the body. Yet Villaclara is not a folksinger here as much as a virtuoso, a camp diva: the grain of her voice works against the normative codes that the dandy listener believes might otherwise curtail his pleasures. The singer is the critic's full-blooded paradox, a personal aporia, inspiring him to his own impossible account amid the rush of his own blood, the tingle of his own spine.

Symons's account appeals to the body as the final court or repository of meaning. Body talk can body forth any number of essentialisms and serve as a foundation for racism. Isn't the "Malagueña" lodged halfway between nature and culture, more precisely in a zone where the sacral has just emerged out of the primeval, carnal ooze? And doesn't Symons appear to locate Villaclara in an emotional hinterland, in the outback where the passions hold exclusive sway? That the native audience matches Villaclara's familiarity and reserve in the face of dark and sacred passions provides further proof that the locals share a proximate psychic location. We might advance the case for Symons's racism further: the song does not overwhelm the audience, perhaps, because it corresponds to truths of the race that the audience intuits.

All these readings substantiate claims for the colonial dandy: but the case must proceed rather selectively to fully convince. Such an interpretation must pass over the special care that Symons takes to situate Villaclara back in the everyday once her performance is finished. The close of the account, with a bored Villaclara, underscores the performer's control and agency. "When the applause was over, she . . . came back to the table at which she had been sitting, dismally enough, and yawned more desperately than ever."

The ability of performers to cross the gap between native character and the everyday is enormously significant to Symons, and I suspect it is intended as a cue for the reader as well. The forays of the performers from normal life to exalted states and back mark the Alcazar as a transformative space, but also as a contact zone. Symons and these performers seem alike in crafting their attitude and stance in a conscious attempt to meet the world with a stance and an attitude. Symons's own self-conscious spectatorship ends with a love of artifice for its own sake and allows him to extract lucid pleasures from his own internal dis-location. Yet Symons must work to get to the level of sophistication that Villaclara has already achieved, not by birthright, but through labor. There are two forms of displacement on display in the essay, and two modernisms. We are trained to recognize one of the modernisms: the statements of the formalizing imagination of a dandy abroad. There are other moderns beside the dandy expert in Symons's account: the dancers of the "Baile Sevillanas," the audience at the Alcazar—at least when they exhibit their carefully modulated attention to Villaclara—and certainly Villaclara herself. Their performance, and above all their distance from the performance, suggests a kindred dislocation, similar to Symons's critical stance; we might say, following W. T. Lhamon, that they both speak "modernism," one doing so in the vernacular.[25]

Symons equates the experience of modernity with the prevalence of new forms of mass entertainment that blur segregated tastes and social groups; further, he seeks to speak for the modern from vantage points not limited to his own. Yet the expert remains aware that by his reckoning he is not the only modern at the Alcazar, for he is not the only one both alert and off-center. His pleasure and unease are enriched by an encounter with folks who might seem, to Symons and his readers, to be primitive. However, the insight that the "locals" are in fact other moderns is at the core of "A Spanish Music-Hall." Camp distance ends with the recognition of fellow experts. These experts signify their distance from and mastery of national codes and signifiers; they are proficient in a vernacular modernism the dandy comes to esteem.[26]

Camp remains with us as a double sign and gesture; it signifies our appreciation for but internal distance from media texts and artifacts; it also signifies our great, excessive, and disruptive passions. Wherever we attend, or love, what the dominant culture encourages us to devalue, neglect, or disrespect, camp rises as a way out of this double bind. We look, but feel we shouldn't. Or we love what others tell us to despise, and love turns curious and queer. As with any practice coming from the margins, it can be accused of honoring the dominant order in the breach, revising taste agendas without confronting issues of power and inequity. That's not to say that camp lacks a politics or even the aspiration toward a collective; indeed, "A Spanish Music-Hall" suggests some of its egalitarian or legitimating powers. Camp doublespeak permits Symons to legitimate himself, clearly, but brings others into this trail of authorization. Camp channels these different experts together: patrons, Symons the tourist, and Villaclara all enter into the modern from varying positions, wielding different kinds of authority. If expertise tends toward a zero-sum game, with room only for the expert, camp taste draws conditional lines between those who get it and those who don't. In "A Spanish Music-Hall," Camp bridges the gap between experts. The close of the essay hints at this kind of mutual recognition when dancer Isobel Santos receives Symons's especial praise as a "professional."[27]

Dance dominates the night's entertainment at the Alcazar, according to Symons's account; there are not many opportunities for the sing-along that was a staple of English music hall. Singsongs, improvisation, ad-libs that broke down the "fourth wall": these were staples of English music hall. A remarkable essay by Peter Bailey elaborates on how music-hall entertainment fostered a self-conscious, plebeian crowd who claimed certain songs and singers for their own, and whose participation in music-hall interactive space allowed them to style themselves as experts within the popular culture forms they patronized and defined. Plebeian expertise was not just a way of knowing but a mode of assertion in subculture style. The youth who yelled the key words and phrases of the song "Pine-apple Rock," "detonating" its sexual depth charge before a hapless Henry Mayhew, laid bare something Mayhew the social explorer would rather have forgotten: the sexual energy and expertise of London's young lumpen.[28] The music-hall crowd's way of knowing would change from this kind of class warfare to something less precise and certainly less confrontational. Plebeian expertise begins to resemble something closer to subculture "cool" or, conversely, the calmer, more orthodox role of "expert," who "signifies competence beyond the formal demonstration of its particular knowledges" through the sly aside or casual implication of her fellow specialists.[29]

Bailey's arguments bear on my own: he closes with a nod to camp (which he tacitly assumes to be an exclusively queer argot) that recognizes its "obvious affinities with knowingness." I share Bailey's conviction that camp needs inclusion in a map of music-hall taste: certainly it resonates in Symons's account of the Alcazar. However, Symons seems after more than securing an advantage over Villaclara; he also wishes to his record his responsiveness, and his vulnerability, as spectator.

What Symons seizes from Villaclara's performance is her indifference to the "local" song she performs. She holds up better than the aficionado on this score, for he admits her song to "pierce" and "torture" him; Symons is compelled to learn the lesson of composure from Villaclara, not to mention from the Alcazar's regular patrons. Peer pressure—or peer review?—sets Symons back on track. The singer offers the dandy a lesson in cool or composure. Symons's emphasis on the singer's backstage poise insinuates that the aficionado realizes he has much to learn from the vernacular modernist about how to strike a pose or deflect the gaze.

"A Spanish Music-Hall" begins with the singular case of the aficionado yet ends in concert with others. The Alcazar is a meeting ground for a league of modernists in the making, who approach the "modern" experience, of dislocation and anomie, from different locations. The aficionado, who doubled as the conventionally literate subject, begins in curious isolation, soliloquizing; the essay ends with the aficionado's eye cocked on another cultural professional.

"At the Alhambra," Symons's last and fullest meditation on the music hall, compacts, or distills, several visits undertaken over the course of several years to a celebrated, upscale English music hall, Leicester Square's Alhambra, one of the premiere sites for ballet in London before Diaghilev revolutionized, and professionalized, the field. Camp and expertise coexist and work toward surprisingly egalitarian ends in "A Spanish Music-Hall"; but in "At the Alhambra," camp taste and expert claims interrogate each other.

Ballet and the Flight from the Front Row

According to Symons himself, the Alhambra's manager, entrepreneur and impresario John Hollingshead, gave the self-styled aficionado backstage privileges in a scene that has the taste of fantasy; as a reward for loyal patronage, Symons gained access to the "secret world" of music hall and to the corps de ballet.

Wayne Koestenbaum memorably argues that backstage views have an inevitable fantasy structure when they are given textual form: the gaze backstage is about the possibility of celebrity attainment and exposure.[30] It proves to be an inclusive fantasy for Symons as well; he seems eager to act as our proxy in the forbidden areas, in the unknown. In a remarkable 1893 letter to fellow aesthete Herbert Horne, insider privilege becomes shared fantasy and camp misrule. The correspondence initially narrates in fragments the author's relations with two dancers (soon after composing this letter, Symons would become involved with a half-caste dancer named Lydia whom he would thoroughly exoticize, leading to jealous fears that culminated in his nervous collapse). The next scene described occurs in the badlands backstage. A tale of flirtation or high jinks becomes a camp tale of heroic cruising.

> The girls who were not on, you understand, had sought refuge in front, and petticoats and stockings sprawled over all the stalls and lounges. On one of the lounges, by the side of the stalls lay three ladies . . . Rosie Dawn and two others. They were coiled inextricably together, somewhat in the manner of a design by Felicien Rops. I was standing in front of them with great dignity, addressing moral remarks to them, when a fatal remark of Rosie . . . precipitated me . . . upon the too tempting seat, and before I knew it my arms were round her waist, and the group was not less extricably, but *I* was one of the group. Rosie's funny little legs kicked in the air; she squirmed with delight, shrieked with laughter: and I need not say the Alhambra—respectable institution!—trembled to its foundation. What is more essential, our little *ebats* were witnessed by far too many spectators.[31]

The letter freeze-frames an exaggerated camp fantasy, and more: the message to Horne is shot through with the kind of coterie references and search for subversion that announce it as a subculture communiqué. For all the brag and bluster, the chance encounter and seduction of the aficionado both publicizes and stylizes sexual behavior. Intertwined with the myth of the frankly salacious chorister there is a fantasy strut of manliness whose primary function seems to be cementing Symons's bonds to Horne. Following a subculture logic, Symons's brag suggests a complex relation between dissidence and visibility; he shrinks from the gaze, from the "too many spectators" he all but exclaims to attend to his transgressions. For all the theatrical flirting here, these private acts seem a play for the crowd, a fantastic notion of "sex" in the service of an equally spectral "politics." The assumption is that a cross-class alliance will somehow bring the respectable world that denies the encounter tumbling down. Symons and Rosie act up under a watchful gaze, in full view of unmentioned and unseen, but scarifying, authorities. The result is a stylized, ineffectual revolt that nonetheless succeeds in reading heterosexuality against the grain, investing the "romance" with all the energies of the taboo or transgressive.

The above suggests that Symons assumed a highly artificial and contentious stance in his forays into the Alhambra. But it also models a confident spectatorship Symons proved unable to sustain or believe in for long. His Alhambra study begins in these moments of stylized revolt, in large part motivated by a desire to outrage an outside world of "straights." Judging from the essay that Symons produced from the "fieldwork" recorded in this letter to Horne, camp poses inevitably led to specific dissatisfaction with camp itself: for "At the Alhambra" takes up camp poses without the requisite hauteur. The result stretches the term to the utmost.

There is a clear sense of camp limits in Symons's portrait of the "front row" men. Their stance and response to the ballet appear to resemble his own; the sum total of their poses offers a composite of Symons's own response to music-hall ballet at different points in his music-hall patronage. Representing other aficionados, objectifying them, allows Symons to figure his own labor as critic as well as the limits of his labor and perception. The variety of these spectators emerges in Symons's account, but, different as they are, they offer a single lesson to Symons. Camp, it seems, requires a rare equilibrium: otherwise its rare sensitivity turns into solipsism. The emphatic declaration of one's desire, a partisan, minority taste, tends to freeze the object of one's desire and both isolates the observer and coarsens his or her sensibility. The front row men begin with a receptive attitude but end up insensible to the performance unfolding before them.

This much is made clear in the description of the Alhambra's regular patrons, men who must sit in the good seats so that they can be *seen* occupying them.

> The front row of the stalls on a first night, has a character of its own. It is entirely filled by men, and the men who fill it have not come simply from an abstract aesthetic interest in the ballet. They have friends on the other side of the footlights, and their friends on the other side of the footlights will look down . . . to see who are in the front row. . . . A running fire of glances crosses and re-crosses, above the indifferent, accustomed heads of the gentlemen of the orchestra; whom it amuses, none the less to intercept an occasional smile, to trace it home.[32]

The men have a "personal" relation to the ballet because, Symons insinuates, they know the women on the other side. The results of this concourse are, I believe, something that Symons treats with suspicion and from which he strives to distance himself. One wary observer in particular mirrors Symons's own poised aficionado, but not necessarily to anyone's credit.

> On the faces of the men in the front row, what difference in expression! Here is the eager, undisguised enthusiasm of the novice, all eyes, and all eyes on one; here is the wary practised attention of the man who has seen many first nights, and whose scarcely perceptible smile reveals nothing, compromises nobody, rests on all. And there is the shy, self-conscious air of embarrassed absorption, typical of that queer type, the friend who is not a friend of the ballet, who shrinks somewhat painfully into his seat as the dancers advance, retreat, turn, and turn again.[33]

The world of the front row is a homosocial space divided as the performance unfolds; however, these men largely share a common invulnerability to what they perceive. The men are also divided subjects, caught between conflicting impulses or desires: the desire to see and be seen, the wish to have one's desire validated in turn by the returned gaze of the chorister or the stoic, jaded musicians in the pit. These are confident men in all cases but one, the "queer" viewer who is threatened and remains passive before the spectacle, yet they share a common inability to connect to what they see.

Where camp appreciation helped meld performer and spectator in the Alcazar, the front-row men seem insufficiently cosmopolitan, even smug. This is the danger of being an insider, Symons suggests, while no doubt aware that this position is one that he too occupies. The wary dandy, able to fend off the crowd, stays outside the network of gazes that circulate here, but gains little else. And even he participates in the strange, stealth masculine heroics that are staged for public scrutiny but remain invisible to it.

The audience and performers become involved in a reciprocal movement of the gaze, at some points the fetish object, at other points wielding the gaze. As glances are held and exchanged, a third party traces back the gaze to its original onlooker. The women become fixed as objects of exchange in a network of exchange; the men too are caught up in the circulating looks. The knowing glances of the orchestra men save the front-row men from simple narcissism, or love of their kind, and authenticate the legitimate nature of these men's passions. Despite all evidence to the contrary, the passage attests, these men do not love each other but other women. The circle of glances Symons highlights is little more than an ostentatious performance of heterosexuality. In subculture style, self-managing techniques and high artifice assert identity; but while this coterie asserts itself in the established network of gazes that comprises these seating arrangements at the Alhambra, something, Symons suggests, becomes lost: namely the ballet itself.

Symons's essay describes in depth only a single performance of the ballet *Aladdin*. By all accounts, including Symons's own, *Aladdin* unfolded according to a predictable Western logic, equating the "Oriental" with the refulgent and opulent. The ballet's staging honored camp notions of the "Moorish" or exotic, full of genies, princes, carpets, and quick changes.[34] As water circulated in the original Spanish Alhambra, heightened visibility, aided by state-of-the-art lighting, marked the Alhambra ballet. But regardless of circumstances and setting, ballet stands for something more in Symons's account: on its own terms it stands as a veritable engine of difference. The possibility of endless vistas and an infinite combination of actions and gestures demonstrate a fluidity counter to the fixed literary text, a static entity that makes for monotony in Symons's evaluation. This is how Symons puts the comparison: "The difference between seeing a play and seeing a ballet is just the difference between reading a book and looking at a picture. One returns to a picture as one returns to nature, for a delight which, being purely of the senses, never tires, never distresses, never varies."[35]

The description of *Aladdin* that Symons provides is brief but significant; he returns to the phrase "transformation": bodies shift and move, costumes change, light changes, and finally the perceived essence of the dancer shifts.[36] Iterating "transformation" in the account hardly amounts to a stammer; rather the word signals Symons's philosophic intent.[37] For the image of ballet that emerges is of a form that deterritorializes bodies, freeing them from practical demands and constraints, in part through the labor of the dancer but also through the use of various technologies, like lighting and stage sets. The body becomes the body assemblage: ballet as form opens the body to new functions and possibilities. Constructed from the organized movement of bodies, ballet transmits a thousand shifting signs that refuse or beggar description.

These signifiers can be processed or mastered, through a pose of camp hauteur, or read formally in the name of certain aesthetic values, such as "beauty" and "unity"; yet Symons's reading of *Aladdin* insinuates that neither the pose nor the technical language quite captures the shape-shifting he witnesses. Since the ballet does not permit itself to be grasped as a totality, it cannot fully be translated into aesthetic terms that depend on a distanced view of discrete phenomena. With the usual maps useless, Symons discards them and begins a series of arduous labors. He traces instead the palimpsest of his memory, embroidering his "thought-events." Symons returns obsessively to the ballet in the process of being produced. Since the event defies the possibility of a full representation, he intensifies his own labor as observer and makes his work visible.

The ballet's own thematization of flow and change in part explains the loose, meditative form of the essay: part realist catalogue or inventory, part nostalgic reverie. It explains why the aficionado keeps moving and why the sectioned essay nonetheless does not order the experience of the ballet in a clear sequence. We have instead a palimpsest of looks and gazes; actualities blur. When memories are differentiated or actions are delineated, they do so along unpredictable axes. So, for example, section 3 of the essay, with its brief, partial reading of a single ballet, provides reasons why the first two sections work as a formal anatomy of the ballet, focusing on the chorister in her various preparations for a performance. Symons's approach in this section hints that the ballet can be comprehended only if approached crabwise, in a ruminative yet exacting account, sensitive to temporal and spatial contingencies. The endeavor to account for the ballet and the power of this performance initiates a decisive break between Symons and the front-row men, and detaches the writer both from his subculture and from their certitudes.

The initial sections of "At the Alhambra" try to redress the limits of camp; the ballet is removed from distanced view and abstract apprehension. Symons makes an effort to represent himself as the observer in search of the quickened perception, concentrating on the tactile surfaces of people, objects, and activities. The desire to provide a multiple account comprises a critique of his former views and of camp spirit. The men in the front row, earlier versions of Symons, fail to comprehend the ballet because they feign disinterest; they move in advance of the experience and without knowledge of the "thought-events" that comprise the subject at hand. So while camp allows the expert to find company in his labor, camp taste, frozen in a superior pose, requires retooling in the latter essay. It could be concluded that camp generates the need to revise its protocols even if it doesn't seem to provide the means.

The opening of the essay highlights this movement away from fellow patrons who are not unqualified but less inclined to represent the ballet. These sections prove elliptical, a veritable seafarer's tale with the attendant digression. Symons pushes off in the essay away from safe harbor among peers in order to access a new territory and, finally, a broader public. "At the Alhambra I can never sit anywhere but in the front row of the stalls," he asserts, but in point of fact the aficionado does not occupy that position generally in the course of the essay.[38] We move with Symons in front of the Alhambra, backstage, side stage, back to the front row, focused on the product of the ballet, which seems to have emerged with delicate care from its hazardous process. Throughout, the essay underscores the expert's own sense of displacement; the recollection of the ballet from a tantalizing, panoptic view of the ballet, collected "from the road in front" where "a brilliant crowd" is captured "drawn up in the last pose," becomes subsumed under other memories, other prospects.

These opening moves reenact the observation of the ballet and leave the questions posed by the performance unresolved. The cogito recognizes things and gets in the details, moving among spaces while invoking and imagining other sights and spaces, prone to illusion and self-deception. "In the general way I prefer to see my illusions clearly, recognizing them as illusions, and yet, to my own perverse and decadent way of thinking, losing none of their charm."[39] This may seem camp presumption, but the underlying passivity suggests that Symons has abandoned his pretensions to mastery and thus avoided the errors of his peers. In sharp contrast, Symons inhabits a nomadic view of the ballet; by doubling as subject and object of his own reveries, the critic is accordingly deterritorialized.

The result, then, resembles a phenomenological account of music-hall space, faithful to the quirks and quiddities of the surfaces of things, confident about the truths of perception grasped by the cogito but never fully committed to recuperating and restoring the thinking subject as transcendent. The intense concentration on detail transforms fact into luminous practice. The recording work that Symons undertakes puts him at risk; he loses the full privileges that inhere in being merely a spectator. He strives to occupy a border zone that disorients the observer: "To watch the ballet from the wings is to lose all sense of proportion, all knowledge of the piece as a whole. . . . It is almost to be in the performance oneself, and yet passive, a spectator."[40] The statement recaps the search for a liminal perspective that opens the essay.

Symons's search for moments of exchange and transaction at the Alhambra bolsters the main aim of the essay: to escape from conventional states of mind and being. For example, in this scene the choristers and their chronicler merge in the act of exchanging news and trading gossip: "I had the honour to know a good many ladies of the ballet, and there was little news, of public and private interest, to be communicated and discussed. Thus I gathered that no one knew anything about the plot of the ballet which was being rehearsed, and that many were uncertain whether it was their fate to be a boy or a girl; that this one was to be a juggler, though she knew not how to juggle."[41] The clap of the stage manager that halts the discussion affects not only the workers but the visitor who records the conversation. Both labor within the same space, admittedly at different kinds of work and under quite different conditions: the pose of mutuality is compelling enough to conceal these differences. Interfering with one worker, the chorister is represented as impinging on another worker, the writer. The exchanges portrayed work to unravel the pose of privileged spectator.

I take these anecdotes for performatives, fashioned in order to level the playing field that includes both performers and recorder. Symons's search to occupy a multitude of stances as participant/observer, including hazardous ones, exhausts the self as it catalogues events. The aficionado becomes etherealized, stretched thin in the rush to describe and interpret. Perception clarifies little, but produces a doubling of wishes and impulses. Contradictory desires find articulation in a pell-mell rush of clauses: "I do not for a minute really want to believe in what I see before me; to believe that those wigs are hair; that greasepaint a blush; any more than I want really to believe that the actor whom I have just been shaking hands with has turned into a real live emperor since I left him."[42] The statement seems simple enough: Symons wants to be a pliant subject before artifice, yet never in fact to lose sight of reality. Yet this is the sort of claim that suggests a fundamental schism in the speaking subject. Which self speaks here, after all, and expresses the desire to be hoodwinked? Which is the self that remains intact? Can an observer maintain his hold on certainty at the same time as he announces his will to be fooled? Once the aficionado leaves behind his front-row cadre, he enters on a truly perilous journey, with the lonely cogito purposely relinquishing its reference points. The aficionado's stance, his body, is left carrying the burden of his unsettling, compromising gazes.

The process is all the more confounding because it seems fully volitional. The systematic derangement of the senses and the turn to method suggest the seriousness with which the aficionado takes his newfound authority. I say "newfound," since the assumed rigor that confers Symons's authority foregrounds the problem of professionalism. The expert begins and ends by assuming a series of exacting responsibilities: this transformation is made all the more surprising by the fact that the journey first followed the itinerary and protocols of camp. The backstage that Symons painted in lurid hues in his letter to Horne becomes a space that denies fantasy in "At the Alhambra"; crowded with workers, it is now painted as a space of lowered expectations, or of sublimated desires. "I have never been disappointed, as so many are disappointed, by what there is to be seen in that debatable land 'behind the scenes.' For one thing, I never expected to find an Arabian Nights' Entertainment of delightful splendour and delightful wickedness, and so I was never chagrined at not finding it. The *coulisses* of the Alhambra are in themselves, quite prosaic."[43]

It would go too far to say that this new patience with limits constitutes a total break with camp, for these claims resemble camp judgment in their fealty to material fact. It is not fully crucial that my reader recognize the aficionado's careful accommodation to the world of ballet, or take Symons's approach to surfaces for the "pure presupposition-less description" of the world Edmund Husserl advocated.[44] Yet I would contend that the dialectical tendency of the essay is inescapable to any careful reader. So is the essay's philosophical conclusion: namely, that camp, apprehended rightly, produces its conceptual other, an unhappy consciousness determined to represent the object of scrutiny with care, from a position outside of events that in fact blurs the line between surfaces and depths. The flight from camp stirs Symons to provide a fuller account of his inscription within an already given system. I take these gestures to be an embrace of theory broadly defined: they constitute Symons's openness and signify his accountability to other potential observers.

It is precisely this newly achieved accountability that underscores how Symons's theoretical work follows a professional logic. And this logic is by no means inherently exclusive or elitist. For in this instance methodological or theoretical awareness is a way of clarifying one's assumptions, and a justification of one's labor before a skeptical public that the recorder internalizes. The move to theory, in this instance, resonates as more than a power grab. Theorizing ensures that intellectuals spin their wheels in public, which makes a spectacle of the intellectual, but also suggests a vulnerability that keeps the practitioner honest.

The aficionado who faces the ballet finds himself in a critical situation in every sense of the word; he grasps for first principles, for the rationale of his labor is now a mystery requiring investigation. This act of self-analysis is conducted in public. All of the above signify labor that honors professional decorum. Symons's interpretive work sets him outside the protocols of his coterie; it is this movement, and the exacting labor that accompanies it, that designates the work as professional activity. For his essay on the Alhambra records Symons's resistance to sights and sounds that normally provoke his desire; the essay accrues authority as a record of resistance. Of course, if the expert effect arises solely from the ascetic impulse, it may be read and discounted as a power play. However, if Symons attempts to accrue authority by shaping experience into a method, the same self-conscious endeavor, he intimates, makes and keeps his labor subject to review. The move away from the coterie and the reliance on an esoteric language and system also constitute an escape from a sanctioned common sense; the new position leaves Symons vulnerable, and therefore accountable, to a host of others.

Symons's search for method allows him a space for self-interrogation; there are discernible results of this effort to achieve critical distance. If on occasion the effort to represent the ballet brings Symons's sexism to the fore, the acceptance of his collective responsibility counters the writer's tendency toward misogyny. The expert function checks some of Symons's fantasies in regard to the choristers, since, in his new role of aficionado, he is no longer at liberty to imagine that their labor or the production requires his presence as spectator. While Symons's biography suggests the poet rarely achieved the distance from his exoticist or misogynist tendencies that might have allowed their revision, the Alhambra, for a time, was a space conducive to changing one's attitudes and stances. While Symons claims the painted women of dress rehearsal combine "the sorceries and entanglements of what is most deliberately enticing in her sex . . . with all that is most subtle, and least like nature, in her power to charm," this banality is soon challenged by the "realist" tableaux of working women that he produces.[45] These tableaux are offered as highly artificial myths that counter the prior cliché, for they provide in compact form a more complex, irreducible image of the chorister. In one of the most striking of the tableaux, "charm" is less present than riddling details; it's a picture of women in the workplace, at rest and labor, that insists on a fractious quiddity:

> The walking ladies are in their walking dresses; and it is with the oddest effect of contrast that they mingle, marching sedately, in their hats and cloaks with these skipping figures in the undress of the dancing-school.

Those not wanted cluster together at the sides, sitting on any available seats and benches, or squatting on the floor; or they make a dash to the dressing room upstairs or to the canteen downstairs. One industrious lady has brought her knitting. It is stowed away for safety in some unused nook of the piano, which is rattling away by my side. . . . Another has brought wool work, which is almost getting too big to bring; several have brought books; the works of Miss Braddon, penny novelettes, and yes, some one has actually brought the "Story of an African Farm."[46]

The women at work and play here constitute an irreducible community; this is less charm or seduction than a mock epic of labor and leisure, caught in process. In the cliché about painted ladies, Symons naturalizes the dancers: they are there simply for his view. However, the effect of this tableau is an evacuation of the observer of the scene; at the very least, the "facts" here are not of the sort that could be put in the service of the spectator.

"At the Alhambra" is also remarkable for its final, and striking, refusal of the usual divide that separates professional claims from public service. I am tempted to use Symons's keyword, "transformation," to explain how expert talk becomes a public account; yet, faithful to the essay's dialectical turn, I have a less mystical explanation for the essay's shift in tone. The pursuit of expertise contains within it an orientation to social responsibility. The exchange that concludes the essay implies that the expert is now more responsive to others, having sundered his or her ties to "nature," whether in the form of a customary spectatorship or the "second nature" of the coterie.

And then there is another reason why one can see a ballet fifty times, a reason which is not in the least an aesthetic one, but on the contrary very human. I once took a well-known writer, who is one of the most remarkable women of our time, to see a ballet. She had never seen one, and I was delighted with her intense absorption in what was passing before her eyes. At last I said something about the beauty of a certain line of dancers, some effect of colour and order. She turned on me a half-laughing face: "But it is the *people* I am looking at," she said, "not the artistic effect!" Since then I have had the courage to admit that with me too it is the people, and not only the artistic effect, that I like to look at.[47]

The exchange between Symons and a "remarkable" woman writer—Olive Schreiner, on a visit to London before relocating in South Africa—seems a powerful indictment of the professional impulse. One cannot fully stand apart or above or beyond the ballet, Schreiner signals in her level view of the event. Symons trots out the language of aesthetics—of form and line—half-heartedly (the only time he does so in the essay), only to be gainsaid by Schreiner, the "naive" reader. In particular their brief closing dialogue counters the expert claim to stand apart or above or beyond.

The exchange would seem to unravel the expert role Symons has spent the essay exploring and in part inhabiting. There might be a part of the reader likely to cheer Schreiner on as she bravely deflates, and humanizes, critical pretension. Yet it seems that Schreiner's naïveté gets certain things about the Alhambra, and about criticism, wrong. As Symons establishes in the essay, the move away from "naive" experience is as risky or compromising a position as that of the amateur. His rejoinder to Schreiner is not given in this account; it resides, however, in the fact that the exchange itself resonates. Schreiner's criticism of critical pretension has expressive power in large part because the ground has been cleared by the expert's prior, exploratory labor. The figure of the amateur and the chastened aficionado are set in clear relief because the background has been delineated by the theorist's labor. The exchange between Schreiner and Symons serves, then, as an apology *for* theory; the prior analytic work means that their dialogue can proceed candidly. Schreiner's naïveté stands as a rebuke to the critic's excessive complexity, yet it is only by virtue of these elaborate maneuvers that expertise can become something public that can receive Schreiner's critique. In Symons's account, expertise is not the transcendent alternative to Schreiner's common sense, but its exacting, and modest, supplement.

"At the Alhambra" resonates for us due to its salutary reminder that two categories we often conceptualize in sharp relief, expertise and service, exist in mutual relation. For experts become linked—in "A Spanish Music-Hall" and "At the Alhambra" both—with images of exchange, their expressive energies enacted in dialogue. Ultimately the passage from camp to expertise, a move that leaves neither category intact, underscores the capacity of the aficionado role. The expert emerges, not as a unique observer and legislator, but as a figure whose function seems to include the reallocation of the cultural capital the critic produces and accumulates. Symons's music-hall essays endeavor, in an incomplete fashion that reflects the imperfect but worldly work of the professional, to open the work of the critic to public deliberation.

3

Spies and Experts

LAURA ORMISTON CHANT AMONG LATE-
VICTORIAN PROFESSIONALS

It remains a scholarly commonplace to assert that Victorian sexuality was dominated by an ever-expanding regulation of the body. Even when the rise of the New Woman challenged gender norms, or clandestine but assertive communities organized around shared homosexual identity, the discursive impact of these movements—according to current scholarly consensus—inevitably culminated in, or capitulated to, dominant social forces of discipline and subjugation. This agrees with a concept of subjectivity as the product of cultural encoding rather than an expression of a deep interiority existing prior to structuring principles. This paradigm also insists that subject formation entails subjugation. Jeffrey Weeks details how Victorian preoccupations with strict moral hygiene worked in tandem with increasing state regulation. A bureaucracy of civil servants concerned with monitoring sexuality generated, in Weeks's words, "intricate methods of administration and management, . . . a flowering of moral anxieties, medical, hygienic, legal and welfarist interventions" with an elitist valence.[1] In a pathbreaking study, Peter Stallybrass and Allon White treat the police and Hudson's Soap as nearly interchangeable agents of "discipline, surveillance, purity"; their work begins with, and expands on, Michel Foucault's suggestion that social and institutional practices found their typical nineteenth-century expression in the "privileged form [of] Bentham's Panopticon," with subjects haplessly policing their own behavior in response to unseen observation.[2] Judith Walkowitz's landmark study *Prostitution and Victorian Society* (1980) traces a surprising historical bloc of antistatists, advocates of personal rights, police officials, and medical authorities, all agreed on the need to regulate the sexual mores of the poor. Even after the repeal of the Contagious Diseases Act (1886), the police enforced the segregation of prostitutes from the laboring poor and promoted "a more rigid standard of sexual stability."[3] Walkowitz ominously concludes that, after the Criminal Law Amendment (1885), "the police had become the missionaries of the new age."[4] For all these scholars—and they are among the very best in the field—the desire to survey and regulate "impurities" in the social body, whether the nonlaboring poor, the "fallen woman," or unpleasant sewer odors, clearly structures the terrain of mid- and late-Victorian culture and discourse.

The controversy that surrounded Laura Ormiston Chant's 1894 attempt to close the promenade of the Empire music hall because of prostitution troubles this scholarly consensus.[5] Born in 1848, Chant taught, nursed, and worked as assistant manager of a private asylum before she became a noted public lecturer on woman's suffrage, temperance, and Liberal politics. She was a member of the National Society of Woman's Suffrage, a merger of various suffrage groups in 1896. Like many women involved in the struggle for suffrage, Chant had ties to social purity movements concerned with regulating sexual behavior. These ties were a legacy of the coalition politics that united moral reformers, medical professionals, and women's rights activists in the aftermath of the Criminal Law Amendment.[6] Chant also had formal ties with the National Vigilance Association, although her efforts to close the Empire promenade were initiated independently from the organization.

That Chant and her cohorts who testified before the London County Council protesting the Empire, the women dubbed by the press "Prudes on

Parade," faced such virulent public disapproval remains something to be explained. Surely a purity reformer's attempt to bring a disreputable space to order would have been amenable to late-Victorian common sense; Richard Dellamora, for example, details how sexual scandal often called forth professionals, activists, and administrators who agreed on the necessity of monitoring and regulating sexual conduct.[7] Controversies in the daily press; the commentary of literary intellectuals like Arthur Symons, George Bernard Shaw, and Clement Scott; the attempt of young Winston Churchill to tear down the partition blocking the Empire's promenade: all suggest the failure of Chant's protest to reassert sexual decorum.[8]

The disparity between our retrospective certainties in regard to fin-de-siècle sexual conduct and the libertarian opposition to Chant suggests we have greatly oversimplified late-Victorian gender politics. The controversy stirred by Laura Chant's attempt to close the Empire promenade quickly shifted from a civic dispute to a crisis over authority. In the words of the London social and theatrical review of current events, the *Sketch,* the Empire battle was "a great fight . . . waged with a war of words, a battery of correspondence, and a skirmish of sketches."[9] We cannot fully grasp Chant's reception by the public unless we consider the difficulties female philanthropists faced when they sought municipal reform.

The libertarian ideology that fueled the opposition to Chant also held that vice was best controlled if regulated, and that regulation required that vice remain visible; the worse crimes were those that somehow remained unseen. In the case of the Empire, male professionals dictated that prostitution was best managed under visual surveillance. Business at the promenade was naturalized by many in the literati as obeying a fully respectable aesthetic of order and comely elegance; vice had never looked so good, or so stylish. The calm poise of the aesthete observer further managed, and accordingly neutralized, the dangers of proximate vice and moral misconduct. To the pure Victorian male, all things, it seemed, were pure. The reading public that avidly followed the Empire licensing dispute was alarmed by Chant's challenge to this disciplinary regime; worse, they feared that, as charity worker, Chant had access to dangerous, "hidden" knowledge concerning prostitutes and the men who consorted with them. The conflict over the Empire quickly became a struggle over credentials: over who had the requisite expertise to utter authoritative statements on sexuality, prostitution, and public amusement. The late-Victorian discourse of regulation and surveillance was, in certain respects, a closed shop, in the hands of almost exclusively male professionals.[10] The resistance Laura Ormiston Chant encountered from a coalition of journalists, literary intellectuals, and "freeborn Englishmen" results from her entry into the gender-exclusive terrain of Victorian professionalism.

Of course, the growth of the professions, including a new trained, managerial class, rendered it increasingly difficult to reach consensus on such matters as the "nature" of popular amusements. Among so many aspiring experts, who had the proper training to lay claim to the arbitration of propriety and taste? In 1890, four years before Chant's complaint against the Empire, the London County Council newly instituted the Theatres and Music Halls Committee, with attendant inspectors licensed to impose fines on music halls for violations of public morality and safety regulations. Constantly criticized by music-hall managers, these new inspectors were criticized for their lack of training, for their supposed amateur status.[11] J. L. Graydon, manager of the Middlesex Music Hall, suggested these inspectors received too little pay to work impartially: "[I]t is inconceivable that men earning 10s 6d a night . . . could possibly be either competent or have any uniformity of opinion apart from the obvious temptations to blackmail or bribery."[12] Throughout the 1890s, municipal workers, proprietors, and audiences disputed over who was best qualified to supervise popular amusement; relations between music-hall proprietors and municipal authorities remained especially tense.[13] In testifying before the London County Council, Chant knew she had assumed authority on contested terrain. "I am quite aware," she testified, "what a serious charge [I bring] & also what a serious matter it is to state that a woman is a prostitute, but I think before I have finished you will see I have good grounds for making the accusation."[14] Her complaint against the Empire could be vindicated only if she demonstrated expertise on a variety of subjects: popular amusement, prostitution, and civic reform. In the end, Chant's perceived threat to the Victorian formation of surveillance discredited her, and her vocation as philanthropist received the stigmatized label of amateur labor. Instead of holding her as an expert, the public branded her a "spy," a meddler too self-interested to receive recognition as a professional.

The Empire Controversy

The Empire Theatre of Varieties opened in 1887 under the management of George Edwardes; prominent in the music hall was a large promenade contiguous to the lounge. A London County Council report estimated that nearly five hundred people, in a hall that normally seated around thirteen hundred, routinely utilized the promenade.[15] On October 19, 1894, Laura Ormiston Chant and six others brought a complaint against the Empire music hall before the London County Council, claiming "that the place at night is the habitual resort of prostitutes in pursuit of their traffic, and that portions of the entertainment are most objectionable."[16] Statistics concerning Victorian prostitution notoriously vary, but there is evidence to suggest that Chant's protest against the Empire promenade was not a simple moral panic. Tracy Davis characterizes the location of the Empire in Leicester Square as a crucial site in what she dubs the "geography of sex"; she notes the hall's proximity to "thoroughfares of vice," claiming it was "a vital nexus of West End immorality involving prostitutes, alcohol, variety theaters, supper clubs, dancing halls, and gambling houses."[17] In 1892, noted music-hall proprietor John Hollingshead claimed that "the sweepings of Hamburg and the low Countries own the right of way" in Leicester Square and designated the area as "the prowling place of demireps."[18] Accounts of the Empire that acknowledge the conspicuous presence of prostitutes in the promenade are too numerous to mention.[19] Even a staunch defender of the Empire confessed, "Every sane man knew vice had been prominent in the Empire promenade."[20] When the London County Council temporarily closed the promenade in support of Chant's suit, casual reports remarked on the migration of prostitutes to the nearby Alhambra variety theater. The *Sketch* editorialist noted sardonically, "The daughters of the Empire seem to have been lifted up like the prince in the 'Arabian Nights Tales,' and dumped down in the Alhambra," adding that, "you could not move an inch without hearing remarks about the humour, one might say absurdity, of such a state of things."[21] Although celebrated literati Arthur Symons and Theodore Wratislaw defended the Empire against Chant, both depicted erotic encounters at the Empire in their poetry that belied the accounts they presented to the public in the media.[22] The testimony of literary intellectuals disdained any empirical account of the halls in favor of an aestheticized view of music hall as pure spectacle.

Chant received complaints in early 1894 from an anonymous pair of American men about being "continuously accosted by night and solicited by women" when they visited the Empire—at Chant's own recommendation—to hear Albert Chevalier's coster songs.[23] Chant, accompanied by fellow suffragette Lady Henry Somerset, conducted her own investigation of the Empire. She made five visits to the music hall and paid more care to her physical appearance, clothing, and deportment on each occasion. She claimed that "on the first three occasions of her visits she dressed quietly, and on the fourth and fifth occasions gaily—that was to say she wore her prettiest evening dress in order that she might get her information more readily."[24]

Chant's effort to change her wardrobe to suit her surroundings must be read as a practical concession to the space, based on an interpretation of the Empire as a homosocial space and a launch pad for predatory males. Accounts of the Empire uniformly assert that the music hall was, in J. B. Booth's words, "as it justly boasted, an Englishmen's club."[25] A prime example of the "variety theater" entertainment that was to replace more plebian halls, the Empire was a gathering place for men of leisure. The music hall permitted the divergent vectors of English colonial expansion to converge in a privileged site of leisure suggested by the hall's very name. As Booth puts it: "Britishers prospecting in the Klondyke, shooting in jungles, tea planting in Ceylon, wherever they gathered in cities in Africa, Asia and America would bid one another goodbye with a 'See you at Empire one day when we're back in town.'"[26] The Empire offered entertainment at a price slightly prohibitive for working-class patrons, although working-class audiences—besides the estimated three thousand workers directly affected by the hall's closing— were among the most vociferous critics of Chant's reform.[27] The Empire, however, remained within the buying power of middle-class men who desired to mingle with an upper-class demimonde of men and women.[28]

Theater historian W. Macqueen-Pope stresses the importance of the Empire promenade to men in search of illicit "attractions": "And the attraction was the cream of the frail beauties of the town. . . . middle-class young men rejoiced to pay their five shillings . . . to have the daring and Bohemian thrill of a night spent in the Empire Promenade, to watch the wicked ladies as they floated—none of them seemed to walk—to and fro; wonderful women wonderfully dressed, . . . overwhelmingly alluring in their known 'naughtiness.'"[29] Stage entertainment gained the extra frisson of sexual possibility because of the Empire's promenade. The women that Macqueen-Pope surveys here are canny entrepreneurs "quick in summing up anyone who meant real business." Young men could boast of an encounter with them "for weeks and be regarded by their less reckless companions as desperate blades." Macqueen-Pope covers a utopian world of male desire with the patina of nostalgia, admiring the opportunity the hall offered middle-class men to solicit women from a sophisticated demimonde who, even if they rebuffed the rake, nonetheless augmented his cultural capital. The

Empire, in this reading, allowed men the chance to interact with "dangerous women" with "very little harm." Martha Vicinus observes that the music-hall environment appealed to male audiences chiefly for these possibilities: "[F]or many young men, cooped up in an all-male office or warehouse all day, close proximity of women, drink and smoke made a giddy and inviting atmosphere of women that broke down their natural shyness and difficulty in speaking to women of their own class."[30] Macqueen-Pope frames the Empire as a masculine haunt, and his "wicked women" primarily signify aristocratic leisure. The same point is underscored in another account of the hall, in which Macqueen-Pope asserts, "[T]he women of the Empire were the aristocrats of their 'profession.'"[31] The Empire offered aspiring middle-class men everything that Vicinus observes and more: an imaginative participation in aristocratic culture.[32]

Chant's testimony before the London County Council challenged the voyeurism represented by these accounts. She displayed the relatively new mobility of middle-class women in urban spaces, exerting control over the Empire as an authoritative observer. In a mock flourish, George Bernard Shaw praised Chant's individual skill and considerable acumen in presenting her case: "You can't have a better example of democracy than the Empire case. Here is Mrs. Chant . . . and she flounces in and floors the whole County Council."[33] Shaw's praise of a strong individual, however, overlooks the respect for collectivist politics, of a sort that Shaw championed, that clearly motivated Chant's protest. Further, her argumentative skill was not a fluke of temperament or a sign of entrepreneurial zeal. She looked to the London County Council, as many municipal reformers of the period did, because she wished to intervene in the council's general project, the administration and rationalization of a sprawling urban culture. Like many of her peers in reform work, and Shaw himself, Chant looked anxiously to the state, or centralized authority, to execute genuine, far-reaching reforms.[34] As self-declared expert, Chant attempted in her testimony before the council to influence fellow administrators, to share a specialist's knowledge with the municipal body regulating London's cultural life.

Chant's deposition features a careful reading of the Empire promenade, locating signs of the "fallen woman" and carefully organizing them into a narrative. In her words:

> There were very few persons in the promenade, but bye-and-bye, after
> nine o'clock, I noticed to my astonishment, numbers of young women

> coming alone, most of them very much painted, and all of them more
> or less gaudily dressed, numbers of young and attractive women. . . .
> [T]hey did not come into the stalls, but either sat on the lounge sofas or
> walked up and down the promenade or took up a position at the top of
> the stairs and watched particularly and eagerly who came out of the
> stalls and walked up and down the promenade. I noticed that in no case
> were any of these young women accompanied by gentlemen or accom-
> panied by others, except of their own type.[35]

Amid these suspicious-looking women, Chant noticed "a middle-aged
woman" who introduced a gentleman to the young women. She testified, "I
noticed she came and tapped him on the shoulder and I followed them. She
introduced him to two very pretty girls who were seated on a lounge . . . one
of them very much painted and beautifully dressed. . . . I saw this man and
this girl go off together, . . . an attendant call a hansom for them."[36] Afraid
that quietly dressed women draw attention to themselves in the Empire (she
overheard an Empire attendant warning one woman, "You had better mind
how you behave to-night as there are strangers round"), Chant secured her
evidence by taking up a "disguise." As an outsider in male spaces, Chant
dressed "gaudily" enough to "pass" at the Empire. Much was made during
the hearings of the unintended effects of this subterfuge, since Chant herself
was approached in an inappropriate manner by a gentleman when she assumed her "disguise."[37]

Chant relied more on her prior work as a philanthropist than on her
undercover work on the promenade to bolster her account. She repeatedly
referred the council to inside knowledge she had gathered from her informants among the women on the promenade.[38] These women disclosed to
Chant that the Empire "is the best place where they can carry on their trade.
One and another have told me they could not do without the Empire."[39] She
reiterated that "[t]heir testimony, absolutely frankly and candidly given, is
that they go to the Empire . . . because they . . . can make better bargains."
Chant's observation of women in the Empire promenade was not her sole
encounter with "fallen" women; she regularly brought prostitutes into her
home whom she met on the streets and who expressed the desire to reform.[40]

Chant's testimony, and her rescue work on the streets, suggested what
many men feared: that female philanthropists "saw more than men."[41] As
Martha Vicinus describes, female philanthropists exerted considerable au-

thority in urban spaces: "[T]he streets of the slums, away from upper-class men's eyes were theirs."[42] Chant's deposition places the hidden work of the prostitute on display, and this ability underwrites a tremendous authority for her among members of her own class. While no booster for Chant, the editor of *To-Day* grudgingly respected her achieved expertise in regard to the social consequences of the trade in women: "[A]fter twenty-years of rescue work, Mrs. Chant knows more of these things than many men about town, and when she spoke of them, there was the ring of truth and sincerity in every word."[43]

Chant's charity work played into the dominant cultural imperative for members of the middle class to understand and control the sexuality of working-class women. Elizabeth Langland, following the work of Nancy Armstrong, Catherine Hall, and Leonore Davidoff, stresses that middle-class women "cooperated and participated with men in achieving middle-class control though the management of the lower class."[44] Insofar as Chant made the secret machinations of prostitution more visible, and thereby subject to control, her work supported a social discipline enforced by panoptic surveillance. However, Chant's interviews with the urban poor put an emphasis on unmediated contact, not specular control. Rather than the impersonal regulation of bodies, Chant sought to achieve interpersonal relation with the urban poor, and, moreover, did so in a manner that disturbed exclusive male control of London streets.[45] Her venture into the promenade on behalf of "the women of England"[46] disturbed the otherwise orderly production of male spectatorship, and the male gaze, at the Empire.

Chant's Protest

That Chant did not play a simple version of the surveillance game is best demonstrated by her later responses to the press, in which she targeted wealthy men as the real malefactors at the Empire. Answering the charge that closing the Empire promenade would force prostitutes into nearby streets, Chant asserted: "It is not the streets which furnish those who fill the ranks of fallen women. The poor souls fall at such places as the Empire and then parade the streets afterwards."[47] In a paternalist fashion, Chant denied agency to working-class women; she did so, however, for tactical reasons. Casting the working woman as victim made the Empire's more affluent patrons seem the true and conscious culprits in the social scenario of vice.[48]

Chant responded to the complaint that "the working men of England object to have their amusements interfered with" by asserting that "working
men . . . will admit that the Empire is no resort of theirs."⁴⁹ This proved a
presumptuous claim about the Empire's audience, but it followed from her
general suspicion of the Empire's more privileged habitués. Chant's class antagonism was likely informed by the "Maiden Tribute" controversy, the *Pall
Mall Gazette's* inflammatory account of aristocratic men seducing young
working-class girls. Her reading of the Empire is similarly shaped by melodramatic convention, with images of innocent women victimized by jaded,
remorseless, and essentially villainous rakes. Melodrama explained the Empire for Chant, although the prostitutes on the promenade represented a relatively affluent, and minority, demimonde.⁵⁰

The reformer was resolute in finding class enemies against her reform
even after the Empire controversy faded; she detected the conspiracy of
moneyed men behind the newly elected, more centrist, London County
Council. The new council, she charged, undermined the previous council's
reform of the Empire because its election had been made possible "mainly
by the money of two classes, the wealthy profligates and the gamblers."⁵¹
Chant's reading of hidden interests protecting the promenade sets the Empire's responsible bourgeois and working-class patrons against an irresponsi-
ble bourgeois ("gamblers") and the degenerate rich. As the controversy played
out, the Empire's middle-class patrons increasingly disregarded Chant's insistence that social divisions and inequity characterized the hall's audience; they
remained comfortable participating, even if only vicariously, in the "spectacular" diversions offered by the pleasure palace.

Laura Chant's belief in a conspiracy of privilege affects her reading of
performance at the Empire. Her major criticism of the Empire centers, not
on the ballet or the "living pictures" performed there, but on the affluent
men who consumed the entertainments. She charges that jaded sensation-
seekers sustained the "degrading" conventions of ballet costume. In her
words, "[Ballet dancers] cannot see that the absence of clothing is an offense
against their own self-respect. They do not realize that they are exhibited well-
nigh undressed for the men in the lounge, men so used up they could not be
attracted by a less sensational form of spectacle."⁵² Chant anticipates later critics of fin-de-siècle ballet such as Amy Koritz, who details how English ballet
privileged the male gaze, and Tracy Davis, who examines how ballet dancing
was specially coded as libidinal fare for men.⁵³ Chant's pronouncements care-

fully exempt the working class from the male gaze, imagining these patrons as her potential allies against the "men in the lounge."

Chant's deposition against the Empire amounted to savvy self-promotion, if not calculated self-fashioning; she deftly presented herself as a daring, yet trustworthy, social investigator. She pointedly demonstrated her credentials and her power over complicated areas of experience. Her rhetoric transforms the space of the promenade into a special field, of which she claims to possess esoteric knowledge that proves the competence of her judgment and acumen, as well as her charisma. The testimony amounts to a compelling account of the deep, mysterious forces behind the confusing blur of appearances that constituted the spectacle of the promenade. Chant's description of the space competed with other powerful, purposely competitive narratives for popular approval. Throughout October 1894, London newspapers circulated the dispute over how to read the Empire, with the *Daily Telegraph* offering its editorial and letter pages to the controversy for almost the entire month.[54] Numerous letter writers marshaled English common sense against the perceived extremity and moral fervor of Chant's reform. H. A. Bulley's letter in the *Pall Mall Gazette* (the *Gazette's* own editorial quoted Cromwell against the puritanism of the social purity workers) dubs the purity crusade "an organized Puritan conspiracy against the liberties of the English people."[55] A correspondent in the *London Times,* signed "Freedom," complains about female government: "If the Vigilance Society is to rule over our lives, and constitute itself an English *Police des Moeurs,* by all means let us have an Anti-Vigilance Society with the Englishman's motto, '*Imperium et Libertas.'"*[56] As a writer to the *Pall Mall Gazette* inquires, "Shall Britons be 'slaves' now more than they used to be?"[57]

Meanwhile the literati began to weigh in on the issue. In the *Saturday Review,* Arthur Symons defended "human nature" against legal fetters: "Does any one really think that by closing, not the Empire alone, but every music hall in London, there will be a single virtuous man the more? . . . In the normal man and woman there are certain instincts, which demand satisfaction, and which if merely restrained and fettered by law, are certain by some means or other to find that satisfaction."[58] The poet's assertive claim for the cause of the Empire also demonstrates the ease with which an Enlightenment-style demand for the respect of individual rights could underwrite male license. Arguments that stressed the inviolability of "human nature" had the practical effect of keeping the Empire available for heterosexual cruising. Such libertarian sentiment does not invalidate the argument that Foucauldian discipline dominated fin-de-siècle sexuality; laissez-faire attitudes toward personal morality could nonetheless coexist with an anxious administration of private conduct.

Libertarian support for the maintenance of the Empire coexisted with a taste for the beautiful and orderly. In like manner, the disciplinary gaze is indistinguishable from the male gaze. The Empire offered itself as a ready solution to the "social evil" of prostitution, and accounts like Symons's eagerly took up this cause. With the London County Council's official regulation of the Empire, the music hall appeared to offer what many medical professionals hoped for: the toleration of prostitution alongside its regulation, with a minimum of government involvement.[59] As a licensed music hall with respectable patrons, the Empire allowed the "safe" harboring of prostitutes, providing a space where prostitution received moderate supervision, rather than overt repression or strict regulation. Chant's protest competed with a political rhetoric that found overt intervention in sexuality "unBritish." Instead the liberties of the true-born English gentleman, secured by historical precedent against meddling women, were maintained. Chant challenged a consensus that believed prostitution was neutralized if it remained a spectacle.

Chant's efforts to establish herself as an authority on prostitution also struck at popular conceptions concerning professional character. A debate over what constituted a true professional emerged in the press, elicited by a consideration of the Empire case. A correspondent in the *Daily Telegraph* asserts that Chant and "those who push themselves forward into the administration of licensing laws" had "no sort of special training as a guarantee either of judicial fairness or practical experience."[60] T. Werle offers a specific complaint regarding Chant's qualifications: "Will someone be good enough to tell me why it is that the evidence of any volunteer as to the propriety of the entertainments given should be, as seems to be the case, accepted?"[61] Werle asserts that "when a witness represents some performance not to be in good taste one may well enquire why a mere self-accredited *arbiter elegantiarum* is allowed to be regarded as a judge in the matter"; he presumes that Chant's arguments can be trumped by the making of a credential check. The *Daily Telegraph's* editorial raises questions about the relative competence of female philanthropists compared to already recognized authorities. The editors insist, "The public has a perfect right to ask the question—of what use are the paid inspectors whom the County Council employ to see that music halls and other haunts of recreation are well conducted if their reports are to be thrown on one side?"[62] The editorial laments that "amateurs 'on the prowl' are listened to while the professional advisors of the Council are thrown overboard." The *Telegraph* attempts to naturalize what Chris Waters observes was a contested point in licensing disputes throughout the decade: the expertise of the "paid inspectors" of the London County Council (LCC). Here, the supposed disinterest of these men is evoked as a counter to Chant's own claims of authority.

The same *Telegraph* editorial expresses the fear that social surveillance by the "prudes" would lead, by way of the slippery slope, to the ritualized misrule of "petticoat government." Hence, the next, inevitable victims of Chant's vigilante efforts would be those authorized to keep public assemblies controlled and orderly, the police. As the next object of Chant's surveillance, the police might be hindered from performing their sworn duty to uphold civic order. In the editorialist's opinion, "It requires very real courage for an officer to come forward and boldly speak up for the hall when he knows that the spies of Vigilance Societies may, in consequence, constantly dog his footsteps in the hope of detecting him in the great unpardonable sin for which Scotland-yard extends no pardon—drinking on duty." The *Daily Telegraph* intimates that the effort to close the Empire promenade would lead to unseemly reversals, with capable authorities now under the watch of amateurs. Let men police men, the editorial suggests. Fears of such inversions, of unmanned policemen and masculinized "prudes," elicited letters like that of "An Ex-Police Inspector," who argues that professional police should take jurisdiction of the Empire away from the LCC.[63]

The struggle between "unauthorized" reformers and recognized authorities, between those who made dubious attempts to pry into sexual practice and those truly capable of monitoring indecorous behavior, was highlighted in the many caricatures spawned by the controversy.[64] One of the most notable, *Punch's* sketch "Mrs. Prowlina Pry.—'I Hope I Don't Intrude'" represents Laura Chant as an unwanted intrusion in a safe, regulated space under the guard of legitimate authorities (figure 3).[65] The caricature depicts Chant discouraged—or barred—from entering a place where masculine pleasures are already sought and found in relative tranquility. The Empire is portrayed as guarded by a stout, prepossessing doorman, who protects the men (and a solitary woman, whose bare ankle the viewer can make out behind and between the legs of the doorman) from Chant. The caricature portrays Chant as an unattractive spinster, in keeping with the iconographic war against public women that extended, as Lisa Tickner documents in *The Spectacle of Women*, to the representation of Edwardian suffragettes.[66] The doorman's hand draws attention to a sign reminding the onlooker that "3000 employes will be thrown out of work if this theatre is closed by the L.C.C."; however, the sketch itself makes an implicit statement. The Empire is depicted as a bright, well-lit place in contrast to the dark, dour, "fancy dress" clothing of Chant. Further, the doorman's visible alarm at Chant's attempted entry suggests she is an unwanted presence, an interloper among the Empire's regular clientele. The caricature brings home to *Punch's* readers the ludicrous nature of Chant's claims to be a disinterested investigator; this woman with drab hat and opera glasses could never spy on the Empire without drawing attention to herself. The shape of the feather on Chant's hat further visually underscores the dubious nature of Chant's police action. Above all, the sketch accumulates visual cues that "demonstrate" the incapacity of women, particularly this woman, to escape the confines of their biology. This "grotesque" figure can never hope to attain the universal vantage point occupied by true professionals. Since it is nearly impossible to locate a visual repertoire that might figure a woman as a professional, the sketch artist takes an easy way out. He presents her instead as a ludicrous meddler, attempting to bring order to an already decorous space. In the process, the sketch transforms the Empire into something of a paradox: a naturally tidy space that is at the same time a testament to the virtuous principles of sage management.

The sketch also turns the debate into a matter of taste and a concern for the body. The two concepts are conjoined, of course, in aesthetic discourse. As Terry Eagleton observes in *The Ideology of the Aesthetic*, aesthetic discourse coordinates a long history of scattered philosophic reflection in the West on relations between mind and body. Aesthetics formalizes the correspondence between sense impressions, the stuff of lived particulars, and the supposed universal truths arrived at through reasoning.[67] Aestheticism privileges an ideal, harmonious relation between the mind and the body of absolute equanimity and order. Such premises authorize certain body images to stand in for the beautiful, as agreed-on images of order and decorum. These body images exude good taste. The *Punch* caricature broadcasts the message that Chant has the wrong body for her line of work. The reformer's "rude" and unshapely body disqualifies her from assuming the role of taste arbiter, or spokesperson for ethics and decorum. The caricature sanctions skepticism toward the compatibility of reason, or taste, with inappropriate female figures. The humor depends on a hard kernel of ideology: the dog-

Figure 3. Spies are not experts: "Mrs. Prowlina Pry." From *Punch*, October 27, 1894, 194.

matic belief that dubious bodies produce questionable taste. With the wrong figure, and gender, Chant lacks the requisite authority to undertake a police action on behalf of the state; rude figures are relegated to vigilante status. They lack the required credentials for social work.

The sketch, then, visualizes an argument about Chant's sensibility, or lack of it; her body conclusively proves her failed taste. This failure occurs not solely on account of her gender, but remains tied to corporeal matters. Chant's assumed lack of fashion sense and the features of her face: both disrupt the achieved harmony, and awesome self-sufficiency, of the Empire. Amid the measured elegance of these surrounding, the reformer is visualized as a drastic contrast. *Punch* comes dangerously close to suggesting that only the beautiful can be reasonable and thus contribute to a discourse about the commonweal, and that only the attractive have good taste.

The accompanying poem, "Mrs. Prowlina Pry," suggests the hazards of careless meddling by aesthetic misfits in civic matters; "Reformers must not act like gutter-boys / Who rake up mud, stir each malodorous puddle," *Punch* warns.[68] The verse also emphasizes the dangers of emptying "vice" from a properly regulated space into areas where it can spread unmolested. Reformers grub around a safe haven "[u]ntil the foul infection loads the gale, / And pestilence stalks boldly in the high-way." The lampoon instills a fear of unregulated prostitution: "What if, free, / They [prostitutes] carry foul contagion through a nation?" The poem threatens contagion, associating Chant's reform with the assertiveness of the New Woman: "Petticoat-government, PROWLINA PRY, / Of this peculiar sort will scarcely suit us." The poem displaces anxieties about Chant's reform into a general aversion toward women who exert improper authority.

Above all, *Punch's* caricature suggests the Empire is an area already under expert control. "Another Englishman" makes the confident claim in the *Telegraph* that the Empire, as an "intelligent and liberal provider of innocent recreation for the metropolitan public," is "so admirably conducted as to be a model of what such establishments should be."[69] Praise for the Empire takes a decidedly Foucauldian tone in a *Daily Telegraph* editorial, which lauds "the acumen with which the commissioners of the Empire and cognate places of entertainment 'spot' or detect women who are likely to be troublesome in public."[70] Another *Telegraph* editorial extols the Empire for its "efficient control and supervision" of indecorous behavior.[71] *The Music Hall and Theatre Review* claims that the Empire was "under the closest control and the strictest surveillance of the authorities."[72] Such statements echo Michel Foucault's assertion that in the disciplinary society "visibility is a trap."[73] Allowing prostitution in a well-regulated space is preferable to placing it out of sight, in urban areas where contagion spreads unchecked.

In practice, closing the promenade would mean the women of the Empire would no longer be contained within a specific space or visual field. The imagined escape of the demimonde from surveillance elicited some very anxious commentary. "The suppression of the promenade," the *Telegraph* warns, will create a "howling wilderness of brazen-face soliciting women and male profligates of every grade, and ere long we may have to hear of nightly police raids on illicit dens of vice rivaling the depravity of the old night-houses of the West-end"—referring to haunts such as the Coal Hole, patronized by aristocratic "rakes" in the 1850s.[74] Fears were raised of an unholy and destabilizing alliance among bold women; there was also anxiety about the promiscuous mingling of men of "every grade." "What is the pollution of the three-shilling promenade compared to the omnipresent microbe of depraved sexuality in Piccadilly," the *Sketch* wonders.[75] The *Lancet* asks, "Is it the least likely to suppress the 'strange woman' to turn her from all popular places of amusement and relegate her to the streets?"[76] Would she not, the paper warns, "be found more frequently and dangerously in the way there [in the streets] than elsewhere?" Suppressing the Empire would transfer vice from a safe zone of surveillance into spaces beyond police control, stretching regulatory apparatus beyond their effective bounds.

The dispute over the Empire encouraged patrons to construct their own private ethnographies to counter Chant's informants at the promenade. In one of the most intriguing reactions to the controversy, "A Londoner" turned to the authority of the prostitute herself. "A Londoner's" correspondence to the *Telegraph* utilizes an interview with a prostitute to uncover the real story of the Empire. The writer goes to considerable length to verify the authenticity of the account, and displays the anxiety over authorization that Chant's protest provoked:

> As a guarantee of my good faith, I enclose my card, and I offer you my positive assurance that I have only set down, as nearly as possible from notes taken immediately after our talk, the views she herself expressed, with much intelligences, and in moderate but forcible terms. She said, in effect—and I might almost say in the precise language I am recording— the following; and she added that if the managers of the Empire cared to produce her as a witness, she would report before any body of officials all that she stated to me.[77]

The account begins with the assertion, "I am a freeborn Englishwoman, and I claim the right to live what life I please so long as I behave myself." Such claims take their place alongside the assertions of individual liberty that proved a focal point in the Empire dispute. This "Englishwoman" declares that individual liberty has priority over "any social reformer, in petticoats, in trousers, or in divided skirt." The congruence between the laissez-faire individualism of the "freeborn Englishwoman" and her chronicler should urge a reader's caution: if "A Londoner's" interview enables a voice from the margins, the anonymous prostitute uses the opportunity to speak on patriarchy's behalf.

Contrary to Chant's depiction of the Empire, the interview presents the promenade as a zone of female autonomy. While Chant staged the Empire promenade as a melodrama—with virtue despoiled by callous rakes—"A Londoner's" account cajoles its male readership. The "Englishwoman" he interviews asserts her moral superiority over female philanthropists, boasting: "I don't go about peeping and prying after nastiness and feed my imagination on foul stuff. . . . I should like to ask the lady who pretends to have seen such a lot—and yet she is so innocent!—how she knows that the ladies she saw in that place were there for the purpose of meeting gentlemen." Again, the accusations focus on the concept of expertise, or the lack of it: Chant is charged with reading the Empire badly while pretending to "see" a great deal. "Englishwoman" alleges that Chant makes the obvious mistake of the amateur: she cannot rend the veil of appearance and make genuine distinctions between professionals with status and a lower-class labor force. Chant is criticized for being unable to recognize the telling differences between "the common street-walkers who make Piccadilly circus hideous" and the Empire prostitute: a difference that matters, it seems, to middle-class men. Chant's lack of discrimination weakens her reading of the Empire and, by implication, her interpretation of other civic assemblies. The ability to recognize these distinctions authorizes "Englishwoman" at Chant's expense. Logically, she concludes, "I am a better judge of what is going on in the world than Mrs. Ormiston Chant."

Finally, the "interview" reveals its genuine purpose: to impugn Chant's motivation as reformer. As the Englishwoman testifies, "[I]t is my belief that Mrs. Ormiston Chant and all the rest of the women who display such wonderful curiosity as to our kind of life are acting only like spies, and would give the world to know what the men really say to us." "Englishwoman" *really* knows what Chant can only vainly desire to discover about the real world of men. Her greater proximity to men indicates her greater access to knowledge and prestige. The account of "Englishwoman" is intended to leave the lingering suspicion that mere power hunger lurks behind all of Chant's claims of expertise in regard to the promenade. In turn, "Englishwoman" engages in a power struggle with Chant over the relative access of both women to social power, believed to reside largely in the knowledge of men and male society.

"A Londoner's" account discloses the hidden fears raised by female philanthropists. "Englishwoman" denies that Chant knew male secrets, but many feared that Chant had gained this illicit knowledge from her reform work. Other women were anxious to separate themselves from female philanthropists, whom they alleged to be in thrall to the will to power. One correspondent declares, "I have found 'women' my cruelest, most memorable persecutors, and always under the guise of the desire to purify society and root out evil."[78] The writer stresses the unrelenting nature of female surveillance, with remorseless moralists undoing a husband's generosity. The correspondent equates this disciplinary action with Chant's attack on the Empire:

> When sixteen I fell into the hands of a scoundrel who lured me into a bigamous marriage. Too late I discovered my betrayal. Eventually a professional man, of good social standing, knowing my history, made me his wife. I thought my wretched past was obliterated. . . . [A]ll went well with us until, in an evil hour, I encountered a woman, personally a stranger to me, but by whom, however, I was recognized. This highly respectable, conscientious lady, whom I had never injured in the least, held it her duty to "unmask" me, and to put a stop to the "contamination" of my presence in society.

The correspondent details the painful separation of husband and wife caused by "respectable" women. Like the writer's nemesis, female philanthropists manipulate secret knowledge to their own advantage. Victorian surveillance worked on the principle that vision produced social knowledge; Chant dangerously works with what usually goes unseen. The results are "petticoat government" gone amok.

Both "A Londoner's" interview and the autobiographical account above attack the work of women "spies." The image of the female spy was a convenient counter to, and apparently a more accommodating image than, that of the female professional. In this rhetoric, the female spy is not in thrall to the higher authority of the state; rather, she stands as a cautionary case of unrestrained self-assertion. While the new professional is, as Burton Bledstein notes, believed to do more than "exclusively pursue a self interest," the spy represents expertise tied to anarchic self-regard.[79] In other words, the spy signifies an expertise sundered from any consideration of ethical means or the social good.

The spy also combines the pursuit of self-interest with an unattractive ignorance of her deepest desires. Constructing Chant as a spy spells out a public misconception of the philanthropist and reformer, especially the female social worker. Since it was commonly believed that women reformers could not approach their work without self-interest, it was not difficult to add to the charge and allege that their services were motivated by an unconscious will to power. The spy seemed to figure the real "desire" of the aspiring woman expert. It is a small leap from these suspicions to the direct allegation that female philanthropists were solely motivated by power hunger. Jerome K. Jerome's editorial in *To-Day* takes special aim at the "evil thinking and evil-speaking meddlers" who have "grown like evil mushrooms in our midst":

> Lately a case was brought to my notice in which a poor and most respectable girl, utterly alone in London and working hard for her living, was deliberately hunted down from house to house by one of these wretched societies. That she could live by herself and be respectable they would not believe. They practically threatened every respectable landlady who gave her shelter, till at last they drove her to hide herself in a neighborhood where lodging-house keepers were less nervous of their reputations.[80]

These complaints about ruthless reformers reveal fear of the power that the reformer was believed to exert, an alarm over the "new breed of governing and guiding women" who wielded control over London and its environs.[81] Indeed, Jerome charges that female "spies" now dominate the city, complaining that charity workers "for years past . . . have practically had the ruling of society."

The charge of spying not only imputed venal motives to the reformers, but masked a deeper fear that they had already attained considerable power over men in late-Victorian London. It was more soothing for male elites to believe that Chant and the reformers were women on the prowl than to believe that they exerted power in the city, or that they provided real services for the city's indigent women. "I have been to the Empire many times," states a *Telegraph* correspondent, and the entertainment "does not shock the average Englishman half so much as the spectacle of this elderly woman dressed in 'her prettiest frock' vainly endeavoring to be 'accosted.'"[82] At a public meeting at the Prince of Wales Theater to protest the LCC's decision to close the promenade, a music-hall manager charged that the witnesses against the Empire were indecent: "one of the women said she went to the Empire three times quietly dressed, and was not accosted [laughter]—and hence she went again, gaily dressed and was, as she alleged, then accosted. Probably the fact was so conspicuous that she was chaffed [Loud Laughter]."[83] Such derisive laughter narrowed the distance between Chant and the women at the promenade; it reminded readers that both prostitutes and the middle-class expert strove to solicit the care and trust of the public. The jest assumes a structural resemblance between these various "professionals."

The *Sketch* editorialist maintains the same ideological project, erasing the difference between Chant and the women in whom she took a professional interest. Women such as Chant, the *Sketch* claims, "who stand up in public and say what these women have been saying," are already "indecent in the true sense of the word."[84] The Empire, the editorial writer wryly notes, must indeed be wicked if it holds men "who shall dare to accost gaily dressed Mrs. Chant out alone at night, even if her dress and her position shall seem to invite solicitation." The *Sketch* recognizes little difference between Chant's reform work and the prostitute's vocation, as far as the police are concerned. As the editorialist points out, "if Chant behaved in Paris as she says she has behaved in London she might have risked being taken in charge by a *sergent-de-ville.*"

Professionals and the State

The Empire controversy circulated in correspondence columns, a forum that, as John Stokes observes, was widely considered as the "ideal structure for democratic debate."[85] Chant's protest created instant authorities on popular amusement, the Empire, and prostitution even as these readers inveighed against supposed experts and authorities. Yet the controversy revealed a fear of democracy as well. The newspaper and periodical debate over the Empire suggests that the public looked primarily to "real" professionals—sometimes the police, sometimes the LCC inspectors, occasionally the Empire's managers—to maintain order. And, while we traditionally think of experts as shutting off access to specialized knowledge, Chant's maligned expertise was closely tied to democratic possibilities. Contrary to charges that she concealed dangerous secrets or dubious motives, Chant made "hidden" knowledge irrevocably public. Her efforts to publicize the "social evil" threatened elite control of these issues.

Considering the social effects of Chant's protest, *To-Day*'s Jerome K. Jerome recalls the example of "Mr. Stead's famous 'Maiden Tribute' articles":

these exposés of vice began as "perfectly legitimate pieces of work" but became dangerous when they fell into the wrong hands, that is, when they reached the general public.[86] "The Truth that is excellent food for thoughtful men and women may be as harmful to the young and weak as brandy and beefsteaks would be to babes," Jerome observes; when Stead's accounts were "greedily devoured by shopboys and schoolgirls, they did incalculable mischief." Likewise, Chant wrested the debate over the promenade from "thoughtful" men and women and placed the matter in untrained hands. "I do not care to see the details of the social evil," Jerome complains, "presented in an attractive guise in the pages of a newspaper that can be bought for a penny." Jerome reminds us of the dangers experts could present to the dominant order when they attracted publicity, acting as conduits for the spread of unauthorized knowledge. Jerome is alarmed by the possibility of achieved democracy, with an entire populace in the know. Through the engines of the press, Chant threatened to provide the public with access to "details" about a "social evil" that they could not be trusted to process.

The responses to Chant reveal an apprehension over the very real power Chant wielded as reformer, a power not limited to visual power or the panoptical apparatus of the promenade. Chant was an intruder in male spaces who was believed to know too much; her field of expertise was too dangerous to permit her to be generally recognized by a male elite as an expert. Her maintained ties to dissent presented another obstacle to her recognition within the managerial class she aspired to join, for the members of this class were increasingly trained to respect secular protocols of knowledge. In contrast, Chant countered the scientific fatalism that dominated the opinion of medical professionals on prostitution, which claimed that it might be regulated, but not eradicated. She assigned a determinate point of origin, and blame, to men for the perpetuation of the "social evil." Her modes of social investigation—assuming a disguise, personal contact with prostitutes— seemed mistaken or counterproductive to a segment of the managerial class, and unseemly assertions of feminine power to others.[87]

Still, we might be able to reconstruct with some fairness what Chant hoped to achieve with her investigation of the Empire, even if her proposed reforms were never actualized. In "State and Society," Stuart Hall and Bill Schwarz elaborate on the increasing tendency of state policy to turn to the regulation of culture and amusement in the years between 1880 and 1920, and delineate mass culture and civility as the conceptual products of statist power. As Chris Waters details, the late Victorians witnessed a fateful marriage between mass culture and state organization; theirs was "an era in which the state and the municipality [intervened] more directly in the field of popular culture than had hitherto been the case."[88] Chant took the London County Council's initial decision to close the promenade not as a personal victory but as a momentous public event, similar to "the signing of the Magna Charta [sic] for public amusement."[89] Her dramatic appeals before the still novel, and often feared, LCC suggest her understanding of the Empire battle as her contribution to a new interventionist state and the "modern" administration of culture in the metropolis.

Chant suggested that the demeanor of Empire manager George Edwardes when she cross-examined him during the LCC's hearings demonstrated the progressive tenor of the times. "In former days," she reminded the press, "if a woman had got up to cross-examine a man upon such matters ribald laughter and indecent suggestion would have been hurled at her."[90] Edwardes's behavior suggested that millennial change—or at least major civic reform—was close at hand. Against these apocalyptic expectations, the total abolition of the trade in women seemed possible, even foretold by historical precedent. In Chant's words, this abolition would not be "more Quixotic than the actions of those who agitated for the abolition of the slave trade." It should be remembered that Chant was a Congregationalist and a pioneer advocate of a woman's right to speak from the pulpit.[91] Her claims here again reveal her occasional discomfort with an increasingly secular discourse of management. They also suggest her personal distance from an administrative or disciplinary apparatus geared toward the management of souls rather than their cure. Her millennial fervor proclaims her confidence that reform, management, and dissent were closely allied. While the new managerial class was often trained within dissenting traditions, and circulated their message through the printed and pedagogic organs of dissent, many new reforms were separating the exercise of managerial power from Christian practice.[92]

A large component of Chant's protest was the achievement of a secular brand of recognition, the enhancement of her cultural capital within a broader social network. Cultural capital, as elaborated in Pierre Bourdieu's careful anatomy, exists in a variety of forms. In Beverly Skeggs's useful gloss, such capital exists in "the objectified state, in the form of cultural goods; and in the institutionalized state, resulting in such things as educational qualifications."[93] Yet, as Skeggs adds, all forms of capital—economic, social, cultural, and symbolic—require public recognition if they are to profit their owner. In her words, "Legitimation is the key mechanism in the conversion to power. Cultural capital has to be legitimated before it can have symbolic power." A fierce, protective discourse of partisanship, exemplified in one mode by the true-born Englishman, and in another by the aesthete, denied Chant's claims to legitimacy. Partisan discourse became hegemonic, a species of common sense that now incorporates a strain of hedonistic consumerism.

This is not to say that Chant's desire to attain symbolic capital, inherent in her desire to be recognized as an expert, situates her within the more culpable middle-class project of attaining full hegemony over subaltern groups. Chant refused to conceptualize her expertise according to a traditional logic, in which experts speak from above to the lowly crowd below. She spoke for the popular in a relatively tolerant and generous manner. Chant believed in the role of mass culture within a renovated civic life. This aspect of her public pronouncements was often overlooked, and sometimes derided, by the media. However, in a lengthy interview conducted by the largely critical *Pall Mall Gazette*, Chant has much to say about the functionality of mass culture for the reformed society. "I stand, perhaps, rather apart in this from my colleagues, for I am passionately fond of dancing, and exceptionally fond of acting, and I look upon dramatic representation both as an amusement and as an education. I regard it as being the great power of the future. It is because I want that power on our side, and not against us, that I am so anxious to safeguard the stage against impurity."[94] Chant speaks of the popular and also seeks to represent it. Like her imagined peers on the London County Council, she hoped to foster "a more interventionist strategy with regards to the nation's culture life."[95] This optimistic progressivism was gainsaid by Chant's failure to close the Empire promenade once conservatives were elected to the LCC; nevertheless, her concern to elaborate on the service element within professional culture complicates a simple explanation or unmasking of her activities.

In spite of Chant's presumptuous attitudes toward working-class men and women, her attempt to gain a measure of "feminine" control over homosocial spaces clearly deserved a more complex response than the monochrome derision and opprobrium it in fact received. Her bid to shut down the public display of vice, which entailed augmenting the power of a centralized state to intervene in cultural life, was a provocative effort to refigure London's "geography of sex." Chant's fortunes in the media, at the hands of the circulating press, indicate that she failed in the articulation of her reform to the forces of consumer and professional culture with which she identified. It appears that a largely vocal male consensus in the press, rather than Chant's "regressive" politics, was the primary reason that her attempts to articulate her reform to these forces failed.[96]

Professional culture, as well as Chant, lost in the public debate. As Bruce Robbins reminds us, "professionalism need not be a zero-sum game in which professional knowledge establishes its authority only by eliminating the knowledge and authority of someone else."[97] The victory of Chant's opponents ensured that a simplistic notion of professionals became consensual, resulting in an impoverishment of our public culture, then and now, since professionals remain largely misunderstood and roundly disparaged. For many male observers and most music hall connoisseurs, it seemed clear that recognition for Chant required a disavowal of their own authority: as men, fans, citizens, and experts. It was a sacrifice most men were unwilling to make. Chant's opponents treated the dispute over the Empire as a kind of zero-sum contest for authority and expertise.

It is certainly time to extricate Chant from these simplified images. Reading her protest as another species of Victorian discipline overlooks a crucial point: that an apparently normative, moralist appeal to public reform failed to take with the general public, especially with a vocal segment of the Victorian managerial class. Chant's attempts to speak on the public's behalf worked within existing systems of social hierarchy. The result was a compromised endeavor that will not please those social critics who prefer that critique occur at a safe, antiseptic remove from power.[98] To simplify Chant's motivations in the Empire affair compounds the injuries done to her a century ago, when she publicized her claims to be a professional.[99]

Aesthetic Professionals

Why is the "Prude on the Prowl" like a poor art critic?
Because she objects to the pictures that are well-limbed.

The jibe is from the *Music Hall and Theatre Review*;[100] the punning conflation of "limbed" with "limned" looks at Lady Somerset's public efforts to censor the Living Pictures (live models re-creating high art tableaux) at the Palace Theatre of Varieties, just as Laura Chant worked to strip the Empire of its license. The joke tells us a great deal as to how the temperance reformer was figured in media controversy. The urban professional was figured a puritan; by definition, puritans are unable to think in sophisticated terms about art, or appreciate art for its own sake, outside reference to a rigid, strictly defined moral code. Chant's dissent against class and gender privilege was framed as a tasteless endeavor, a violation of the aesthetic decorum respected by the polite middle class and the aristocracy. The opposition was marked by an entente between two class factions that otherwise existed in tense relation during the period, but who fell in together as natural allies on this occasion, sharing a common desire to protect masculine prerogative. The alliance between upper-middle-class and aristocratic patrons of music hall was based on the shared predilection to preserve the privileges of flaneur-style mobility for male citizenry of the metropolis.

In contrast, Chant belonged to a group of nascent state intellectuals and progressives who were reconfiguring the public sphere, hoping for a more efficient administration of metropolitan life, guided and transformed by the work of trained and certified experts. Like Chant, these other experts had proved themselves in the maelstrom of the city; they knew the city's ills and ailments, and worked at projects for the large-scale renovation and renewal of urban life. Chant believed that music hall at its best produced "rational amusement" for the improvement or solace of the masses. Yet this tenet of faith was maintained by Chant with a generosity not shared by a large segment of public opinion within the managerial sector.[101] Ironically, in comparison with many of this class, Chant, the so-called sanctimonious puritan, evinced considerable faith in the possibilities of mass culture to improve the public. She suggested that the theatrical arts and music hall had the capacity to uplift, as much as the museum or municipal art gallery, the primary choices of the managerial class for productive technologies of cultural enhancement.

Chant's desire to be recognized as an expert on mass culture may appear to be so much middle-class aggrandizement, or to correspond with an elitist narrative of expertise. Yet she entertained a fluid conception of the public she represented, and framed her postulates about popular taste in an attractively tentative fashion. Unlike many of her colleagues in the temperance and suffrage movements, Chant often took pains to emphasize in her public pronouncements the relative autonomy of art and amusement from a heavy-handed moralism. The woman designated by the print media as the "Puritan on the Prowl" spoke in favor of art, but often divorced the experience of art and pleasure from the exclusive idiom of taste that governed the discourse of the professional spokespersons for belles lettres. Chant issued

provocative statements such as this during the height of the Empire controversy, according to the press: "No doubt some of the entertainments thus
provided [by the halls] might be vulgar, but she had no more fit to quarrel
with a vulgar entertainment than with a vulgar bonnet."[102] Possibly the most
controversial aspect of Chant's protest against Victorian gentlemen was her
ability to occupy a class-specific taste idiom, while at the same time refusing
to police aesthetic hierarchy. The reformer did not appear to be honor bound
to reform or combat public "vulgarity."

In marked contrast, aesthetic professionals, such as Arthur Symons, routinely relied on a construction of the fully autonomous, well-regulated, and
properly aesthetic space in order to counter Chant's intervention. The Empire as an aesthetic artifact had more authority than meddling reformers,
and was above the social fray. It also existed outside a potential feminist critique. Chant endeavored to avoid associating training with exclusive power,
the representation of popular taste with a compulsory tutelage of the public. In contrast, aesthete defenders of the Empire often worked unabashedly
to authorize their amoral views of prostitution as common sense and just
public policy. For example, Arthur Symons's correspondence to the *Pall
Mall Gazette* finds the poet assuming the role of cultural expert to defeat
Chant's own claims to know the popular. He takes especial aim at the reformer's professed knowledge of aesthetic values. In Symons's estimation,
Chant made the mistake of a novice viewer before a complex, nuanced experience; she imposed a moral prejudice on a space and practice that required
proper perspective, attainable through careful training and self-imposed discipline. Despite the modest disclaimer that the poet/critic provides, that he
cannot pretend to know "all about the music hall of every continent,"
Symons claims to have well researched the issue at hand. "I have made special study of music-hall entertainment, and visited music-hall in Paris and
throughout France, in Belgium, in Germany, in Italy and in Spain, and I can
only say that, in my opinion, the Empire is, as a place of entertainment, the
most genuinely artistic and the most absolutely unobjectionable that I know
in any country."[103] This confident, expansive declaration positions the cosmopolitan aesthete against the more provincial, and therefore less discerning, views of the visiting prude. The aesthete speaks in the capacity of the
self-appointed, self-authorized music-hall inspector whose work entitles him
to speak for the form from a universal viewpoint. Symons, the music-hall
professional, demonstrates his authority through ready recourse to his vast
knowledge of the subject matter of music hall. Professional rhetoric is linked

with a position on the relative autonomy of the aesthetic. A well-regulated space is a "genuinely artistic" one, and therefore beyond the criticism of untrained interlopers.

Symons's letter to the *Pall Mall Gazette* moves the Empire debate further from the "presence or absence of 'loose women'" in the promenade toward the more specialized topic of aesthetics, which the poet can address with a confident, and convincing, authority. Cultivating the Empire as an aesthetic concern means breaching with a conservative moralism, often associated with conservative views in cultural matters. Aestheticism is made to serve the ends of liberalism and an accordingly "progressive" position on the issue of prostitution. "By closing the promenade you take from the Empire, which is a music hall, its privileges as a music hall and reduce it to the level of constraint and discomfort of an ordinary theatre. . . . Now one of the chief charms of the music hall would be gone at once; for the great secret of music hall's success is that . . . you are not obliged to sit solemnly through a whole evening's performance but can take your pick of the programme."[104] The rhetoric of insider knowledge convinces in part because it honors a professional decorum; it imagines the music hall according to special, or specialized, definitions. Symons writes in the special language of the trained expert, who, as Burton Bledstein observes, marshaled "esoteric knowledge" and "a special understanding of a segment of the universe."[105] Chant, by comparison, appears the mere amateur, motivated by moral considerations that set her at odds with a space organized according to esoteric, complex, aesthetic standards. "Prudes," the connoisseur intimates, are culpable for their neglect of the aesthetic properties of music-hall space, and for ignoring the rules that trained observers realize are actualized in the structure of the entertainment. The controversy is evacuated of its potential social significance, and the orderly promenade comes to "naturally" represent essential qualities of decorum.

Paradoxically, the meddling prude threatens to rid "music hall" of what in principle it could never lose: its essence. The promenade is imagined to be the supplement necessary to secure the aesthetic character of the Empire. As Symons warns the *Gazette*'s readers, the effect of closing "the space [of the promenade] would be, not to place the Empire on the footing of the Tivoli and the Palace [music halls], but to deprive it of every outward characteristic which distinguishes a music hall from an ordinary theatre while giving it no advantage as a theatre." Chant and kindred reformers are guilty of reading the promenade by solely moral criteria, rather than properly formalist ones.

Symons's correspondence on the Empire controversy strives to save the matter from what he considered a significant misreading of music hall by the "prudes," a reading perpetuated in the debate over its legality. For the aesthete, music hall must be appraised like any art form, by a consideration of its properties, form, and function; the entertainment must be read according to the "aesthetic disposition" described by Pierre Bourdieu.[106] The amateur overlooks the structural function of the promenade that distinguishes Symons's idealized, integral "music hall." Naturally, these errors of omission are to be expected of the novice; the proper aesthetic disposition and the correct reading of the space remain the exclusive property of specialists—those who, in Symons's own words, "talk about music hall for a living."

Arthur Symons's correspondence on the Empire revises some aesthetic doctrines from within the discourse. He displays an unconventional notion of the high/low cultural divide in the casual comparison between theatrical entertainment and music-hall amusement drawn in his correspondence against Chant published in the *Gazette*. The poet parts ways with authorities such as Henry Arthur Jones and William Archer in finding significance and a degree of pleasure in the distractions that accompany the music-hall experience in contrast with the more concentrated, and, by implication, more cognitively challenging, pleasures of the drama. Yet if Symons appears to trouble one tenet of good taste, he maintains a key taste axiom intact. His definition of music hall in structuralist terms serves to mark off territory from untrained observers, from those believed incapable of attaining the distance from the entertainment that might allow them to formulate a precise, and therefore authoritative, conceptualization of the form. Nothing less, it seems, can ground an adequate reading of the Empire. Symons's quarrel with the work of Chant and her "prudes" is in contrast with the later entente he achieves with a woman he recognizes as a peer and fellow literary professional, Olive Schreiner. The critic demonstrates a willingness to revise his taste protocols, even critique his expert stance, in "At the Alhambra," an essay he publishes two years later. There he will cede the high ground of a "trained," formalist perception to the opinions voiced by a woman "novice." The dialogue between them encourages Symons to abrogate his achieved authority. In the controversy raised by Chant over the legitimacy of the Empire as a "true" music hall, Symons assumes a more conventional stance: that of the paternalist, juridical intellectual. In his public pronouncements on the fray, he works to correct the untrained misconceptions brought by amateurs like Chant to a special field too complex, it is insinuated, to be mapped by mere novices.

While marshaling their forces against Chant's perceived inability to distinguish between artistic spaces and dangerous urban zones, literary and theatrical professionals alike endeavored to aestheticize the Empire. In their accounts, the promenade became associated with order, autonomy, and a freedom of movement that, in Symons's case, signified the imaginative freedom that was believed to be a hallmark of aesthetic experience. Others suggested that the Empire offered the disinterested consumer a similarly distanced apprehension of the "beautiful," achieved through a vision of available, but removed, femininity. These constructions of the Empire had at least two discernible effects: first, they cordoned off the Empire from "interested" social groups such as philanthropists, setting the Empire under the control of more capable—that is, aesthetically discerning—professionals. Second, they had the subsidiary effect of demoting Chant's social critique to incurable "bad taste."

It was suggested in the pages of the *Sketch* that the final word on the entire debate would belong to artists, to those who crafted visual responses to Chant's public protest in the press. Sketch artists, as we have seen, found Chant's project an appealing subject, a veritable incitement to representation. The *Sketch,* for instance, coupled its coverage of the civic controversy with illustrations taken from Raven Hill's sketchbook *The Promenaders,* which provided twenty-two full-page drawings depicting the dispute over the Empire and the promenade.[107] The *Sketch* describes three Hill sketches satirizing Chant and praises his depiction of the Empire, which it printed on the facing page. The editorialist in fact happily follows Hill's lead in glamorizing the promenade according to the conventions set by sophisticated continental painters of consumption such as Degas and Manet. Hill's sketch frames the controversial promenade as a controlled, impressionist landscape, rather than the spectacle of vice (figure 4). The *Sketch* editorialist, perhaps inspired by Hill's example, goes the artist one further, admitting that the Empire promenade is a meeting place for rough trade, for promiscuous assignations between the demimonde and male patrons, yet insisting that it remains, in his words, fully "tasteful."

Nearly forty years later, the distinguished publisher Grant Richards would confirm in his memoir the *Sketch*'s early prediction that the Empire dispute would be "won" by men of taste, not meddling reformers. Richards recounts the controversy from a fully aesthetic, that is, a moral and asocial,

Figure 4. Music hall as high art. "'The Empire'—The Decline and Fall." From *Sketch,* October 31, 1894, 9. (By permission of the British Library)

perspective. He relies on metaphors from the exclusive world of painting and portraiture, the locutions of high art practice, to frame the routine experience of closing time at the Empire. Long after the event he frames the Empire as high artistic endeavor, part of a complexly imagined and elegantly impressionist vision: "The scenes at the moment of closing-time outside these various places of resort would astonish people to-day, but they had the quality of being picturesque. Manet might have painted one or other of the little groups—Manet or Toulouse-Lautrec or Felicien Rops."[108] Richards goes on to extol the Empire—safely situated as high art—with "its dark

Whistlerian wall decoration" and with "women [if] not all beautiful" at least "fitted more or less beautifully into their background."[109] In his memoir, the Empire controversy loses its social referents and becomes reterritorialized within the aesthetic.

Richards's retrospective view of the Empire controversy takes its cue from the caricature of Chant that proliferated in the period; he recalls how Chant "and her devoted busy-bodies" had "the worldly press against them and the graphic artists who dealt in amusement." The account concludes with a nostalgic lament for the loss of "colourful" spaces in the city where men of privilege could meet in open, yet clandestine, fashion with "decorative" women. In his reckoning, the actual closing of the Empire promenade after World War I only further sublimated an already sublimely elegant reality, transforming it into a safe and decorous ideal. Sexual impulse sublimated into an airy phantasm: this was a tried and tested modality of the aesthetic imagination. As a result of the reforming impulse, fortunately vanquished in Chant, but renewed by martial fervor, the encounters permitted in well-regulated spaces such as the Empire were "driven to frequent the museum of the artists' fancy." Richards's account inscribes Chant and the Empire into a series of images and representations existing at a considerable remove from material facts.

Hill's sketch, Richards's painterly metaphors, and Arthur Symons's "formalist" music hall: these images of the Empire all imagine the space as a resonant particular of the truly cultured life. They also serve to keep the "reality" of the Empire at a considerable imaginative distance. The Empire is a safe and elegant space for these men in theory, if not in actuality. Theoretical constructs are marshaled against Chant's melodramatic reading of the music hall. For all these men, she stands first and foremost as the untrained amateur who misreads complex social forms because she lacks the requisite skills and taste to interpret them. Chant gets inserted into the abject term of taste discourse: the place of the uneducated "other." Perceiving the Empire aesthetically lifts the debate out of the public realm and sets it under the purview of an elite. The reforms that Chant and her charity worker peers argued for lost the day against a formalist reading of the Empire mobilized by male professionals and circulated by means of the press. The links between men of taste from the professional middle class and segments of the aristocracy strengthened in defense of the Empire. This coalition stood behind a formalist reading of the Empire that became, for a time, hegemonic.

The difficulties the "Prudes on Parade" faced in the attempt to challenge the common sense of their culture gives us a sense of how consensual even extreme statements of aesthetic autonomy proved to be, even in a culture that often mocked and vilified the aesthete. At least before the Wilde trial, the avant-garde had sufficient symbolic capital to win consent for their belief in the autonomy of art from moral judgment. Chant's failure to reform the Empire was assured once that space was defined as a matter for experts and a matter of taste (and class).

Professionals and the Public

The controversy over the Empire is a significant event for this study, since it provides the clearest example of the generative rhetoric that coalesced around the London music hall by century's end. The London halls boasted their own discursive history, a figural, expressive embellishment that existed alongside their material manifestations. Spaces like the Empire were imagined and articulated as "mythological" realms, in the sense Roland Barthes elaborates; they existed as a collective representation, an ideological locus of commonsense propositions, and part of the "decorative display of what-goes-without-saying" within Victorian bourgeois culture.[110] The Empire, as word and image, came to signify things in excess of its plain sense, in the late-Victorian public sphere. This book elaborates how late-Victorian music hall received its own elaborate semantic coding through the efforts of intellectuals and culture workers; "music hall" was a generative semiotic in a city that proclaimed its own extensive, pedigreed history within linguistic inscription. A language of fussy partisanship, rooted in a proprietary fan-based relation to the form, was cultivated by aspiring and established aesthetes to defend the Empire from outsiders. This partisan rhetoric became a constitutive part of the discursive music hall. The Empire controversy also reminds us that a major portion of music-hall discourse was centered on the rhetoric of expertise.

The conflict over the Empire allowed many defenders of a marginal, upscale discourse of aesthetic values to express their potentially unsettling views in public venues. When high aestheticism went public, a constitutive, internal tension in aesthete discourse became apparent: between exclusive, closed-circuit taste communities and a more egalitarian language of urban expertise, also disseminated in the licensing debate. Of course, professional conduct has its exclusive aspect and mystifying tendencies, as Burton Bledstein diagnosed.

"Professionals," he observes, cornered the market on knowledge in an uneven playing field, in which "only the few, specialized by training and indoctrination, were privileged to enter, but which all in the name of nature's universality were obliged to appreciate."[111]

The liberating potential of expertise may be a chimera, rather than an expressive inventory of material possibilities. Yet for Chant, the late-Victorian culture of expertise no doubt seemed preferable, more inclusive, than a culture centered around the service of an exclusive elite or the supposed, inviolable liberty of true-born English subjects, verities that still circulated in a degraded half-life in newspaper columns throughout the metropolis. Bledstein claims, with no small irony, that Victorian professionals had a distinct and "unusual advantage" in the age of genteel culture, for "the radical idea of the democrat as autonomous professional had only socially conservative consequences."[112] Chant, as I have noted, made special claims for her knowledge of the "social vice," working-class women, and the streets: these were sometimes presumptive, classist claims. Yet she also expressed a desire to participate in a genuinely civic-minded culture. However, this aspiration got lost in the public clamor over her efforts to gain public respect. As a perceived threat to the masculine monopoly over expertise, aesthetic and otherwise, Chant's protest suggests the insurgent potential of a genuinely inclusive professionalism. Contrary to Bledstein's ironic treatment of reformist professionals, the Chant case suggests some common ground between the aims of professional culture and radical democracy.

Chant's work and rhetoric mark her position with the managerial class. George Bernard Shaw may have been too eager to read Chant as an exceptional individual, as she testified before the LCC, rather than a participant in a collective culture of professionalism, although he recognized the democratic impetus behind her claims to cultural expertise. Professional structures offered women like Chant a measure of authorization, legitimation, and power. Her protest confronted the claims of the supposedly universal subject of aesthetics. The discourse of professional authority, built on symbolic capital, seemed more accommodating to agents desiring social change.

Laura Chant's dramatic representation of her own social investigations demonstrates the capacities of a canny provocateur, capable of capitalizing on the new possibilities for public life offered to women in the expanding, imperial, capital city. She clearly recognized in the London County Council her real allies: those trained and concerned with civil service, versed in the administration of municipalities, confident in their ability to somehow bring the capital city under some rational survey. Chant took considerable care to affiliate her philanthropic enterprise, including the Empire case, with the officials of the newly elected, ambitious London County Council, seeking to modernize the capital city. She sought to gain popular support for her work and sought the aid of urban professionals in her campaign; this course of action alienated another brand of expert, confident in his or her ability to recognize and differentiate among items in the cultural marketplace. And Chant's efforts to reform a music hall were countered by the discourse of gentlemanly leisure that sought to gain allies in the press for its claims that male privilege and prestige were coterminous with real culture.

Chant's attempts to publicize class and gender inequity in the heart of London were effective, but never fully popular, despite her efforts to enlist working-class constituencies for the cause of municipal reform. The alliance she sought, between segments of the laboring class and the managerial class, was in large part prevented by a vocal cadre of men from different ranks and stations determined to retain their prerogatives as flaneurs. These would-be strollers and privileged spectators of the cityscape were comfortably middle-class, Oxbridge-trained aesthetes, but they were also journalistic profession-als and lower-middle-class music-hall patrons. The discursive construct of music hall won over the real space of the Empire: its space signified natural properties of taste and elegance. In the name of taste, music-hall connois-seurs also ratified their "innate" caste and privileged autonomy as men; they marshaled a residual but powerful discursive force against the new ethos of administration and reform, which was honored by many of the new city's professional class and briefly brought to bear on London music hall.

Insofar as the music hall itself became a mythology, an ideological complex à la Barthes that linked urban entertainment with exclusive male privilege, Chant was provided with an afterlife in English representations. As the repre-sentative image of the killjoy nonconformist conscience, she shadowed partisan accounts of the halls for years to come, troubling the unalloyed male pleasures evoked in music-hall chronicles by Macqueen-Pope, Colin MacInnes, and James Agate. The myth of Chant the uncultured busybody, the woman who didn't know better, proved as resilient as the discursive music hall, both of which significantly outlasted the "real" thing. These myths have had an unfor-tunate effect for social and cultural historians; they have obscured Chant's place, and the role of the music hall, in the Victorian culture of expertise.

The gender divide that Chant encountered at the heart of the city, and in the center of the Empire, marked other social domains of the age. In the

1890s, a segment of literary intellectuals began fictionalizing the music-hall experience, filtering that experience through the lens of gender, and bearing a fascinated obsession with the agency of performing women. At the same time that Chant was denied the authority to reform music hall by some within her class because of her status on the outside of music hall, it seemed to some that women on the "inside" of the halls were gaining a new charisma and authority. The fiction of Walter Besant, Hall Caine, and Henry Nevinson, centered on music-hall performers, constitutes a complex, if not generally capacious or generous, commentary on the status of the female professional. In the next chapter, I analyze the ways they pit their anxious, reactionary representations of feminine professionals against new, charismatic images of aggressive manhood.

4

Tales of the Culture Industry

PROFESSIONAL WOMEN, MIMIC MEN, AND VICTORIAN MUSIC HALL

In previous chapters, I have focused on the different ways the halls were represented in various media, in the pronouncements of journalists or on the correspondence page of daily papers. The controversy over the Empire demonstrated that urban spaces and heterosocial crowds were subject to heated public debate on their use and abuse. The stakes for these regulatory conflicts were high: to describe the Empire promenade as a male space could in effect determine how the space was utilized, or at the very least its discursive significance.

This chapter examines the various representations of music hall provided in literary work at the end of the 1800s. In a crucial particular, literary portrayals of the halls and their performers display a remarkable agreement: they all focus on the spectacle of women assuming new and powerful roles. By the 1880s and 1890s, the music hall had become a public space that was no longer subjected exclusively to a strict male control or dominance; as Judith Walkowitz details, the century's close saw the end of male, middle-class hegemony over London's public areas.[1]

Of the texts I examine, Walter Besant's *Dorothy Wallis* (1892) has the most optimistic, even meliorist tone; Besant propagates the message that it is possible for single working women to find both a career and vocation within the spaces of metropolitan London. Besant allows for the possibility that a woman might take to the stage and assume a major subject position in regard to the culture. Yet he remains markedly ambivalent as to whether middle-class professionalism, with its attendant emphasis on discipline and self-restraint, can sustain itself against forces that compel performing women to lead disreputable lives and direct them back down the class ladder. In contrast, Hall Caine's best-seller *The Christian* (1897) works as a cautionary tale against public women like the novel's heroine, Glory Quayle. The novel expresses overwhelming alarm in the face of the fact that women, potential dupes and stand-ins for consumer culture, might attain a measure of control outside traditional, patriarchal institutions. Hoping to bring Glory back under his paternalist solicitude, the protagonist John Storm actually attempts to murder the actress to prevent her final decline into vice.

These writers encountered, and often conflated, two different but equally threatening forms of the "feminine" at music halls: the presence of strong female performers, many of them challenging male stereotypes through song, and the "feminizing" allure of mass culture itself.[2] Andreas Huyssen details the ways in which popular entertainment was stigmatized by male observers as sentimental, hysterical, irrational—traits that "serious" male artists associated with women. The literature of the hall in the 1890s is largely a reactive formation, a masculinist endeavor to take back a mass culture form to healthy, manly, and middle-class norms. The writers discussed below—Walter Besant, Hall Caine, and Henry Nevinson—attempt to dissuade women from a career at the halls, reducing them to largely subordinate roles. We will see that Nevinson concludes his music-hall fiction "Little Scotty" (1894) with a powerful image of a new kind of expert: a working-class man who finds his identity, and his sovereignty, by taking to the stage. The stage also redeems working-class manhood from a supposedly degrading feminization.

These music-hall fictions conceive the space of the halls both as a cultural site, where audiences are influenced and occasionally inflamed, and as a workplace. This dual focus presents intriguing problems both formally and in terms of content. The ideological content framed by these tales is double voiced, even when these authors endeavor to be programmatic. Besant and Caine both read the halls through the moral dilemmas posed by the figure of the actress; in this respect they share common ground with works more familiar to Victorian scholars: Henry James's *Tragic Muse* (1890), Oscar Wilde's *Portrait of Dorian Gray* (1890), and, earlier, George Eliot's *Daniel Deronda* (1878). Yet detailed comparisons between the novels are difficult to sustain. For example, in Besant's *Dorothy Wallis*, the presence of women in the labor force is a social fact that cannot simply be escaped either by maintaining a deep suspicion of performing women (as is the case with George Eliot) or through the critique of a culture industry believed to inevitably sacrifice an artist's integrity (as elaborated in James's *The Tragic Muse*). Walter Besant's reputation as a social explorer—he scrutinizes "Unknown England" in his 1884 best-seller, *All Sorts and Conditions of Men*—informs his detailed account of Dorothy Wallis's experience as a struggling actress.

Fictions of the music hall were often less indebted to high literary models than to the sensational forms popularized by the ongoing sociological exploration of darkest London, the East End.[3] As chronicled, Dorothy Wallis's experience of backstage life displays a marked continuity with the interviews with the poor provided in Henry Mayhew's midcentury *London Labour and the London Poor,* a model that dominated journalistic exploration of London, particularly of its East End. Whatever the marked duplicities in Besant's role as reformer, his experience as a social investigator compels him to recognize the economic imperatives that encourage women to enter the workplace; such material constraints organize his account of an actress's life. On the face of it, Dorothy's narrative reconciles middle-class values with the theatrical profession: but the fear that women might take up these roles in greater numbers leads Besant to double back on the opportunities he offers in theory to women. In an odd, rhetorical maneuver, *Dorothy Wallis* suggests that in spite of the success of its protagonist, women wishing to retain their class status and stay "respectable" are best off avoiding a career in music hall.

Virtue and Virtuosity

Discussions of late-Victorian texts about performing women have commonly overlooked Walter Besant's *Dorothy Wallis*, the account of a young East End woman who chooses to become an actress. Consequently, scholars have neglected a serious endeavor to understand the forces that led working-class women to take to the stage. Besant gained his reputation from popular novels chronicling London's East End and his own effort to "civilize" the working class through the suasion of tutelary philanthropists. His most celebrated work, *All Sorts and Conditions of Men*, ties an exploration of "the great and marvelous country which we call East London" to the imperatives of a romance plot.[4] *Dorothy Wallis* carries on Besant's tradition of an imaginative mapping of East End culture. Unlike more canonized fictions about actresses and performance, Besant's novel is not given to accounts of deep subjectivity or in any respect psychologized. The psychic costs that accompany public display for performing women are not Besant's primary focus: a woman's choice to go on stage is constructed, at least initially, as simple economic imperative. The novel, in contrast with Besant's other work, considers how feminine expertise can find validation and, more specifically, how the theatrical vocation might receive sanction.[5]

Dorothy claims at the outset, "I can hardly dare to hope that I could ever be a great actress. In fact I do not consider it at all likely."[6] Yet, along with this recognition comes this statement of purpose: "Still, I believe I have such a fair amount of natural aptitude as with time and care will enable me to attain a certain point. It will not, perhaps, be a high one, but it will be respectable. I need not be ashamed of it. And in the work that is near to our heart there are compensations even for comparative failure." Besant imagines how a woman performer, even if not "naturally" gifted, can still maintain a respectable profession in the theater; *Dorothy Wallis* fits comfortably with the semitransgressive project of recuperating middle-class theater as a respectable culture form.[7] Despite the degrading environment Dorothy performs in, she remains, as Besant writes in the preface, a "gentlewoman."[8]

Such imaginative identification with a struggling worker perhaps motivates Besant's swerve away from the romance narrative that typically frames his stories of "slumming." Instead, *Dorothy Wallis* is presented as "an autobiography," prefaced by "an introduction by Walter Besant." Reviewers easily saw through the disguise, yet Besant's personal emphasis and empathy are worth noting. Besant personalizes this tale of a working woman "who resolved to win for herself, by her own exertions . . . an honourable position in the profession for which she felt an irresistible call."[9]

For Besant, the importance of Dorothy resides in her representative status; he stresses the similarities between Dorothy's narrative and the experience of other women in a crowded labor market: "There are thousands of girls like Dorothy in London: not all trying to become actresses, it is true, but all trying somehow to live. They would write; they would paint; they would act; they would become typewriters, clerks, cashiers, anything and everything." Dorothy's daily routine as clerical worker is given in great detail; her first job as a clerk is work that can "never bring large remuneration because, as it requires no special training, it is greatly in demand among the unskilled workers who are legion." As Dorothy recognizes, "[the] supply of this sort of labour is so enormous, that the rate of this wage is reduced to the lowest limit"; she adds that these "unskilled workers" are primarily women.[10] Such passages hearken back to the controversy over "redundant women" that alarmed journalist William R. Greg midcentury; instead of "spending and husbanding the earnings of men" (Greg's words) Dorothy searches for employment.[11]

Unlike Greg, who believed that working women led "an independent and incomplete existence of their own," Besant appears to countenance working women with comparative calm.[12] Nevertheless, Besant's portrayal of women workers evidences discernible conceptual weaknesses. He uses Dorothy's "case" to further the notion that low-paid workers remain both unfailingly respectable and cheerful in the midst of drudgery. Like the East End poor who retreat to the shelter of the People's Palace in *All Sorts and Conditions of Men*, Dorothy's fellow workers are happy despite the routine work they perform and the low wages they receive. The protagonist recounts, "[T]o me it is truly wonderful how these girls retain their cheerfulness. Some are even merry." Besant's preface to Dorothy's narrative stresses how "girls like Dorothy never do complain"; as in many narratives concerned with East End workers, the working class in *Dorothy Wallis* evidence decidedly "English" traits and, even more consoling to middle-class readers, are "resigned to exercise them in even the most unpromising of circumstances."[13]

Besant's solicitude for outraged virtue keeps working women under his anxious, chivalric gaze. While his introduction censures male harassment of working women, professional women remain under his paternalist gaze. "[I]n the history of a girl who lives such a life, protected only by the companionship of another girl, many things have to be suppressed; many insults which such girls have to encounter must be passed over. . . . [T]here is a certain class of reptile who sits at the entrance of every profession or calling taken up by girls. All that we need to say of him is that it is a pity he cannot have his multitudinous carcass rolled into one for a single comprehensive flogging."[14] The introduction also expresses the hope that all the working women Besant invokes "have their lovers, one hopes, in due time, their hus-band." The tales of all these women end as Dorothy's own autobiographical fragment does: with Dorothy waiting for the return and tutelage of her ab-sent boyfriend.[15]

Although *Dorothy Wallis* is cast as a woman's autobiography, it is not concerned with tracing or positing a deep, feminine subjectivity, such as George Eliot portrays with the troubled, complex character of the Alcharesi, or with the "double consciousness" often manifest in the accounts authored by nineteenth-century actresses.[16] Dorothy's story is instead an account of her rigorous self-discipline and self-control. This asceticism is apparent from the outset, with Besant's own assurance that Dorothy's desire to be an actress was "no sudden fancy such as comes to many women, springing from a desire for the admiration, the applause, the splendour, the costly raiment that belongs to the successful actress—it was a resolution, fixed and deter-mined, grounded on such a perception of the Art as is given only to those who have the genius to practice it."[17] With this description, Besant detaches aesthetic values from Dorothy's work: professional concerns require a total renunciation of frivolity.

It is here that we can see the limits that mark Besant's account of Dorothy; her life and circumstances must continually underscore her beleaguered but essential "respectability." While respectability is a social construct, Besant figures it as an innate aspect of Dorothy's character (not her interiority). As with contemporaneous autobiographical texts of noted actresses such as Madge Kendal and Marie Bancroft, Besant endeavors to "domesticate" the theatrical life. Madge Kendal, like Besant, urges actors and actresses to "lead such lives that those who have regarded the Stage with a suspicious eye will at last give it its proper place in the world of Art."[18] Such public statements were designed to exonerate the profession from the charge of moral laxity; Kendal and Bancroft imagine acting as demanding labor in order to assert compelling claims about the professional status of actors. Likewise, Besant legitimizes Dorothy by establishing her difference from women who take to the stage for the wrong reasons. While name actresses commanded increas-ing respect for the profession in the 1890s, their own respectability and prominence did not extend to all performing women; the uneven nature and effects of individual authorization for a community of women are un-derscored by Dorothy's own moderate success. The contradiction is ex-tended in her representation, for the fortunes that attend her career are portrayed both as something the earnest aspirant to bourgeois status must expect and plan for and, at the same time, as exceptional and fortuitous.

Dorothy's account begins with her move to London, a move that quickly leads to calamity. Her Uncle Nathaniel is a Fagin-esque career criminal who encourages her cousins, Rachel and Daniel, to commit theft. Her cousin Daniel, who steals Dorothy's jewelry, is placed under arrest while Uncle Nathaniel escapes into the nether regions of East London.[19] Rachel and her younger brother Oney move into another East End apartment, and the women take low-paid clerical work to support themselves.

It is in the midst of these events that Rachel introduces Dorothy to an actress who had previously lodged in Uncle Nathaniel's apartments. The actress, Mrs. Wardlaw, presents her own labor as both secular career and sacred vocation. Aesthetic demands merge with claims of civic duty: "It was in the theatre that we saw life in its joy and sorrow and the artist showed us how we felt and lived. Oh, it was a beautiful thing to be an artist. An artist lived two lives. One life was public, the other private. . . . An artist was the friend of the public, more, their brother or sister."[20] The public-minded aesthetic Wardlaw espouses captivates Dorothy: "I listened intently. It was all so new and strange, so delightful." She is even more taken by Wardlaw's private drawing room performance, witnessed by both her and Rachel. Here the brutalities of working-class life are suitably sentimentalized. Wardlaw recites "a little piece about two ragged children, one of whom stole in order to give the other bread," and who die "when there was no more bread to be fought for or stolen because one would not let the other sin."[21]

Dorothy's account of the recital is noteworthy for what it reveals about Besant's own aesthetics of performance:

> As [Wardlaw's] eyes grew bigger and intenser and her hands trembled and moved with each change of feeling, the very presence of these waifs came upon me. I saw them distinctly before me, eager, hungry, imploring. I heard their voices, so earnest, hopeless, and sad. And the ring of death was in them. When the last words died away, I sat with parted lip and dimmed eyes staring into vacancy. Before me lay two children ragged, dirty and blue, huddled up in the snow, dead.

The performance detailed here is clearly intended to be exemplary and produce the emotions it imitates in captivated spectators such as Dorothy. Mrs.

Wardlaw's sister, who also witnesses the performance, assures the overpow-
ered observer that she "had shown the artist the highest compliment possible in the tears [Dorothy] was ready to shed for the sorrow [Wardlaw]
had depicted." The passage intimates the crucial role the performing artist
played in transforming the London poor into a sentimental discourse: a tale
of poverty ends not in discontent but with a demonstration of the unflagging
virtue of the "deserving" poor. As with Besant's own fictions of "the people"
(as opposed to the working class), Wardlaw recasts class experience into
something universal, which rids itself of its own class particularity. The actress's vocation is linked to the imperative to moralize economic need in the
East End.

After witnessing the performance, Dorothy defines her own aesthetic in
great detail, elaborating the importance of natural activity and clarity.[22] For
Dorothy, acting receives its justification as professional labor when it imposes an austere discipline. "The beginner," Dorothy claims, "still [clings] to
identity"; it is only "when the artist has completely involved body and soul
in his work that he can . . . snatch a mighty conception from the mind of a
great master."[23] Dorothy's own idea of the artist is aligned with the traditional aesthetic language of timeless greatness and the masculine "master."

Surprisingly, it is this masculinist artistry that gets passed on from woman
to woman in *Dorothy Wallis*. Dorothy's ideas about acting are gained from
watching women perform; it is an anonymous leading lady who suggests to
Dorothy the joys of aesthetic professionalism:

> The leading lady was standing at the wings. Her face was beautifully se-
> rious. It had a glow almost of rapture on it. She looked as if she saw
> something a long way off, a great glory, in light of which she fell back
> awed. There is something almost reverential in this unveiling of the
> inner chambers to catch a reflex, however faint, of the glory of its revela-
> tion. To the careless and indifferent it never comes. Of the deep secret
> joys of mystic communion only the true lover can taste.[24]

Dorothy's aesthetic raptures inevitably lead into a separation of an artistic
elite from the rabble. When Rachel attempts to recite a poem, Dorothy concludes: "I fear Rachel is deficient in imagination. Her conception . . . ex-
ceedingly feeble." Further, when Rachel worries about taking to the stage
because "there is no money it," Dorothy interjects, "Never mind, there is
plenty of art."[25] Rachel's desire to follow Dorothy on stage because Rachel

"does not care what work we do as long as it is honest" earns only Dorothy's derision: "Fancy speaking of Art in that way!"

In contrast to Rachel's, Dorothy's ardor is tested through exposure to degrading surroundings such as impoverished theaters and the halls. She is especially sensitive about performing in the halls: "One thing I object to in halls is the loss of that private and often snug region of the stage designated 'behind the scenes.' . . . In halls there are no proper dressing rooms. . . . It is not pleasant to have to rush out and disappear up a stone passage as rapidly as possible, followed by curious eyes. One feels as if half the enchantment were gone, and as if one must have looked horribly painted under the bold scrutiny."[26] Working at the music hall entails a close proximity to the audience, and the crowd threatens to disrupt the proper distance aesthetic value requires. Such close scrutiny, Dorothy fears, invalidates claims to the aesthetic; it also troubles the distance required by Besant's own conception of genuine professionalism.

Specifically, professional categories require an assumed, conscious distance from the audiences that performance is meant by Dorothy and Wardlaw to serve. Distance and remove are valued because such attitudes repress unseemly emotion. The very ambition that success in the profession requires fosters the self-discipline that the working class need to better themselves. As Dorothy proclaims: "Let us encourage all poor girls to be ambitious, for the girl who believes in future has a double safeguard. For the sake of a name in that future which be untarnished she will keep straight. Ambition rivets the armor of the good and true."[27] Ambition promotes a rigorous moral hygiene among working girls. Dorothy learns that affect must be restrained in order for aesthetic values to be preserved. As her theatrical group presents Shakespeare at a provincial music hall, a young actor in the company regulates Dorothy's emotions. He complains to Dorothy about the lack of "dignity" evident in behavior backstage: "What is there to keep a man straight who goes on roughing it year after year and sees no prospect of advancement? . . . It is not art, not ambition alone that will keep a man from making a beast of himself and sinking into the ranks for whom there is no hope. . . . I have kept what I am because I respected myself too much to be what some men are."[28] The young actor's advice tempers Dorothy's aestheticism even further. She concludes that her calling demands "that respect for ourselves which would make us better than ourselves."[29] The young actor's resolve keeps the sovereign self aloof and uncontaminated even in precarious conditions; the young man remains "calm, cold and seemingly indifferent to all

inconvenience," although "underneath that callous exterior burned a vol-
cano which no one suspected."

Besant allows Dorothy to articulate a notion of the professional that underscores the vast difference between those in a managerial class and those
outside its parameters. He links professional conduct with an ideology of
self-control and restraint available only to a select few. This barely concealed
elitism suggests why, for a text that demonstrates the economic hardship that
leads working-class women to find work on stage, *Dorothy Wallis* nonetheless
cautions novices and amateurs from casting the performing life as an escape
from the most arduous work and self-discipline.

Besant's novel is not alone among the works of his contemporaries in the
confusing messages it offered working women attracted to theatrical life; the
same ambivalence is often echoed in the counsel given by successful actresses to the novices. In Madge Kendal's *Dramatic Opinions* (1890), a collection of professional shoptalk and advice originally published in theatrical
journals, we see similar double-edged counsel given to women hoping to
enter the profession. Kendal claims, "I do not think that there is a thing in
the world that a woman could be better than an actress," before she hedges:
"I do not say there is room for all, but those who have the ability will naturally come to the fore."[30] Even this window of opportunity snaps shut: "[O]f
course there must be a large majority who will go to the wall, poor girls!"[31]
With increasing frequency over the course of Besant's novel, Dorothy's examples of the amateurs she meets at work are women. One hapless woman
makes the mistake of confiding to Dorothy that she has taken to the stage
solely for the money, and that she believes that "having a really splendid
wardrobe, I ought to get on pretty easily."[32] Dorothy and the rest of the troop
find this speech and sentiment beneath comment; her response is coy silence and complete condescension: "We smiled and did not try to enlighten
her as to the difficulties of the profession."

Dorothy Wallis illustrates strangely divergent intentions toward the stage,
in part because of the difficulties Besant has in reconciling an aesthetic enterprise with the late-Victorian ideology of philanthropy. Performance is
presented as an opportunity for self-help and an expression of autonomy,
even for working-class women. Yet performance remains allied with notions
of aesthetic competence that are exclusive by definition. As Dorothy complains: "Girls have a weakness to the stage because they imagine it requires
nothing but a pretty face. If they do get on it they find how greatly they have

been mistaken. The manager wants workers like every one else. And art is different from mechanical work. Every one cannot even attempt to do it."[33] Besant's work with the People's Palace and his pronouncements about the East End demonstrate his concern that workers receive "a little more of the pleasures and graces of life."[34] However, his social policy to democratize art is in clear tension with Dorothy's own pronouncements on the rarefied world of aesthetic professionalism, which seems fully exclusive.

On one hand, *Dorothy Wallis* broadcasts the message that unemployed young women should consider taking up acting as a means to secure a respectable livelihood; on the other, Dorothy's attitude toward art remains fiercely exclusive, and the pressures of the marketplace on performers are continually dramatized.[35] Dorothy sustains her own claims to expertise by denying the achievements and integrity of her competition. Several women in her theatrical troupe voice their resentment when Dorothy is cast in what they believe to be superior roles, and Dorothy strikes back: "Perhaps no women are so madly jealous of another's attractions as in this profession. It is certain not many women love each other in it. . . . An old actress may admire a young girl whose triumph she imagines to be partly her own, but even here you see there is a touch of personal vanity again."[36] By the end of the novel, negative accounts of the profession dominate; Dorothy's own voice is interrupted by personal monologues that express the "real feelings" of performers. Here Dorothy's account intersects with Besant's own interests as social investigator, and the text resembles the "universal interview" with a prominent social "character" of the type pioneered by the new journalism.[37] One unnamed actress tells of how theater life ruined her domestic life; the complaint concludes in the style of advice literature, a style that increasingly characterizes Dorothy's narrative: "Let no girl think lightly of going on the stage. What can she know of it? Can she realise what life will mean to her in a few years' time? It may seem pleasant, but the flowers have a poisoned perfume."[38]

Dorothy's account of her acting career does not extend much past her tour of the provinces; on returning to London, Dorothy takes on a small role in a London theater. Rachel's worst fear, the return of evil Uncle Nathaniel from the deep recesses of the East End, occurs; but confronted by Dorothy, Nathaniel has heart failure. The account ends with the expected return of Dorothy's boyfriend, Alec. While Dorothy's work as an actress may continue, *Dorothy Wallis* closes without answering whether marriage will end her acting career. And, although some reviewers suspected that Dorothy would continue her career, others made quite different speculations.[39] Theater critic A. C. Deane praised the work for "neither magnifying the faults nor exaggerating the advantages of life on the stage" and warned that unrealistic novels "possibly do some harm by temporarily attracting deluded persons to a vocation which they imperfectly understand, and for which they have no real fitness."[40]

In common with other voices in the culture—the new journalism that popularized the acting profession through personal interviews with actors, the praise of literary professionals for the theater, and autobiographical accounts of actresses themselves—*Dorothy Wallis* suggests that the actress can behave in public and private. Yet, as the wife of a touring manager assures Dorothy, for every good actress there remains a "rowdy set" of women whose fate will be to end up as disgraced music-hall artists.[41]

The music hall stands throughout Besant's novel as what eventually resists the improving influence of professionalism. Throughout the novel, the halls appear as a place of male license that refuses an easy assimilation into middle-class protocols. Dorothy's delinquent cousin, Daniel, patronizes the Empire; he extols "the girls who danced [there]" to Dorothy and even considers entering the music-hall business as an entrepreneur.[42] Through Daniel, the halls and hooliganism are suggestively linked and mutually disparaged. And if a Dorothy Wallis can be encouraged to perform under strict guidelines, Besant actively dissuaded women from performing at the halls a year after the novel.

In "At the Music Hall," an essay signed "Dorothy Wallis," published in *Longman's Magazine,* Besant visits the women backstage at an anonymous hall. Passing under Dorothy's name for readers of the magazine, Besant desexualizes the backstage visit: putting "Dorothy" to rhetorical use, he gives readers an "insider" glimpse of what women do backstage, away from public scrutiny. The essay begins with a picture of a disorderly crowd, a "performance . . . greeted with screams of laughter by the house, who began also to stamp their feet and shout, completely drowning the voice of the singers."[43] Backstage, "Dorothy" encounters similar confusion: "a moving crowd of girls dressed and undressed" in which "everyone is in a desperate hurry, and seems to be looking for someone or something."[44]

Besant's essay turns this crowd into something surveyed, subject to "Dorothy's" anonymous but controlling gaze. Amid this fearful disorder, Dorothy's interviews impose order. Yet "she" faces a clear and unequivocal danger, for the actresses disclose their unmitigated antagonism toward, or failure to respect, the strictures of married life. "I don't think there is much money to be made on the halls, but I only do it for fun," one actress confesses: "The worst of the profession is that it makes me forget my house-keeping so. I often don't remember whether there's anything for supper or not till I get home. I hope my baby's all right and that the servant will give her medicine. I quite forgot to tell her. I came off in such a hurry. . . . [M]y old man will be so tired and cross."[45] This backstage confession appears to confirm the worst fears of Besant's readers that working women are forced to neglect their domestic duties, so that their labor inevitably produces dysfunctional households.

The performer's monologue turns into a full-scale attack on domestic labor, as she recounts the reasons why her husband wishes her to quit the stage: "[H]e wants to know why I can't give up going on in the halls and stay at home in the evening till he gets back; but I'm so dull and miserable by myself all night, I can't. I'd do a great business to get on the halls, but he just can't say 'no' to me when I've really made up my mind to a thing. So I went and learnt dancing and all, and used to shut myself up in a room trying to do the American twist and the Rocks, and clean forgot meals and everything else." These backstage glimpses are clearly intended as a sensational revelation; the labor of performing women has the *necessary* result of disrupting the home and challenging male prerogative. These working women talk back to the patriarchy in sensational fashion, troubling masculine (primarily working-class male) control of the household and, by extension, of the city.

Dorothy's reportage expands on a theme shared by Besant's novel: that of an overcrowded profession, offering a minimum of available opportunities. One woman complains: "I can't see why folk are rushing off the stage on to the music hall. . . . It's just their fancy that there's more money in it!"[46] An anonymous worker backstage admits, "[W]e can't give everyone an appearance. Seems to me girls are all dying to get on the music hall."[47] Another expresses alarm over the surplus production of culture: "There's too many [sketches] about just now, and too many people of a sort, that's it." The essay closes with the manager complaining, "[W]e are overdone with people asking for extra turns" and murmurs from the women:

"Can you put me on next week?," she asked eagerly.
"And me?"

"And me?"

It was a chorus.

The manager put out his hands entreatingly.

"Ladies," he said, "I will do what I can, but you see how it is with us. I can promise nothing."

A general murmur followed.[48]

For Besant, the music hall is, despite his conciliatory interest, a culture of resistance that circumvents both aesthetic control and philanthropic maintenance. The fierce autonomy of the performers Dorothy encounters backstage is not easily aligned with any moralizing schemes or meliorist design. It is no surprise that Dorothy/Besant stresses that the halls are a shop closed to other laborers. Besant represents the strong individualism of the performers according to prevailing models of laissez-faire thinking. These women are finally punished with glutted markets, increasing scarcity, and unremitting competition.

Dorothy's depiction of the final skirmishing between these performers backstage is a cautionary tale: since these women are unable to cooperate and work collectively, "At the Music Hall" ends in a clash of competing wills. In this way, Besant makes the stage safe for women, but only for professionals like "Dorothy."

Men Take the City Back

If Besant's novel and "Dorothy's" essay act as cautionary tales for working-class women, Hall Caine's *The Christian* acts as a full-fledged narrative of male backlash. Caine revels in the opportunities to dramatize the moral havoc brought on when women take to the stage and men lose control of the city's spaces. *The Christian* sets the story of a successful female entertainer at the music halls against an image of a divided London, a city segregated between wealthy and cynical West Enders and "outcast" East Enders. Caine's novel intervenes in one of the issues that clustered around these potent images of divided spaces: the efficacy of philanthropy to promote the cultural and moral reform of the underclass. It is not too surprising that Caine sees the music hall as a threat to schemes for improving the poor. Caine's novel suggests another way we can appraise the cultural work of the hall: it stands, like the business of philanthropy itself, for the feminization of social spaces, and for this reason must be resisted. *The Christian*'s attack on music hall is part of a larger endeavor to regain control of two different places in which women's presence was manifest and women's labor was recognized: on the music-hall stage and in settlement houses.

The dual plot of the novel narrates the careers of two protagonists: John Storm, a minister from an aristocratic background who becomes isolated from his peers because of the strength of his religious convictions, and Glory Quayle, the beautiful granddaughter of a Manx clergyman who travels to London in order to become a nurse. The seduction of a nurse by an aristocrat forces Quayle, working at a Hyde Park hospital as a nurse, and Storm, assigned as an Anglican minister to the same hospital, to leave their respective jobs in protest. Quayle becomes a prosperous music-hall performer who gains access to the wealthiest circles in society; her story serves as a stark contrast to Storm's gradual fall from West End society and transformation into an East End charity worker.

Glory's position in the novel is fully overdetermined by her gender. On a surface level, her success in the West End represents the growing commercial and popular success of women stars. But Caine also uses Glory to represent the moral decay of the West End; she eventually signifies all that resists the ministrations of Storm's philanthropic project. *The Christian* details how Storm overcomes the threat that successful performers pose as he remakes London. Glory is almost a literal casualty of Storm's endeavor to clean up the city: in a critical scene, Storm cracks under the strain and attempts to kill her when she refuses to leave the music-hall stage. Her success is presented as a practical obstacle to Storm's goals to reform the East End's "Devil's Acre"; but as exemplar of woman performers at the halls, she comes to stand for an entire culture industry that exists in startling autonomy from religious values.

John Storm's express difficulty in gaining authority over the city is depicted as part of a general crisis in masculine authority and privilege. Storm comes from an aristocratic heritage, the son of a peer and nephew of the prime minister. But the seduction and subsequent suicide of Polly Love, a nurse whom Storm meets while conducting charity work, forces Storm to become a class traitor, according to the terms set by the novel. More accurately, the incident empowers Storm to assume the manly role of policing the morals of his class; he accuses the seducer, Lord Robert Ure, and, by association, attacks the lax mores of the aristocracy. Although Storm's target is upper-class men, he focuses on women as the cause of male license. In Glory's account of Storm's sermon, Storm emphasizes that men are "generally as pure as women require they should be; and if the lives of men [are] bad it [is] often because women did not demand that they should be good."[49] Demanding that middle-class women take up custodial care of male sexuality, Storm blames the victimization of lower-class women on the failed tutelage of bourgeois wives: "Tremble, ye women that are at ease, and say why you allow your daughters to marry men who in fact and effect are married already. Strip you, and be ashamed for the poor women who were the first wives of your daughters' husbands, and for the children whom such men abandon and forget." Storm's sermon is a complexly situated speech in regard to gender, in part because of the dense overlay between philanthropic discourse and the nascent feminism of the age. Storm's call to women to assume control over the sexuality of middle-class men keeps with the contemporaneous claims by purity workers and temperance reformers, who similarly believed that domestic women must gain control over unruly male libertines.[50] However, Caine also places the responsibility for male license on middle-class women, and largely exonerates men in his assignation of agency and blame with regard to sexual misconduct.

Storm's sermon, in other words, both relates and significantly revises the discourse and politics of late-Victorian philanthropy. Storm's attempts at social reform steer him away from realms of privilege into a territory that was coded largely as feminine. By the 1880s, female charity workers had, as Judith Walkowitz observes, "reimagined the cityscape of London, particularly the slums, as a place appropriate for women in public."[51] Middle-class men such as Samuel Barnett, who established the Toynbee Hall settlement, reacted against the success of female philanthropists and attempted to claim charity work as a male endeavor. Barnett barred women from Toynbee Hall in the fear they would take control of the settlement from Barnett himself.[52] Storm's reform efforts similarly appropriate ground claimed by women: the dereliction of female control over their husbands' conduct, castigated by Storm in his sermon, demands that men take up the moralization of the city.

Storm's reform plans for Soho's Devil's Acre is itself a militant act of chivalry. He vows to "make an attack on the one mighty stronghold of the devil's kingdom whereof woman is the direct and immediate victim: to tell Society over again it is an organized hypocrisy for the pursuit and demoralization of woman . . . to look and search for the beaten and broken who lie scattered and astray in our bewildered cities, and to protect them, ... because they are my sisters and I love them."[53] Mrs. Callendar, the Scottish matron who hears this speech, appropriately responds, "That's spoken like a man." Indeed, with its feminization of the poor and its courtly ethos, Storm's declaration forcefully affirms patriarchal prerogative.

Storm's effort to gain financial support from his uncle for his new settlement home singles out working women as the locus of his efforts, and he recognizes the counterculture that ruins them: "My experiment would be made on a social basis, and first of all in relation to women. . . . Three halfpence an hour was the average wage of a working woman in England! . . . Ruin lays in wait for them, and . . . enticing them in the shape of dancing houses and music halls and rich and selfish men."[54] In reward for Storm's devotion to his "sisters," he gains a tremendous charismatic power over working-class women. When Storm is later arrested for inciting a riot, "a strange crowd" gathers in his support, consisting "for the greater part of . . . the priestesses of society, who are the lowest among women."[55] Although Storm renounces traditional forms of prestige and cultural authority, he remains "master" of the city. His philanthropic work indicates how the aristocratic male can regain authority over the unruly metropolis.

Caine clearly privileges Storm's vision of London, East and West Ends, unified by a common moral contagion. The fissured city is imaginatively restored when Storm's apocalyptic predictions about a biblical destruction of the city gain newspaper publicity and spark riots. His predictions, anxiously scrutinized in newspaper editorial pages, provoke fear and trembling when they circulate among the West End elites Storm renounces. Max Beerbohm expressed his distaste for Caine's novel as a "false, garrish farrago about life in London"; but its best-seller status indicates Caine's success in intervening in the cultural politics located around the late-Victorian working class.[56]

If Storm's philanthropy and feverish religious visions indict and symbolically unite London, Glory Quayle's tale suggests the nature of the forces that resist the paternalist imagination. Her success in the East End halls places her in close proximity to the working class that Storm desires to reform. Even when she becomes overwhelmed by feelings of contagion, her opening performance suggests her power in this new world: "After the first thrill of success the shame of it all came over her and she saw how low she had fallen, and felt horrified and afraid. The clamour, the clapping of hands, the vulgar faces, the vulgar laughter, the vulgar song . . ."[57] Glory's rhetoric represents her commercial success as an unequivocal moral disaster, a "fall" that brings immediate recriminations of guilt that we must assume the author believed fully justified. The burlesque singers who surround her in the dressing room are characterized as a "noisy, merry, reckless, harmless race, free of speech, fond of laughter, wearing false jewellery, false hair and false complexions."[58] "Harmless" is the least charged word in this description; the links between an unreclaimed working class and a degenerate upper class are further suggested in the dressing room talk of the idle rich who obsessively follow every performance of certain female performers.[59]

John Storm is drawn in to the hall where Glory is performing by "supernatural" compulsion, and although "tired and ashamed, . . . he could not bring himself to go away."[60] Storm's initial impression of the East End crowd, and the girls who "look into John's face with a saucy smile," amounts to sympathy overlaid with condescension: "God forbid that I should grudge them their pleasure! It's all they have poor creatures." His attitude toward harmless pleasure quickly becomes more critical; Storm becomes repelled by the audience's "inarticulate squeals" in response to a female artiste's song. The working-class audience is portrayed as responding with sexualized abandon to the performance onstage: "[E]very face was red and hot, and grinning and grimacing."[61]

Glory's performance of a song with special childhood associations for her becomes transformed and vulgarized by the act of performance, primarily by her proximity, which the text renders and sensationalizes, with the unruly crowd. Another song detailing how drunken fishermen are put to bed by their sweethearts with a kiss has the entire crowd making kissing sounds, with Glory leading the luridly described call and response: "The singer smiled and kissed back. . . . Somehow she conveyed the sense of a confidential feeling as if she were doing it for each separate person in the audience. . . . It was irresistible, it was maddening, it swept over the whole house." The interaction between audience and performer is unavoidably personal and sexually charged, leading to the inevitable conclusion that it is Glory's performance that creates the riotous moment of shared sexual intoxication. It is her work that sexualizes the audience and contributes to a vulgarization of the poor, not insisted on in Caine's portrayal before Glory sings. Storm finds himself "tightly wedged in by a wall of faces—hot, eager, with open mouths, teeth showing, and glittering and dancing eyes."[62]

Storm imagines his own philanthropic effort as in direct competition with the halls' degradation of the poor. He outlines his alternative to debased entertainment in a letter to Glory: "Foreign clubs, casinos, dancing academies, and gambling houses are round about us. . . . Let us go down . . . and disinfect them. They want music and singing; give to them. They want dancing:

give them that also, for God's sake, give it them in your churches, or the devil will give it them in his hells."[63] In a scheme modeled on Walter Besant's plans for a People's Palace in the East End, Storm reclaims a clergy house as "a club for working girls" that will offer its settlers wholesome pastimes rather than unruly entertainment. It seeks to replace residual culture forms with a brighter, more rational amusement, imposed from above. Such plans are the ideological focus of Caine's work, as his later stage adaptation demonstrates, with an added scene in which Soho boys and girls "danced and boxed" in the chapel's vestry under Storm's approving gaze.[64] Immediately after the children perform a musical number in the stage adaptation, Horatio Drake enters the chapel to inform Storm of his plans to tear down the church and enlarge the neighboring music hall, where Glory performs (a similar confrontation occurs in the novel). Glory's career directly competes with Storm's efforts at urban planning and civic renovation. The barely repressed violence Storm feels toward competing cultures is further demonstrated in Caine's stage adaptation, which lingers on his attempted homicide of Glory when she refuses to leave her profession: a literalization of the desire to kill off the competing form.[65]

Glory relinquishes her career, after much hesitation, once working-class toughs rough up Storm after the divine retribution of his apocalyptic predictions fails to rain down on London. The romance plot speeds the final assimilation of Glory; she becomes a subsidiary to his project for urban renewal. The history of Storm's barely repressed violence toward Glory suggests the fiercely exclusive, borderline murderous rage thinly concealed by his claims of meek Christian altruism and self-sacrifice. His impending death and his deathbed marriage to Glory finally inspire her decision to relinquish her career and become a charity worker. Caine underscores that Glory's succession of Storm will not substitute feminine sensibility for male hegemony; she insists on her symbolic thrall to Storm, and casts her assumption of power in a submissive posture. Glory assures the dying man: "[I]n the further time people will come to me and say—girls, dearest, brave, brave girls, who are fighting the battle of life like men—they will come and say: 'And did you know him? Did you really, really know him?'"[66] Glory renounces her success, vocation, and West End connections in order to vanish into Storm's mission and perpetuate his cultural authority. Instead of recognizing Glory, the working woman of the future will memorialize Storm's own achievement in the Devil's Acre. Glory succeeds Storm's rule, but she is allowed to do so only on ironic terms: as a degraded reminder of a once glorious kingship.

Caine's novel endeavors to bring together the sundered halves of London, but under the proprietary control of men. If *The Christian* reclaims the city from a feminized philanthropy by asserting male prerogative, men of letters used other means to imagine a reinvigorated male control over the spaces of the city. In contrast with Caine, fiction writer and esteemed journalist Henry Nevinson conceptualizes the halls themselves as a necessary pedagogical force for the sustenance of identity and the spiritual renewal of working-class men. The halls allow a way for these men to defend their masculinity against moralizing forces from outside the neighborhood and within.

East End Boys, West End Reformers

Henry Nevinson's "Little Scotty" is a forceful attempt to protect male authority in a realm in which it is perceived as endangered: London's East End. The music hall is conceived as a force that counters outside, emasculating forces working against the sturdy English manhood of the worker. Nevinson's tale of a working-class boy whose natural talent for mimicry leads him to the music-hall stage portrays the halls as a natural support for working-class masculinity. The story suggests that, despite the endeavors of municipal workers and philanthropists to regulate the halls and to administrate working-class culture, music hall exists intact. Further, it suggests that the "unreformed" music hall performs the most valuable kind of cultural work: it reproduces male supremacy and a gendered hierarchy.

The late 1880s and 1890s witnessed the rise of a set of powerful concerns centered around the uses of culture and the dangers of "amusement," primarily focused on the antagonistic social space of London's East End. Nevinson uses his short tale of East End halls to intervene in this tangled politics of working-class life and philanthropic reform. "Little Scotty" subtly disparages the many ameliorative schemes that proliferated in late-Victorian London, schemes that endeavored to bring "real" culture to natives of darkest London.

Nevinson experienced life at both Oxford and Whitechapel, taught English literature in Hackney, and accompanied rent collectors on rounds through slums.[67] A socialist who turned to practical social philanthropy, Nevinson, with his wife Margaret, took part in Canon Samuel Barnett's effort to acculturate East Enders at Toynbee Hall, the celebrated Whitechapel settlement house. As Margaret Nevinson recounts, Toynbee Hall brought "all the most eminent in literature, art and politics . . . to pour out their wisdom to the poor of Whitechapel"; the list of luminaries included Walter Pater, Leslie Stephen, Henry Sidgwick, Charles Booth, and S. R. Gardiner.[68] Henry Nevinson's fiction, however, is profoundly critical of philanthropy and moral reform; in opposition to efforts to "civilize" workers, he extols the self-sufficiency of proletarian culture.[69] Nevinson takes care to portray East End music halls as an autonomous zone, a frontier outpost of cultural resistance, persisting in the face of the forces of moral uplift. "Little Scotty" also intimates that the halls have a necessary and conservative effect on East End life: they serve as vital support for working-class manhood.

Nevinson's "Slum Stories of London"—collected in *Neighbours of Ours* (1895), the volume that includes "Little Scotty"—are linked by the presence of an active, interventionist narrator, Britton, an East End native. His name, of course, emphasizes how crucial representations of the working class were to the articulation of English national identity. In the nineteenth century, the Cockney came to stand for an essential English hardiness and masculinity, and this image bears heavily on Nevinson's Britton. In a useful and comprehensive study of working-class images and representations in late-Victorian London, Peter Keating touches briefly on Nevinson. He extols the East End of Nevinson's portrayal, affirming it as an authentic community linked by a complex network of familial relations, language, and custom. He commends Britton's character as a means to establish "a central working-class viewpoint" and suggests Nevinson imagined that working-class community constituted a "culturally homogenous community," vital and productive despite its depleted resources. This community, unified and integral, represents "a distinctive affirmation of shared values: humor, compassion, and gentleness."[70]

Evincing more skepticism toward the notion that working-class communities share essential values, Regenia Gagnier praises Arthur Morrison's contemporaneous slum fiction, particularly *Tales of Mean Streets,* over Nevinson's tales of community. Morrison's fictional world is circumscribed, in Gagnier's estimation; class, race, and gender remain "determinant social factors in characters' identities."[71] In contrast, Gagnier asserts that Nevinson's sentimental humanism vitiates his portrayal of working-class life, robbing it of realism. In her reading, Britton serves an interpellative function within the narrative, bringing the rhythms of retrospection and introspection to Nevinson's stories and imposing a fundamentally false, middle-class subjectivity on the realities of East End life. Gagnier characterizes Nevinson's working-class fiction as overly obsessed with the "introspective, self-conscious, self-interested" aspects of working-class character; his East Enders are hardy individualists who present no substantial threat or discomfort to Nevinson's middle-class readership. They seem readily glossed by reference to traditional, Liberal values.

However, Nevinson's curious tale of the rise of an East End music-hall star does not harmonize with a portrait of the East End as an organic, "knowable community"; nor does it unfold in agreement with the tenets of (Nevinson's own) Liberal humanism. Ben—known by those in the neighborhood as Scotty—and his successful career amount to a spectacular Cockney success story. Unlike Nevinson's other protagonists, Scotty breaks out of the neighborhood; in so doing, he encounters some of the threats that Nevinson insinuates pose a danger to working-class manhood. Scotty is the essential Cockney star, or will become one, but he is portrayed as an exception to typical Cockney manhood. His talent for mimicry is not freely developed but fixed, innate rather than a "hardy" working-class adaptation to environment. Britton grasps Scotty's talent for mimicry in the same terms in which he apprehends Scotty's singing ability: "As for singin', too, [he] seemed to have it born in 'im, same as a cage-bred lark as 'ill start singin' some mornin' just like other larks."[72] This metaphor of Scotty's natural talent seems carefully chosen. Nevinson figures Scotty's talent as a natural essence, not as a craft. The talent is something inborn that is also presented as beyond his control. For most of the tale, his abilities set him at odds with his community, his class, and even his own self.

Gagnier's claims, then, require some modification in the light of "Little Scotty," since the hapless protagonist bears the weight of determining forces on the biological level, if not within a social matrix. Nevinson portrays Scotty as having a talent that serves as an essence: the ability to imitate and represent others. Yet this curious essence does not fix or even form his character. Most of Scotty's self is seen to reside in unconscious impulses he cannot bring under control. Scotty's mimicry talent is portrayed as an expression of his essence, but it does little to determine his gender. Here, Nevinson imagines the music hall as a cultural form to play a beneficent role, for music-hall performance sets Scotty right and normalizes what might otherwise be a crippling eccentricity. In "Little Scotty," the East End halls, with their songs of costers and swells, and achieved hypermasculinity, sustain working-class manhood outside the purview of moral reform or philanthropic control.

Although Scotty is "born" to sing, it requires a great deal of cultural work for him to become a "natural" at the halls. "Little Scotty" centers on the conflict between Scotty's pursuit of the music hall and the Evangelical grandmother who raises him, Mrs. Macrae. The contest here is pitched not only as a conflict between moralities, but as a clash between masculine identity and domestic values. The domestic order maintained by Mrs. Macrae stands as an essential part of neighborhood lore. As Britton puts it, "But as to 'er bein' clean, all of 'em give in on that, there bein' no denying it. . . . For there's nobody livin' ever found a speck o' dirt anywhere in 'er place, not so much as a smear of mustard on the tablecloth."[73] Mrs. Macrae's cleanliness is the envy of other working-class women, although it also marks her difference from her neighbors; as Britton remarks, "The rest don't love 'er none the better for that and kept throwin' it up at 'er as she's got nothink to look after, only one boy of a grandson."

If Mrs. Macrae represents a mania for cleanliness more representative of bourgeois order than Cockney manners, Scotty at first appears to stand for the irascible, energetic misrule of the East Ender, a carefree nonchalance that middle-class readers expected and largely esteemed. An expert at mimicking the speech patterns and bodily carriage of others, Scotty constantly mocks his schoolteachers. In the playground, children "set 'im up . . . to take off somebody as all of us knowed, such as the coppers in the 'ighway or the parsons 'e'd heard preach. We'd only got to say the name, and 'e did the man we wanted."[74] These imitations do not express an insubordinate spirit. Scotty does not imitate in order to mock or critique authority; it is not, in Britton's words, a case of "makin' game of the teacher," a Salvation Army captain, or Scotty's grandmother, all of whom Scotty emulates well enough to unsettle their pose, and poise. Britton emphasizes that Scotty's imitations are compulsive; what he produces is taken for parody but issues outside his intentions. In Britton's words, he "just did it 'cos 'e couldn't 'elp it, 'e not winkin' at us, nor laughin."[75] His mimicry of authority is not a send-up of authority; his "parodies" are neither a display of manly prowess (although they entertain schoolboys) nor an expression of deliberate dissent.

This unconscious production of parody distinguishes Scotty from his peers, but not as a rebel temperament. Scotty's behavior reveals his eccentric, misfit selfhood. Britton also observes that Scotty fails to participate in the rituals of working-class boys: "So 'e didn't never join no gang, nor band, nor rode be'ind trams, nor came cat-'untin', or saw life. And nobody wouldn't 'ave thought nothink about 'im, no more nor if 'e'd been a girl, but for 'is bein' able to make us fair die with laughin' whenever 'e liked, and 'e keepin' 'is solemn little mug all the time." The natural-born singer never gets the joke, largely because he appears to lack any ability to reflect on his actions, let alone master his speech, mannerisms, or manhood. Scotty appears "at home" only within the domestic order constructed with great care by his grandmother; he spends most of his time "listenin' to 'er reading in 'er books." Britton cannot situate Scotty among the working-class activities and exploits in which the other boys participate; his ties to male companionship are brittle, based only in his ability "to do the police" in different voices. Scotty's ties to other boys in the neighborhood rely on skills that he is not believed to consciously control or exploit.

While mimicry makes Scotty noticeable to other boys—indeed, it's all that distinguishes him among the crowd—it troubles his gender identity. His formidable prowess at mimicry is never described without being feminized. Typical are Britton's comments as he listens to, and carefully watches, Scotty perform "Comin' through the Rye" at a church function: "But the moment 'e started singin,' you'd 'ave sworn 'e'd changed 'isself into a girl . . . , full of 'ankin' artful little ways, with a look this way, and a look that way, and smile down the middle."[76] Britton specifically links Scotty's abilities to his grandmother's influence. When Mrs. Macrae scolds Scotty for singing, his riposte is revealing: "All right, gran, . . . but it was yourself as taught it me." The notion that Scotty's natural talent might have a proximate social origin is also raised by Britton himself: "[I]t's certain she must 'ave been given to singin' 'erself at one time, for there wasn't nobody else could have taught Scotty all the queer songs he knowed."[77] In this alternative account, Scotty's talent and character are shaped by his grandmother and domestic values rather than by his relations with the neighborhood boys or older men.

Nevinson hedges on the origin of Scotty's talent, renders his character an ontological puzzle, and puts a question mark to the boy's gender identity. The ambiguity that accompanies the question of Scotty's nature only serves to make his eventual triumph at the music hall the more significant as an affirmation of his virility: a late but undeniable achievement. The halls offer entry into a man's world, and the trajectory of Scotty's career ends up scripted by masculine values.

The young man's uncontrollable mimicry proves a liability in the workplace, and soon Scotty is forced out of the navy for unintentional insubordination. Scotty drops out of the neighborhood, and outside of Britton's purview, until he is spotted one day on a poster. Britton spies "Little Scotty, the Star of the East," advertised at a hall in East London's infamous Mile End. Accompanied by his friend Lina and an anguished Mrs. Macrae, Britton attends Scotty's music-hall debut.

Nevinson's evocation of music-hall performance begins with the complex semantics of Scotty's stage name. "The Star of the East" evokes the symbolism that haunted middle-class reformers and charity workers. For many, East Enders signified as London's own, indigenous "dark natives." As Judith Walkowitz remarks, the conflict between London's East and West Ends "took on imperial and racial dimensions, as the two parts of London imaginatively doubled for England and its Empire."[78] Nevinson's music hall stages this complicated doubling of ideological codes. When Scotty's friends and family witness a minstrel show before Scotty appears to sing, Mrs. Macrae's horrified response to minstrelsy doubles for the contemporaneous critique leveled by many on the Left at music hall as nationalist, racist, and militarist, a critique that must have been familiar enough to Nevinson for him to internalize it.[79] Mrs. Macrae stands in for a "civilized," sophisticated criticism of music-hall performance; but she also stands in for the ineffectual nature of bourgeois self-critique. For the success of "Little Scotty," as well as the resolution of the gender cipher that stood at the core of his identity, stands as a rebuke to the reforming impulse. Scotty is an instant success with his audience: significantly, the performance is a triumph both for Scotty and the working-class men he entertains.

Onstage, Scotty puts on the various guises of working-class masculinity; his fluid identity finally coalesces into a character. When he first performs as "a ragged cross'-sweep," Britton recognizes in Scotty for the first time the figure of the besieged but winning Cockney male: "'Is nose and eyes was all pinched and screwed up with cold and 'unger, and yer coul' tell by the way 'e kep' lookin' round 'e'd only just escaped from somethink and was still scared almost out of 'is life. But there was a kind o' smile on 'is little mug, oh so artful."[80] Scotty's song portrays the casual laborer as Everyman, an image with powerful resonance for late-Victorian audiences. As Patrick Joyce observes, the Cockney figure depicted at the music hall worked to affirm a working-class presence within the city to working-class audiences and others, as well as attested to the prominent role played by the worker in the nation's own self-mythology.[81] Scotty's Cockney renderings served to remind Nevinson's middle-class readers of their hidden ties to outcast London. However, as Roger Henkle suggests, the Cockney also assimilated working-class "otherness" into something more compatible with middle-class desire, insinuating that workers were "individualistic, spirited, jingoistic, hard-playing, blunt, beef-eating, beer-drinking, and for all that, ultimately law abiding."[82] The Cockney affirmed class identity in ways that subtly confirmed class hierarchies: in breaking with middle-class moralism, the figure still circulated mostly reassuring messages about proletarian character. Certainly, as Scotty goes on to portray his working-class community, East End patriarchy comes to have more than a family resemblance to its middle-class counterpart.

Still, Scotty's presence begins to suggest something of a critique of middle-class moralism as much as its subtle recoding. In a world in which working-class masculinity was placed in crisis by the demands of casual labor, in which working-class women had de facto control of working-class households, Cockney swagger could also fly the flag of embattled male privilege.[83] As Britton continues to detail Scotty's performance, Nevinson suggests that Scotty's songs have their function. They bring Britton and the working-class men in the audience together in a mutual celebration of their difference from middle-class men. Scotty's performance glorifies a working-class aggression difficult to assimilate into middle-class moralizing: the Cockney that Scotty portrays gives notice to the pretensions of the philanthropic work that both Henry and Margaret Nevinson undertook in their time at Toynbee Hall. As if to mock the ineffectual nature of these endeavors to impose culture from above, Scotty's first song emphasizes the distance between working-class misrule and middle-class domestic order. Scotty's song about the neighborhood broadcasts the message that, in the normal run of events, working-class men *naturally* beat their wives, women *always* fight other women, and the Irish batter each other for profit:

> If yer want a bit o' quiet, destitoot o' noise or riot,
> Why, yer'd best come down our alley, and I'll show yer round,
> For there's Nelligan a-sayin' as Macarthy's self wants flayin',
> And 'e's doin' business on 'im as'll cost ten pound:
> Then there's blue-eyed flaxen Lily as is knockin' Susan silly,
> And there's Jemmy Gren just leavin, off from stampin' 'is wife:
>
> . . . .
>
> And if yer ke' a churchyard, why, yer'd see more life![84]

Here the underclass is imagined to live and breathe within a nexus of violence, perpetuated by men. The lyrics of the song amount to a compensatory fantasy for imperiled working-class masculinity. The rousing performance of the song, which elicits the greatest cheers from the audience, suggests that

Scotty has finally found a way to turn mimicry to his advantage, as well as to the profit of his community. The song affirms a virile, impossibly alive, working-class community, thriving outside bourgeois moral codes.

The performance not only confirms Scotty's ability to act like a man, but also effectively severs his ties to the domestic world. Scotty's act serves to distance him from his grandmother and allows him to escape her guidance. During the performance, Scotty's songs incite a running commentary from Mrs. Macrae that Britton does his best to tune out. Her criticism is primarily directed against the audience's approval of Scotty. From the outset, Mrs. Macrae is depicted as an unfit audience for music hall's rough fare: not because the fare is indeed too rough, but because she fails to esteem this toughness. Britton notes that the crowd enjoys the minstrel show before Scotty's performance as coarse spectacle: "The people fair loved them niggers, and roared with laughin' at 'em for lookin' like guys and makin' such queer noises."[85] Yet he also notes that Mrs. Macrae responds to the minstrelsy with a suspect—in these putatively "mean" surroundings—empathy for the enslaved women: "When a lot of darky savages, mostly women, came on, and started throwin' their legs about, and makin' as if they was killin' each other, she looks up a minute, and I 'ears 'er sayin': 'O Lord, O Lord, it's poor women-creatures like mysel', and all bought with a price!'"

Mrs. Macrae's reaction to Scotty's lyric evocation of neighborhood assault and battery is even more pointed. In response to his song about the neighborhood, she retorts, "It's lies, all lies he's sayin'. He's lyin' with lyin' lips."[86] Scotty's song about going on "'oliday at 'Ampstead 'Eath with Nannie and Fanny and Jane and Sue and Polly, all at the same time"—the best time the singer recalls since "'is 'ole pile of relations got blind drunk on th' day of 'is grandfather's funeral"—sends Scotty's grandmother out of the halls.[87] As Nevinson frames it, Scotty's performance has a ritual function in these surroundings: it isolates and marginalizes Mrs. Macrae and the values she represents. It also gives shape and heft to an imagined community organized around the aggressive display of masculinity and the repudiation of domestic values. In marked contrast to the distressed Mrs. Macrae, Britton is fully captivated by Scotty's performance, and Lina "'ad a mind to turn up 'er work at the ropes and take to the stage."

Despite Lina's positive response here, the narrative goes on to insinuate that neither she nor any woman can be fully at home in the music hall, nor are they intended to be. The form is not for them, the tale proposes. Later,

Lina's recollection of the evening causes her to denounce the very community Scotty's songs help sustain. She and Britton follow Mrs. Macrae home to find Mrs. Macrae upbraiding Scotty: "[B]ein' an 'auld wife, I've indulged ye l'ow 'er much. But the Lord, Ben, He will na indulge ye."[88] As Mrs. Macrae preaches to Scotty after his performance, Lina aligns herself with the values represented by the older woman. After the scene, Britton laments, Lina "didn't seem to care about love-makin', and the proper sort o' things." Instead, as Lina confesses to Britton, she is deeply unhappy with her lot in life: "I'm thinkin', Jacko, the kind o' life me and you lives in sometimes seems right enough, and sometimes it looks poor, some'ow—bleedin' poor." Lina's assent to the values espoused by Mrs. Macrae escapes Britton's regard; he responds to her lament with the insouciant, "'Ye're right,' says I, 'but thank God tomorrow's Sunday, and we can stop in bed all morning.'"[89] Britton's stoic resolve is given the last word over Lina's expression of "middle-class" scruples.

The different responses to Scotty expressed by Lina and Britton suggest the fault lines in the story are aligned with gender, as they are in Besant's tale, and Caine's. While Lina feels alienated by the working-class life Scotty presents, Britton's imagined community of manhood receives validation. The story closes with Scotty moving to the West End, gone on to conquer the West End music hall. Although neighborhood gossip hints that Scotty's grandmother saves the money Scotty sends her in the hope he will eventually leave the stage for the ministry, Britton knows better: "[B]less yer soul, Scotty ain't such a born fool as what that comes to."

The move away from the neighborhood seems to set Scotty's functional role for the community at risk, as well as endangering the links the tale posits between music hall and working-class ritual. Yet the reader is positioned to conclude, from the representative night of Scotty's performance figured by Nevinson, that the singer's gender identity, his manhood, has been secured, and exists safe from either his grandmother's strictures or Lina's more gentle rebuke. "Little Scotty" suggests performing at the halls resolves gender trouble, changing boys into men; more important, Scotty's work proffers a coherent and assertive masculine identity to other working-class men. Scotty's rise at the halls reflects the conflicted politics involved in representing London's East End, as well as the supposed pressures a working-class culture of resistance exerted against moral, "feminizing" influences brought in by middle-class charity workers. Above all, the success of "Little Scotty" situates the music hall outside a rhetoric of reform or Christian moralism. It is worthwhile to note the discrepancy between Henry Nevinson's portrayal of music halls and the "real" gender inclusion that began to dominate music-hall performance in the period. "Little Scotty" plays a subtle part in the backlash against the female performers who increasingly dominated the halls and the growing number of women—particularly single, working women—who were beginning to make up a substantial portion of music-hall audiences.[90] Judith Walkowitz observes how female comic singers played a crucial role in redefining music-hall style; these women nightly deflated the pretensions of the "swell," the popular figure of the young, lower-middle-class man who traversed the city's pleasure zones with inimitable style.[91]

"Little Scotty" neglects the reality of prominent women at the halls as, in their own ways, do the narratives produced by Besant and Caine. If, as Walkowitz suggests, "no clearly hegemonic gender message" emerged from the volatile collective nightly assembled at the halls, Nevinson's story attempts to concentrate these disparate energies.[92] It seeks to provide music-hall performance with a unified and univocal meaning. The narrative asserts that the halls performed a cultural task in response to the gender-specific needs of their working-class audience: they stabilized male identity and patriarchal prerogative. In "Little Scotty," the halls also secure the performer's own unstable identity. The music halls are imagined as a safe zone in which men can be men and reclaim manhood, and resist the moralism imported into East End communities by middle-class reformers. Nevinson's narrative seeks to assert the integral importance of music hall to working-class culture, while at the same time significantly simplifying the expressive range of this culture. Gareth Stedman Jones asserts that late-Victorian music halls resisted "bourgeois tutelage" despite their compromise with nationalist values; certainly Nevinson wished to believe in and express the autonomy of music hall from tutelary intellectuals, and "Little Scotty" expresses faith in the ever-resistant powers of music hall.[93] Certainly, as I suggested in the case of the music-hall lament, the unsettling power of music-hall performance was a credo espoused by many literary intellectuals, and it served to ground an entire discourse that imagined the form's freedom from commercial assimilation and middle-class cultural appropriation. The defense of music hall could be framed as a powerful separatist message: in outcast London, the working classes have an entertainment that works according to a different logic than middle-class order allows. "Little Scotty" insinuates that what troubles middle-class female sensibilities about music-hall performance can redeem a threatened working-class manhood.

The texts I have examined imagine the music hall as a strong cultural force that makes over and transforms working-class culture. Insofar as these writers suggest that music halls reduce working-class culture to criminal activity, the halls themselves symbolize a dangerous species of mass culture. Yet while these fictions by Besant, Caine, and Nevinson gesture toward music-hall culture as participating in the full-bore "homogenization of difference" feared by literary modernism, they also retreat from this generalization.[94] These texts also work to reestablish plausible links between the music hall and working-class community. The performances these writers detail are not simply "spectacle" or commercial entertainment. Partly through their auditory appeal, performers are believed to forge and sustain communal life. To judge by "Little Scotty," the potent flavor of song, including its lyric component, underlies music hall's expressive force for Nevinson, and, to a lesser degree, for Caine. In The Christian, the community that the music hall sustains desperately needs to be uplifted under the watchful gaze of male administrators. Both Nevinson and Caine portray a music hall that expresses working-class character in an almost unmediated fashion. Nonetheless, these authors also suggest that working-class culture needs tutelary control of the right sort: experts, either from within (Scotty) or without (John Storm) who can reestablish an imperiled gender hierarchy. In the case of Nevinson's "the Star of the East," the boy without a character, but an innate impulse to mimic and imitate, becomes an avatar of his community and its wild life. His inability to shape his character and assume a man's role gets recuperated as boon for the community. His ability to record and play back Cockney mannerisms helps coalesce a community believed to be under siege by intrusive middle-class reformers. He is fated to repeat the rites of working-class masculinity that he failed to internalize as a young man.

This is to say that Scotty has found that he can establish his masculinity only by embracing its serial repetition as performance. Inevitably the music-hall fictions I examine thematize performance, suggesting, most strongly in Nevinson's case, that cultural truths themselves are fabrications: made, not found. These fictive explorations of performance also imagine the spaces of a burgeoning consumer world, in which images are produced and consumed and "things are inseparable from how they look."[95] My next chapter deals with a form of music-hall performance that literary intellectuals experienced considerable difficulty explaining, justifying, and textualizing: the late-Victorian "Living Pictures." The demand for pictures and images, especially prominent at the most affluent London halls in the 1890s and the early years of the next century, suggest the prevalence of the desire to treat images as commodities, too. Music-hall tableaux in variety theaters like the Empire and the Palace Theatre constituted a signifying economy in which the display of poses counted as highly meaningful semiosis. At issue was a proliferating, abundant display of poses "whose primary function," in Martha Banta's words, "was to incite, and sell, desire."[96] The music hall, along with the shop window, the street poster, and the picture gallery, was utilized as a space where the general desire to produce attractive displays and salable illusions could be given free reign.

Striking a pose during the fin de siècle was a mode of seduction aimed at a spectator who was characterized as, above all else, a consumer. The work entailed in producing and embodying resonant images that could keep an audience was considerable. In the heyday of creative posing, it became impossible to fully distinguish the complex semiosis of posing from the arduous labor that was acknowledged as necessary to produce an esteemed work of art in the visual or verbal realm. The success of the tableaux depended on the skill of the model and impresario not simply to imitate, but to affiliate with, a tradition of high-cultural endeavor. By participating in posing, working-class women transformed their figures into "classical" bodies in order to acquire the cultural and symbolic capital believed to inhere within high-status artistic achievement. Martha Banta discerns in the many languages of posing shared by American women of the Victorian era a broad-based endeavor to rename the body and to "[appropriate] the language of bodily attitudes for their ends."[97] I suggest that similar efforts to renominalize the body motivated the models who acted as Living Pictures on the London music-hall stage. The art of posing connected these women to a major nexus of cultural power with ideals of grace, tradition, and classical norms. The women who struck classical poses embodied, and in some measure appropriated, the mantle of cultural authority. I will consider next the attempts by these workers to annex prestige and a measure of legitimacy for their career and themselves, as well as the efforts of middle-class philanthropists to break the circuits of symbolic power and disrupt the various spectacles of consumer culture.

5

"Spectacular" Bodies

TABLEAUX VIVANTS AT THE PALACE THEATRE

An inspector for the London County Council visiting in 1893 the Palace Theatre of Varieties, an opera house that had been converted into a music hall two years before, duly noted that entertainment at the Palace featured "skirt dancers . . . ballet, etc., which involved the usual display of limbs encased in tights."[1] However, prominent among that evening's exhibitions at the Palace were "Living Pictures," re-creations on the music-hall stage of paintings by Royal Academy artists such as Lawrence Alma-Tadema and Lord Leighton. Edward Kilyani's Living Pictures allowed for the prominent display of simulated nudity, as models draped in muslin performed as still lifes in classical poses. On this occasion the inspector's report for the council demonstrated, as Susan Pennybacker observes, "a remarkable preference for aesthetic concerns over suppression of vice."[2] He found the pictures, or, as they were often called, "tableaux vivants," to be "skillful and artistic living representations of well-known paintings and sculptures."

The inspector used the occasion to consider whether "the nude" could ever be cordoned off into an autonomous realm of the aesthetic: "Some people . . . would simply object to such public and complete display of the female form. It is a matter of difficulty to fix the exact point where propriety ends and impropriety begins. The borderline which divides the legitimate from the objectionable is not well-defined. I have endeavoured to report the facts as impartially as I can, and it is not for me, but for the Committee, to approve or condemn."[3] The inspector's deference to municipal authority sidesteps the vexed question of where legitimate artistic endeavor ends and illicit entertainment begins. Here, the problem of separating legitimate entertainment from spurious pleasures is largely avoided by recourse to what is simply seen: the inspector need only report on what he witnessed.

The controversy elicited by tableaux vivants, a frequent staple of the fin-de-siècle halls, was not to be settled by appeals to the self-evident. Tableaux vivants, or, as they were often called earlier in the century, "poses plastiques," had long been a risqué theatrical attraction. However, the Living Pictures became a special focus of controversy nearly a year after the initial appearance of Edward Kilyani's traveling troupe at the Palace Theatre in late 1893. In August 1894, Lady Henry Somerset, leader of the Women's Christian Temperance Union, entered a formal protest against the tableaux before the London County Council. She was joined in her protest by W. A. Coote, a leading official in the social purity movement in the National Vigilance Association; his organization supported Somerset in challenging the renewal of the Palace's liquor license.

The Palace controversy involved many of the same citizens initially galvanized by the Maiden Tribute controversy and the effort to repeal the Contagious Diseases Amendment.[4] Unlike the similar protest of purity workers over the presence of prostitutes in the Empire music hall in 1894, the dispute over the Palace did not necessarily draw special attention to the authority of women philanthropists or purity workers; nor did it stop the Living Pictures at the Palace.[5] Throughout the decade, controversy over tableaux vivants was often simply deferred, as if no one quite knew how to handle the entertainment. Protests could be quelled through compromise, since managers quickly moved to appease troubled authorities. Although the Palace liquor license was never denied, a member of Parliament wrote to the Theatres and Music Halls Committee the month of Lady Somerset's public protest, warning, "[I]f you wish to conciliate public opinion, which I believe is becoming increasingly hostile to these representations, then *prompt* action on your part is desirable."[6] In response to these pressures, Palace manager Charles Morton quickly dropped what he considered the more risqué tableaux.[7]

Morton's actions illustrate how controversy over the Living Pictures at the Palace could promptly shift from public scandal to uneasy, secret compromises. However, for a brief time in 1894, the debate over tableaux vivants, as John Stokes put it, "reinvigorated the old topic of the 'naked' and the 'nude.'"[8] The dispute over the Living Pictures created a crisis in accepted notions of aesthetic value by addressing feminine spectacle. The purity workers' attack on tableaux vivants placed these entertainments under scrutiny at a moment when variety theater was becoming increasingly supported by middle-class constituencies. The ensuing controversy over tableaux vivants instigated an intriguing exchange, expressed and contested in the public sphere, about women, mass entertainment, and the nature of the aesthetic. The debate over Living Pictures at the Palace illustrates the importance of intellectuals—various experts in culture and taste—in determining the proper boundaries of "entertainment." Defining the borders of the permissible is among the acts "of those experts in culture, who patrol the ever shifting borders of popular and legitimate taste";[9] certainly the controversy over the Living Pictures empowered "experts" to clarify the boundaries the inspector found difficult to determine. What he suggested was a delicate matter to arbitrate was what other authorities were emboldened to define.

This chapter, focusing on tableaux vivants of the period, reexamines how certain images of women become privileged, commodified, and, ultimately, consumed. There is, however, something incongruous about linking the efforts of intellectuals to elaborate common sense with a volatile, potentially libidinal entertainment such as the Living Pictures. Theories of the male gaze have typically argued that visual pleasure turns spectators into passive voyeurs.

In Laura Mulvey's classic discussion of the pleasures of looking in Hollywood film, "Visual Pleasure and Narrative Cinema," the display of women in cinema places them in essentially passive roles beside the activity of male protagonists, whose desire to see without being seen determines the very apparatus of film. Mulvey emphasizes the determinations mass entertainment exerts on spectator response; she stresses how "cinematic codes create a gaze, a world, and an object, thereby producing an illusion cut to the measure of desire."[10] The voyeurism and wish fulfillment that Mulvey finds privileged in mainstream cinema are, as we will see, prefigured in the production of the tableaux vivants at the Palace Theatre of Varieties.

However, the female nude was not linked simply to scopic pleasure for late-Victorian London spectators; audiences participated in a complex production of meaning when they encountered the female body in settings that encouraged aesthetic evaluation. Experiencing the Living Pictures at the Palace meant encountering feminine display in a highly mediated fashion; new stage technologies including lighting techniques and elaborate stage backdrops encouraged audiences to situate the nude in narrative contexts that might assuage any unease caused by display of the female form.[11] Mulvey argues the presence of women in Hollywood film "tends to work against the development of a story line," tugging against the constraints of diegesis and inciting desultory fantasies in male spectators.[12] The reception of the Living Pictures indicates that the exhibition provided careful contexts that situated erotic spectacle. Further, entertainment at the Palace was not simply consumed but also critiqued; the dispute over the Palace's Living Pictures, instigated by Lady Somerset, was an intervention in the production of a mass entertainment. The controversy elicited a public dialogue over the women who performed in the tableaux vivants and their status as workers. This public mediation of events contrasts with the emphasis most theorists of the gaze set on the construction of individual subjects through scopic pleasure.

What the controversy over the pictures suggests is that consumer decision, as Simon Frith and Howard Horne emphasize, is "the subject . . . of moral and political assessment and choice."[13] In its assumption of a passive spectator prone to voyeurism and fantasies, Laura Mulvey's description of spectatorship belongs to a tradition of modernist pessimism about the very act of consumption. While Mulvey recounts how classic Hollywood narrative privileges male observers, her account genders viewers as classically "feminine": passive and prone to nostalgia, daydreams, and furtive desire. These spectators are languid consumers, compliant subjects who willingly yield to the "masculine" apparatus of cinema that informs them of their erotic longings. In this respect Mulvey's analysis corresponds to many accounts of consumers that equate consumption with passivity and focus on easily manipulated audiences.

Although tableaux vivants in the fin-de-siècle music hall staged the female body as spectacle, I do not treat the exhibitions as another example of the "monolith of misogyny";[14] this chapter explores the ways such spectacular entertainment raised questions of class. My focus on the response to the Living Pictures gestures toward something inadequately registered in Mulvey's analysis of cinematic convention: the continuous pressure of class-based tastes on any consumer choice. The history of tableaux vivants and of their response is inseparable from class-bound codes of taste and disgust; an account of these exhibitions does much to illuminate how codes of inclusion, self-regulation, and exclusion function historically.

Fin-de-siècle music halls and the spectacles they displayed cannot be isolated from questions of class. The halls were in many ways a summit in late-Victorian consumer culture. The London music hall provides a case study in how a private, upper-class amusement became a commodity. Music hall was transformed by a series of changes, starting in the 1860s and continuing through their heyday, the 1890s. Such changes, including the routinizing of entertainments, the professionalization of labor, the increasing regulation of audience interaction with performers, the fixing of audience position, and the growth of management, are well documented.[15] For this reason, Guy Debord's suggestions about the expansion of the market into everyday life—into forms of leisure, personal expression, and private desire—illuminate the topic of this chapter. Debord's theory about the "society of the spectacle," dating from the mid-1960s, is primarily concerned with how electronic media have "colonized" everyday life through television, cinema, and advertising in an age of late capital. However, the "spectacle" is not simply about electronic media; in Debord's qualification, "the spectacle is not a collection of images, but a social relation among people, mediated by images."[16] Spectators at the Palace were a target audience for the leisure industry, part of an attempt to incite patrons who would come and watch. Attending the Palace Theatre meant a spectator entered a space designed for mass consumption; in that respect, the experience prefigured the proliferation of the commodity in other areas of social life.

Despite Guy Debord's tendency to read consumer culture as a monolith and his own later quietism, his analysis decidedly emphasizes the social effects of spectacle: how spectacle functions as part of a complex network of social relations, and how spectatorship works as a social practice.[17] Certainly the fad for posing that swept the halls in the 1890s announces a society organized increasingly around spectacle, with images of high art eliciting new needs and desires, if only for more images to consume.

Still, while tableaux helped link the halls to a spectacular consumerism, these pictures also participated in a community of signs and images, an entire set of conventions that spoke powerfully to the dominant order. Further, as Martha Banta suggests of the posing craze that swept turn-of-the-century America, tableaux suggested a tremendous "talent for pleasure" uniting spectators across class boundaries.[18] It seems futile to deny the pleasure of the pose: for many working-class women, posing not only provided economic support but, as we will see, amounted to something like a strategy for the appropriation of cultural capital. The luster of artistic tradition allowed performing women to accrue such symbolic gain while it furthered the distribution of this capital.

This chapter links the triumph of tableaux in the halls during the 1890s to the logic of "spectacle." Still, Debord's critique of spectacle does not fully translate to earlier instances of public posing in the late-Victorian era. Spectacle did not ensure the passive gaze or the full objectification of women workers. For the Victorians, spectacular entertainment did not simply produce the passive regime of looking that Debord anatomizes. Indeed, this chapter suggests that the dominant culture had but tenuous control over the origins and practice of tableaux vivants, as well as over the new subject of leisure that music-hall entertainment appears to have produced.[19]

Background

Tableaux vivants originated as aristocratic diversion, linked to state ceremony; it was not until late in the eighteenth century that they were linked to sexualized display. In 1787, Goethe attended the new, more exclusive tableaux vivants: an upper-class entertainment staged in Sir William Hamilton's Naples residence, where his mistress Emma Hart posed in colored costume within a frame that simulated classical painting. The presentation included theatrical elements such as lighting, costuming, and a makeshift stage.[20] Goethe hailed Hamilton as a genuine impresario, and the tableau as a logical culmination of the aesthetic project. Hamilton privately saw, Goethe declares, "what thousands of artists would have liked to express realized before him in movements and surprising transformations."[21] Genteel private entertainments such as Hamilton's depended on a select audience's acquaintance with classical art; although there were no attempts to reproduce specific paintings, as later tableaux did, classical literacy—and the requisite cultural capital associated with humane learning—was required for spectators to respond properly to the display.

Yet here at the inception of the nineteenth-century craze for posing, we can detect how this brand of spectacle was open to appropriative possibilities. As Martha Banta remarks, Goethe was quick to point out that he regarded Emma Hart herself as a "vulgar and rather boring woman," while, in Banta's words, "the woman he watched in performance was the personification of grace."[22] When Emma strikes a pose, she becomes magically transformed into a type. Goethe is fascinated by Hart's ability to leave behind the accidents of an individual life—and sidestep male prejudice—to become an exceptional form. As Banta suggests, Emma's history as artist's model and fallen woman disappears when she aspires to model the ideal.

Goethe's description of tableaux vivants in *Elective Affinities* (1809) stimulated a vogue for the entertainments. The newspaper *Allgemeine Literatur-Zeitung* in 1810 heralded Goethe's presentation of tableaux vivants in his novel as a signal event in the history of aesthetic discourse: "The fashionable world is also indebted to Herr Goethe for the new kind of pastime which he has invented. After exhausting everything which nature and art can provide in the ordinary way, he has hit upon the idea of getting living people to imitate paintings."[23] Goethe's use of the pictures not only suggested a "fashionable" aesthetic innovation, a new, refined entertainment: it also connected the tableaux to culpable feminine spectacle. In *Elective Affinities,* Luciane and Ottilie's engagement in tableaux vivants confirms a link between spectacle and essential "feminine" character. When Ottilie takes part in a Christmas tableau, "the humility, wonder and happiness in Ottilie's performance are truths of the self," as Martin Meisel observes.[24] Luciane's performance, however, in the staging of Gerard Terborch's *Paternal Admonition,* reveals Luciane, an ambitious and forceful personality, as a character in need of correction. Goethe assumes an intimate connection between mimesis and the truths of feminine character in his presentation of the novel's tableaux; a woman is what she represents. The power of Emma Hart, which so moved Goethe, is exempt from his moral reproof, attesting to the symbolic liberty woman gained from the patriarchy by assuming a pose.

The vogue for tableaux vivants opened them up for use beyond exclusive salons or drawing rooms: no longer limited to private audiences of refinement, they became a staple of mainstream French theater, in which they were dubbed *poses plastiques.* Tableaux vivants were featured alongside melodrama at Drury Lane, which always maintained a loyal working-class audience. They entailed the arrangement of human figures, often against a staged backdrop, and required that these figures remain still until the curtain was drawn. In theatrical performance, the models would often rearrange in a series of displays; music or spoken commentary often accompanied the visual presentation.

Tracy Davis observes that tableaux vivants followed "a circuitous and sordid route to the British stage": part of the disgust the presentations elicited was constructed by class bias. Perhaps it was inevitable that when displays of the body moved from safe, domestic spaces into public arenas with heterogeneous audiences it would raise fears of contamination. If, as Peter Stallybrass and Allon White argue, the "very highness of high culture" is constructed through "the obsessive banishment of the low," tableaux vivants initially must have constituted a defense against the threatening presence of lower-class bodies.[25] The "classical body"—"a refined, orifice-less laminated surface"[26]—embodies certain values that counter the danger posed by grotesque bodies, the bodies that those who lack culture are imagined to possess.[27] When this "classical body" encountered the charged, public space of English stage melodrama, the results could only be volatile. The conflation of feminine display with the norms of classical culture could not be transferred to "vulgar" spaces. Once it left privileged spectators who could read the codes of classical literacy, the private pose embodying aesthetic beauty became degraded display. The contentious history of the entertainment on the nineteenth-century English stage suggests the difficulty of eliciting a proper response to such performances from a heterogeneous crowd. Although advertisements for tableaux vivants often reasserted their claims to artistic value and "classical" status, the display of nude bodies in front of diverse audiences could result only in an unruly spectacle.[28]

For these reasons, tableaux vivants often appeared to have a "grotesque" character—and appeal—to the late Victorians. When Edward Kilyani's "Living Pictures" came to the Palace Theatre in 1893, both Kilyani and the theater manager, Charles Morton, endeavored to present a spectacle that was properly managed and compatible with bourgeois tastes. To do so, Kilyani entered into an immense struggle against the entire previous history of these exhibitions. An entertainment often contaminated through association with a popular audience, tableaux vivants, in their actual practice throughout the century, subjected the "classical body" to a lower-class travesty.

Tableaux took their place among a dazzling panorama of quite disparate display at Leicester Square's Suffolk Home club, where they were only one segment in a dizzying, carnivalesque exhibition of amusements. Bohemian journalist George Augustus Sala recalls the poses plastiques at the Suffolk Home[29] as a part of a bewildering collection of commodities that often included "[s]erpents both of land and sea; panoramas of all the rivers of the known world; jugglers, ventriloquists; imitators of the noises of animals; dioramas of the North Pole, and the gold-diggers of California; somnambulists (very lucid); ladies who have cheerfully submitted to have their heads cut off nightly at sixpence per head admission; giants; dwarfs; sheep with six legs; calves born inside out."[30] Such displays echo the parade of commodities triumphantly exhibited in the Great Exhibition (1852).[31] For Sala, tableaux proved to be a commodity that was difficult to standardize as it was exhibited: his attitude toward the tableaux evidences clear class condescension. He describes them as "clumsy caricatures of good pictures and good statues, enacted on a turn-table by brazen men and women."

Sala's account illustrates the ease with which the cultural capital of classical heritage could become debased currency. For Sala, the foreign actors assuming roles sullied the aspiration of the form to the status of genteel culture. The line between performing in low entertainment and overt criminality is easily crossed, as this account suggests:

> I, your servant, assisted once at a representation . . . where the subject was Adam and Eve in the garden of Eden. Adam by Herr Something, Eve by Madame Somebody, and the serpent by a *real serpent,* a bloated old snake quite sluggish and dozy . . . The most amusing part of the entertainment was the middle thereof, at which point two warriors arrayed in the uniform of Her Majesty appeared on the turn-table, and claimed Adam as a deserter from the Third Buffs; which indeed he was, and so was summarily marched off with a great-coat over his fleshlings, and neat pair of handcuffs on his wrists.[32]

Sala recalls a tableau at another theater that presented "the most magnificent parable in the New Testament parodied into a gee-gaw spectacle—a convention between the property-man, the scene painter, and the corps de ballet": the fear that such performance debased rather than transmitted cultural tradition prompted the otherwise tolerant Sala to call for state intervention. He complains sarcastically about "the charming efficiency of the Lord Chamberlain and his licencers, who can strike a harmless joke out of a pantomime, and cannot touch such fellows as these, going vagabondizing about with nothing to cover them."[33] In Sala's description of the tableaux nudity is of less importance than the productions' deflation of cultural objects. The poses plastiques are unable to embody value; they simply refer spectators back to lower-class citizens who impersonate classical bodies. The failure of poses plastiques to represent the cultural heritage endangered the values of traditional aesthetic display.

When tableaux vivants moved from public, heterosocial spaces to predominantly male enclaves, the cultured pretensions of tableaux vivants were exposed to open parody and ridicule. Poses plastiques were added to the salacious entertainments at Renton "Judge" Nicholson's Coal Hole in 1858 and quickly became part of Nicholson's ritualized male license. Dubbed by theater historian Harold Scott "a convenient resort for journalists and men of letters," the Coal Hole catered to an audience of "Bohemians and intellectuals, considerably removed from . . . lower middle-class patrons."[34] The famous journalist/social explorer James Greenwood complained that the Coal Hole corrupted young men from the provinces who visited London during the Cattle Show season in search of urbane entertainment.[35] Entertainment at the Coal Hole promoted gender and class solidarity among men; the bohemians who attended the Coal Hole were, to their mind, different from the affluent bourgeois above and working-class audiences below; their rituals of leisure demarcated a special realm of their own.

Under Nicholson's managerial control, the Coal Hole offered patrons alcohol, parodic images of transgressive women, and the opportunity to intervene or participate in the evening's entertainment. The Coal Hole had no raised stage dividing audience and performer. The Judge and Jury Society, presided over by Nicholson, staged public "trials" concerned with seduction, divorce, and sexual scandal, recounted with studied coarseness and double entendres. "Witnesses," many of them male performers in drag, were cross-examined before the audience was permitted to join in the banter. Drag performance at the Coal Hole did not circumvent masculine roles: rather it affirmed masculine order. The comic trials routinely burlesqued "dangerous" women—prostitutes, divorced women—normally excluded from the bourgeois symbolic order.

Nicholson's club celebrated impertinent behavior and attacked sacrosanct values. James Greenwood, in an account of a visit to the Coal Hole, describes a "disgusting wretch in woman's attire," who played a prostitute on trial, "and who was supposed to be a native of Germany, importing filthy blunders into his broken English."[36] The sketch that Greenwood relates included this female impersonator, a convict, and a policeman with "his belly stuffed out with hay in a highly humourous manner."[37] Greenwood experiences a visceral disgust at the spectacle: "Assisted by the judge and counsel, the man in the bonnet and petticoats would now and then utter a something that came at one as a rotten egg might, causing a shudder and a sensation of sickness at the stomach."[38] In fact the trial comes to a comic halt midperformance when the "German prostitute" throws his wig in the counsel's face. It is clear from Greenwood's inflammatory rhetoric that in the Judge and Jury sketch, "drag" constitutes not an avowal of gender ambiguity but a travesty of "womanhood," just as the codes of foreignness threaten Greenwood's own sense of Englishness.

Nicholson's introduction of poses plastiques into his Judge and Jury Society performances brought tableaux vivants into a volatile space. Poses plastiques were performed to illustrate a lecture given by Nicholson on poetry and the arts. Women sang out of sight until the curtains were drawn back in a dramatic moment of exposure. The posed women were attired in flesh-colored costumes, simulating nudity. The spectacle was staged after the Judge and Jury performances and broke the homosocial ambience of the Coal Hole; women were invited to attend the performance. As late as the 1870s, Greenwood observed that audiences still noticeably increased during tableaux performances.

From the outset, Nicholson's control over the display of women at the Coal Hole was evident; through lectures, stage apparatus, and the promise of a cultured entertainment, Nicholson worked to control the effects of feminine spectacle. This was a role with which he was familiar; in his edition of *The Swell's Night Guide through the Metropolis* (1841) Nicholson wrote as cultured guide to "temples of voluptuousness." The book advised young swells on where to see French women "in every possible state, from complete nudity to the half-dressed, go through the most voluptuous exhibitions— imitate the classic models—and perform the most spirit-stirring dances."[39] It is difficult to resist finding Nicholson's role as Coal Hole lecturer and as procurer of clients for masculine nightlife in *The Swell's Night Guide* essentially homologous; both activities illustrate entrepreneurial control of feminine display. As tour guide and "host," Nicholson monitors such spectacle and offers it for consumption.

Journalist James Greenwood's description of poses plastiques at the Coal Hole relies on a common misogyny to convey his distaste with the proceedings. Greenwood is unimpressed with the technology behind the display; he describes the first tableau in a disenchanted fashion as "four ordinary and elderly females attired in fleshlings and kilts, hand in hand, and revolving on a pedestal, as though the machinery that moved them were a roasting-jack."[40] Greenwood notes that the tableau of "The Three Graces" produced no effect but a "slight tittering"; otherwise the audience was "unmoved." And "No wonder," Greenwood adds: "Fancy a trio of bold-faced women, with noses snub, Roman, and shrewish, with wide mouths and eyes coarse-footed, having the impudence to represent the graces!"

Greenwood strives to demystify the spectacle of the poses plastiques and take away its glamour, in order to dissuade customers from attending the performances. The Coal Hole is represented as a space filled with cultural rubes and amateur aesthetes, to be avoided by men of culture. The club is figured in the threatening image of a "dragon that has devoured many green men." It is noteworthy that Greenwood, like Sala, is not as shocked by nudity as at the inappropriateness of using "coarse" women to represent classical forms and normative feminine beauty. The social explorer shares with Sala a distinct distaste for the class transgression manifest in the public display of poses plastiques, in which the classical body became tainted when circulated in spaces outside the controlled area of the aristocratic drawing room.

Greenwood's essay attempts to bury both the poses plastiques and the Coal Hole, but his efforts to herald the end of such diversions largely indicate his own anxiety that such spectacles may continue to spread. The *Saturday Review*'s impassioned attack on poses plastiques in 1874, the same year Greenwood's account was published, does not cast the poses plastiques as an innocuous entertainment losing its audience. On the contrary: the *Saturday Review* suggests that the exhibition not only was flourishing but still retained a transgressive charge.

Complaining of a "certain class of performers—not actresses, for they cannot act or speak or sing—who may be called, for want of a better name, exposers of their persons," the journal attacks in particular an unnamed theater manager and her "free and unabashed display of her undraped figure. The exhibition of a big woman who appears to be wholly unclothed except for about a foot and a half round her middle is one which may be commended to the attention of the Censor." Like Greenwood, the *Saturday Review* is less disturbed about the impropriety of poses plastiques than about how the display disrupts the spectacle of the classical, orderly body: clearly the epithet "big" carries the weight of opprobrium in this observer's account.

The manager's exhibition is dangerous because it insolently discloses the gap between real bodies and the classical body of high art.

Worse, the poses plastiques threaten the circulation of proper, tasteful art. "It cannot be doubted," the *Saturday Review* continues, "that it is in the interest of genuine art that resolute measures should be used to clear the stage of the models of the studio, and the lay figures of lascivious poses plastiques." The "lay figures" of tableaux vivants threaten the professionalization of the actress at a historic juncture when social sanction of the theater was broadening.[41] "When a taint of this kind breaks out," the journal concludes, "it has a tendency to spread. It frightens respectable persons away from an honourable profession, it attracts disreputable persons towards it, and it tempts people who have no preference for impropriety in itself to try how far they can go in competition with it."[42]

The account likens poses plastiques to the current practice of displaying actresses' photographs in shop windows. Both provide images of commodified femininity that challenge claims to theatrical professionalism:

> Nothing can be more sadly significant than the representation of the theatrical profession which is exhibited in the windows of the photograph shops. Who are the young persons with fantastic hair and very low-bodiced dresses who are there depicted? Are they actresses capable of articulate speech or of the faintest kind of histrionic personation? . . . In many cases they are women who find in this sort of publicity a useful advertisement of another trade.[43]

The professional features of the actress are played off the physicality of women on display; the comparison to prostitution suggests itself immediately. The editorial clearly establishes a binary of corrupt physical display and commendable rhetorical ability. Although, as Peter Fryer observes, the poses plastiques continued their popularity in London theater throughout the 1870s and 1880s, journalism marked them as a degrading spectacle that threatened the genuine aspirations of theatrical professionals to respectability.[44]

As these examples suggest, tableaux vivants were largely associated by the end of the century with an unsavory brand of spectacle. The difficulty with the exhibitions lay not only in their simulated nudity but also in the discrepancy between the cultured body and the working-class performer who represented the classical form in front of heterogeneous audiences. The approbation of the classical body meant the purposeful exclusion of what the bourgeois would "[mark] out as low—as dirty, repulsive, noisy, contaminating"; this cultured ideal needed a substantial amount of policing in order to be maintained as a hegemonic standard.[45] In poses plastiques, women outside the symbolic economy of bourgeois decorum might represent the classical body. Tableaux vivants often used models employed by professional artists; the new technology, however, permitted the class markers of the body to be erased. The effects were literally unreal.

Kilyani's Pictures

Edward Kilyani's troupe of Living Pictures, whose tour visited the Palace Theatre in 1893, performed complicated ideological work in order to secure its acceptance, let alone its success, with a popular audience. Kilyani's entertainments had to secure public consent for a performance that was largely linked to inappropriate, indecent display. The success of Kilyani's troupe demonstrates how an entertainment form not only achieved financial success for an economically troubled theater, but also constructed an audience that would steadily support the exhibition.

Kilyani's success lay in the unprecedented technology he designed for his Living Pictures, which, unlike the poses plastiques of twenty years before, reproduced paintings with realism. Technical advances in lighting led to the marshalling of quite literally spectacular effects: sophisticated lighting could even make models appear as if they were cut from marble.[46] Reviewers praised the lighting techniques for securing an unprecedented "softness of tone and absence of shadow" in figures. Special illusionist techniques were used in the display of "Venus de Milo"; as one reviewer observes, "the arms of the woman personating the armless figure were draped in sleeves of the same color and texture as the background." "The illustration was so perfect," the reviewer adds, "as well-nigh to defy detection." Kilyani's design for a revolving table, divided in sections, with removable backgrounds led to a remarkably rapid change between different tableaux. The degree of attention given to matters of verisimilitude in background and scenery, and to musical accompaniment for the Living Pictures, was considerable.

These advances in illusionist technique allowed for a remarkable control over the nude figure on display; they also offered new possibilities to aestheticize nudity in displaying and controlling the spectacle of the female body. The new technology Kilyani developed for the display of tableaux vivants is best understood as constructing new forms of knowledge about the body, connecting the desire to see and know more about the human figure to the pleasure of visual spectacle. Kilyani's Living Pictures partakes in what film historian Jean-Louis Comolli has called the "frenzy of the visible" that "dominated the latter half of the nineteenth century." Comolli draws attention to the proliferation of optical inventions in the late nineteenth century—cameras, magic lanterns, dioramas, biographs—"machines of the visible" that place the body under new, intense scrutiny. Along with the "ever wider distribution of illustrated papers, waves of prints, caricatures," such machinery ensured the "geographical extension of the field of the visible and the representable" during the Victorian age.[47]

The simultaneous development of these technologies places Kilyani's inventions for the Palace tableaux in the proper context. The links between Living Pictures and cinematic apparatus were clear and explicit to contemporaries. Advance notices for Edison's Vitascope candidly made the connection: "By this invention," they promised, "veritable living pictures are thrown upon a screen."[48] Kilyani's exhibitions anticipated the film studies of female subjects that debuted in music halls in the late 1890s; the Living Pictures already linked new technology with female display. The affinity between greater verisimilitude and increased scopic pleasure was made evident in the new Living Pictures.

Kilyani's exhibition also utilized the erotic potential already culturally encoded in the display of women's bodies. The cultural imperative to enhance the visual observation of bodies affected the female nude differently than it affected male bodies. Kilyani's tableaux vivants and the problems the exhibition symbolically resolved are best understood by comparison with other technologies that predated the development of film apparatus. In her analysis of the motion studies included in Eadweard Muybridge's *Animal Locomotion* (1887), Linda Williams draws attention to Muybridge's difficulty in making photographic studies of women appear unselfconscious. Where men could be filmed with minimal props, Muybridge felt compelled to place his female studies among suggestive mise-en-scènes and mininarratives. In effect, Muybridge invented scenarios to make sense of the women on display. Where two men posing engage in activities such as contact sports for the camera, Muybridge stages subtle mise-en-scènes to justify his exhibition of women. In one scene, a woman pours a bucket of water over another woman seated in a basin; in another scenario, a woman suggestively leans against another woman smoking a cigarette. Williams argues that these exhibitions of the female body in scientific motion studies nevertheless "immediately [elicited] surplus aestheticism."[49] The display of the female body using new technologies required an account or a context, something that could contain the problem of sexual difference posed by the spectacle.

Williams's comments are helpful in considering tableaux vivants and how they might have functioned for the fin-de-siècle spectator at the halls. Like Muybridge's motion studies, Kilyani's Living Pictures combined visual pleasure with the sanction of culturally privileged knowledges. In Muybridge's case, science underwrote feminine display; in Kilyani's, the tradition of high art painting. Technological advances in the tableaux vivants helped situate the display of the feminine body; more than previous poses plastiques, Kilyani's troupe at the Palace erased the distinction between real models displayed and the classical body that signified decorum and rationality. Technology helped eradicate the distaste that James Greenwood or the *Saturday Review* had expressed concerning poses plastiques, over "coarse women" playing the Graces or "big" women representing Venus.[50] In Kilyani's Living Pictures, technical innovations worked to legitimate prolonged scopic enjoyment of the classical nude.[51]

For both Muybridge and Kilyani, spectacle called for a narrative or context instead of halting diegesis, as Laura Mulvey has suggested. Kilyani's tableaux offered visual pleasure through the illusion that these "marble" statues might become kinetic; he frequently introduced moving elements in otherwise static representations. Kilyani's nude Aphrodite was "made more real by the dripping of water over the form," a device one reviewer complained threatened to make "the realism . . . a little too strong to be artistic"; a staging of Delaroche's "Pharaoh's Daughter" traveled "through imitation bulrushes to a painted Moses." Lerch's "Will o' the Wisp" was lit in a manner that suggested the model was floating. Technology linked pleasure and knowledge in these exhibitions; the "Living Pictures" produced the pleasure that accompanied the exhibition of bodies that a spectator might see without being seen.[52] Kilyani's pictures became a Foucauldian apparatus for sustained observation, "a continuous incitement to discourse" because of their sensational displays.[53]

Kilyani's living statuary at the Palace Theatre also activated the link between tableaux vivants and the high culture discourse of Royal Academy painting. Ronald Pearsall observes that, for the Victorians, "in a sea of changing values, [feminine beauty] was something permanent; there was a reverence for the naked female body that was reflected in the large number of nudes that were exhibited each year at the Royal Academy."[54] After Kilyani's troupe left the Palace for a New York engagement, lighting designer W. P. Dando continued to present tableaux (most likely under Kilyani's tutelage) with subjects taken almost exclusively from paintings by Royal Academy artists: Luke Fildes, Alfred Glendening, Jean Bougereau, Lord Leighton, and Lawrence Alma-Tadema. The cult of female form in academic painting was, as Pearsall observes, "a cult bound up with perfection, with the elimination of the particular, the ruthless excision of the grubby inessentials."[55] Following this artistic discourse, the new technology of the Living Pictures promulgated the classical body to a broad, heterogeneous audience.

The Palace Living Pictures were a powerful incitement to aesthetic discourse. The *Stage* praised Kilyani's troupe as "perfect in every artistic sense";[56] "to have introduced the famous tableaux to the metropolis is in itself enough to earn the undying gratitude of artistic London," the *Music Hall and Theatre Review* asserted.[57] W. Macqueen-Pope's account of the tableaux vivants at the Palace recalls that "Kilyany [*sic*], a Viennese, had a really artistic touch";[58] similarly, the *Music Hall and Theatre Review* singled out the performers as "distinctly classical, models of feminine loveliness, . . . graceful and artistic in pose."[59]

Aesthetic discourse provided the Living Pictures a mise-en-scène that could contextualize the women on display. The Living Pictures placed models against fully conceived backgrounds with meticulous efforts to represent exact pictorial detail. The technology of tableaux vivants had complex effects on how audiences received the display. The presentation could rely on expectations encoded in the response to artistic objects, on narrative cues that could contain the effects of erotic subjects. The Living Pictures worked both to elicit excitement and reverie and to provide a context that could ease any discomfort such forbidden pleasures might arouse.

One of the most popular tableaux at the Palace (it was later withdrawn after Lady Somerset's complaints), an adaptation of Jean-Léon Gérome's "The Moorish Bath," illustrates how the discourse of Royal Academic art could situate feminine spectacle. A reviewer singled out this tableau, observing that of the night's exhibitions, "[t]he representation of 'A Moorish Bath,' is particularly happy, both in idea and execution, the dusky slave forming a pleasing foil to the voluptuous beauty preparing for her ablutions."[60] The brevity of the comment belies the complicated response the Living Pictures could call forth. Gérome's painting juxtaposes a white mistress with the ministrations of a black servant. Like the original painting, the tableau drew on images of the exotic other, in this instance a serving girl and the "Oriental" setting of the bath, to highlight the eroticized European female. The painting activates a series of distinct binaries: black and white, energy versus languor, the classical body versus the Eastern exotic body, the latter facing us without answering our gaze. In the case of "The Moorish Bath," the proper execution of the tableau underscored the secondary position of the "dusky slave" to the "voluptuous beauty"; as the reviewer hints with his comments on the slave as "foil," the painting even suggests the proper hierarchy in which to situate these women. The women are framed in a manner to suggest a hierarchy and a context in which disturbing sensations can be placed. When a painting such as Gérome's was properly reconstructed at the Palace, the work of high culture was fostered by other means than in the museum or the academy.

The response to such charged tableaux could be quite various; while the *Music Hall and Theatre Review* worked to emplot the "Moorish Bath," "Gossamer," who reviewed music-hall entertainment for the belles-lettres journal *Fun*, stressed the more private pleasures the same tableau provided: "The 'Moorish Bath' tableau is a perfect dream. In fact, I dreamt about it for several nights. The lady stands there clothed in flesh-coloured tights and her native modesty, and a very charming vision she is, too. During the 'Moorish Bath,' the auditorium is also bathed—in darkness, so that your girlfriends cannot see your blushes, or your eagerness in using the opera glasses. This is a distinct advantage."[61] In keeping with an overwhelming popular success, the Living Pictures had it both ways: it was both a "contained" display of aesthetic value, alluding to works of high artistic value, and an incitement to sexual reverie.

Another reviewer's response to a series of tableaux at the Royal Theatre "somewhat on the lines of the celebrated Palace Production" that reproduced with "striking fidelity some of the best known masterpieces of English and continental artists" provides a sense of how closely aesthetic judgments could be intertwined with scopic pleasure when evaluating living statuary. The reviewer finds the artistic effect of the Royal Theatre's tableaux vivants to be secure because "the selection of the ladies taking part in the representations [was] particularly happy."[62] The opportunities tableaux vivants allowed for visual pleasure are apparent in the reviewer's list of the performance's artistic qualities: "There are four statue sets, 'Justice,' 'Psyche,' 'The Toilet of Venus,' and 'Poetry,' in which Miss Travers, a lady with most beautifully molded limbs, is seen to great advantage. . . . Miss Marsden—tall, divinely fair—

makes a pretty picture as 'The Favourite,' and with Miss Lait, in 'After the Bath,' discloses an entrancing vision of female loveliness." The reviewer praises "The Sirens" on formalist grounds—"faultlessly grouped and perfect in form and figure"—yet his description of the tableau as "both voluptuous and artistic" is telling. The discourse the Living Pictures elicited from reviewers made appeals to artistic value and hedonism in ways that were difficult to untangle. Along with the aesthetic values of formal composition, tableaux vivants utilized the sensational pleasures of bodily display.

Most important for the Palace, the seductive discourse around the Living Pictures attracted customers. The success of Kilyani's Living Pictures was overwhelming: when the tableaux initially appeared on the Palace bill in October 1893, there were none advertised in London. By the time Kilyani's troupe left the Palace in February of the next year, a throng of imitators crowded the halls. H. G. Hibbert recalls that the entertainment "became a mania" among "every music hall in town and country"; he also claimed in retrospect the entertainments "marked the turn in the fortunes of the house."[63] Contemporaries said much the same thing: the *Music Hall and Theatre Review* reminded readers that "[i]t must not, however, be forgotten that the present popularity of the theatre is largely due to the beautiful Tableaux Vivants, a form of entertainment produced here."[64] This financial success cannot be considered in isolation from what the pictures offered spectators. The tableaux made a new technology available that could secure the classical body on the music-hall stage; it linked scopic pleasure with the cultural capital of art in a way that poses plastiques had previously failed to. To many male spectators at the Palace the inherent cultural capital of feminine display became a "natural" fact: a reviewer's casual description of two comedians following the living statuary at the Palace as "low comedy [following] high art" was typical.[65]

The Living Pictures succeeded in becoming a "spectacular" entertainment. Spectacle played a crucial role throughout the century in theater and music-hall entertainment; the extent to which popular entertainments were enabled by new technology has been well documented. Novel combinations of lighting, sound, elaborate scene painting, projections, and moving panoramas had become staples of melodrama in the 1830s.[66] In many presentations, special effects quickly became the real show: as one theatergoer put it, "We go not so much to hear as to look."[67] It is in reference to this meaning of spectacle that art critic Frederick Wedmore in the *Nineteenth Century* later distinguishes "the newer and more fashionable" music halls, including the Palace, the Empire, and the Alhambra, from other London halls. The difference, Wedmore observes, lies in the "immense and novel importance . . . assigned to 'spectacle' in their programs." Wedmore specifically invokes the Palace tableaux as heralding this new form of entertainment in the halls: he dubs the living statuary "organized splendours."[68] Wedmore locates the same elements of commodified "splendor" found in the Living Pictures in "the yet greater spectacle of the Dance" at the Empire and the Alhambra, where "the dance [is] organized and performed upon a scale that makes the ballet or the opera a comparatively insignificant thing."[69]

Wedmore's description of "organized" splendors—the search for large-scale effects, overpowering images, and incessant novelty—touches on Guy Debord's later understanding of spectacle as "capital accumulated until it becomes an image."[70] Debord's definition of spectacle focuses on how commodity forms influence cultural styles; Thomas Richards has recently suggested that spectacular theater in melodrama functioned as "a kind of experimental theater for industrial capitalism . . . by making the technologies themselves into a form of entertainment."[71] Spectacle worked in accord with a fundamental tenet of market culture: an expansive tendency that led audiences to expect, and compelled theater managers to provide, bigger, more expansive displays. Spectacular entertainment accommodated this logic of excess; at the Palace such entertainment allowed the affluent a vision of what they might be or what they could possess. It offered those with little the aesthetic compensation of *watching,* of vicarious participation in what the wealthy might experience on a more regular basis.

An important element in the Palace's success was its ability to "stage" its own commercial success; its patrons were encouraged to imagine themselves part of an exclusive elite. The *Era* claimed that tableaux vivants brought the Palace a "brilliant audience," further observing that "the presence of many celebrities in law, literature, and medicine may also be regarded as a proof that a variety entertainment is rapidly winning its way into favour with these classes."[72] W. Macqueen-Pope's retrospective account of Palace audiences also emphasizes the class position of its patrons. Kilyani and Dando's exhibits, he writes,

> drew many people to the Palace who had never entered a music hall before; leading statesmen came, smart society folks and even Bishops. Royalty often visited the Palace to see the Tableaux. . . . The stalls, boxes and dress circle of the Palace flashed with jewels, gleamed with white shirts

and shimmered with silks and satins, no such an audience had ever before graced Music Hall. The Palace became . . . the world's smartest Theatre of Varieties (it never called itself a Music Hall, that would not have done).[73]

As Macqueen-Pope suggests, the Palace audience was an aesthetic event itself, another "spectacle" in the hall: this much is given away by his parenthetical. The audience marked the Palace as a site of privileged consumption where, in Macqueen-Pope's words, "evening dress was the rule and opulence the prevailing note."[74] After the success of the tableaux turned the hall around, Palace manager Charles Morton proudly reported to the shareholders of the Palace Theatre Company, Ltd., that "they could . . . boast of having created a new era in a variety theater, as they had a class of audience unequalled anywhere else. They had in their stalls—not hiding themselves in boxes, as they might do elsewhere—royalty, peers, judges, ambassadors, law officers, and even cabinet ministers, who did not hesitate to bring their wives and daughters [Applause]."[75] Certainly the usual differences between pit and gallery maintained class identity at the hall; however, the Palace's singular success lay in placing its elite audience on display. If, as Guy Debord observes, "The spectacle is the existing order's uninterrupted discourse about itself, its laudatory monologue," the Palace promoted the illusion that, for the price of admission, this discourse was also inclusive.[76]

Conventional thinking about the prestige and cultural capital of high art offered the Living Pictures another means of capitalizing on the utopian desires that spectacle answered: they could advance a high style of representation open to all consumers. As late as the 1907 hearings of the Theatres and Music Halls Committee on tableaux vivants, such exhibitions were defended on the grounds that they allowed a large audience the opportunity to study sculpture and art. This raised the countercharge that, as an LCC member claimed, "the proper place to study sculpture are the museums and the art galleries."[77] Still, the argument that tableaux vivants acculturated as well as entertained was readily at hand in the culture. A review of a tableaux vivants star, La Milo, recorded that art students were "especially conspicuous among the audience" and were "loud in their praise of the beautiful poseuse, whose work they declare to be the most artistic exhibition of the female form divine yet given on the variety stage."[78]

As a consumer spectacle, the Living Pictures at the Palace endeavored to create the ideal patron; on this count, the Palace shared similar goals with other London variety theaters dedicated to extravagant display. It was the everyday work of fin-de-siècle music halls like the Palace to place, in Peter Bailey's words, "the open social mix of the city street in some kind of territorial order."[79] Bailey goes on to observe that class difference in music-hall audiences could "generate a lively drama of individual and collective acts of display and competition, amplified and encouraged."[80] Struggles between class fractions at the halls, however, worked against subtle controls in what was called the "aristocratic" variety theater, which began to flourish during the 1890s. At the Empire music hall, walls were embellished by huge expanses of glass throughout the promenade: John Stokes notes that these mirrors were "so plentiful and so dominating that they could easily reinforce a mood of introspection."[81] The Palace was decorated with an intricate fenestrated screen of brick tiles, in the style of the early Spanish Renaissance.[82] These ornate decors provided cues that a particular kind of consumption—more insular, more formalized—was being offered in these spaces. The very surroundings of a hall militated against overly familiar interchange and the experience of direct, physical pleasures.[83] In the midst of such opulent surroundings, the ideal consumer of sensational entertainment was encouraged to personal reverie and privatized pleasure.

The cover of the *Music Hall and Theatre Review* of February 2, 1894, offers a clear example of what we might refer to as the music-hall imaginary, the repertoire of images that variety theaters strove to evoke in their ideal patron (figure 5). The cover, captioned "Seen in the Mirror," abstracts what such a patron might recall from a performance on stage if the customer remained in the promenade. The Empire's large mirrors allowed audience members to watch performances without leaving the bar, or even without facing the stage. Dancer Clara Wieland, strangely foreshortened, appears in the foreground with five different "Wielands" occupying the background in a surreal display. Empire doormen flank the exhibition on stage. Masculine order demarcates and contains the phantasmic vision of the spectator, half gleaned from the mirror instead of from a direct view of the stage. At the Empire, feminine display was contained, offered for the quasi-private delectation of patrons.

The upscale variety theater presented visions of high style and excess and, especially with ballet and tableaux vivants, of spectacular feminine display. In retrospect, literary intellectuals made ideal middle-class patrons of such halls; most of the decadent poetry with the music hall for its

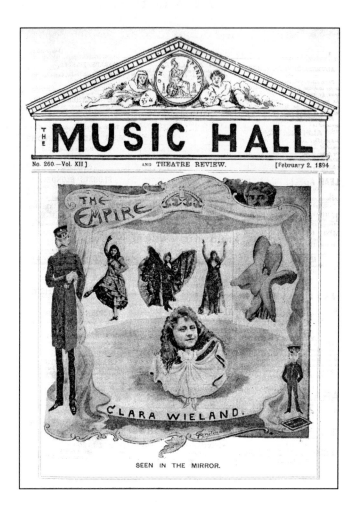

Figure 5. "Seen in the Mirror." From *Music Hall and Theatre Review,* February 2, 1894. (By permission of the British Library)

subject suggests how totally these myths of abundance were absorbed. Literary patrons of the music hall such as Arthur Symons and Theodore Wratislaw responded to the images of women on stage and working women in the promenade by further elaborating on the phantasmic element of sensual luxury that the halls displayed.

Typical of decadent verse in this tradition, Arthur Symons's "To a Dancer" transforms the public performance of a music-hall dancer into a private fantasy of a sexual encounter:

Intoxicatingly
Her eyes across the footlights gleam,
(The wine of love, the wine of dream)
Her eyes, that gleam for me [84]

Another of Symons's music-hall poems, "Behind the Scenes at the 'Empire'" (1894), first published in the *Sketch*, was originally accompanied by a prominent illustration of ballet dancers coming from the green room and going down a stairwell toward the stage (figure 6). The poem itself participates in the conspicuous display of ballet dancers (one of the dancers is in putting on leggings) the picture provides. Feminine display is linked to fantasy images that erase traces of working-class association with performing women's bodies.

The little painted angels flit,
See, down the narrow staircase, where
The pink legs flicker over it!
Blonde, and bewigged, and winged with gold,
The shining creatures of the air
Troop sadly, shivering with cold.

· · · · · · · · · · · · · ·

All wigs and paint, they hurry in;
Then, bid their radiant moment be
The footlights' immortality! [85]

Although he notes the vulnerability of these performers—"shivering with cold"—Symons's poem catches the ballet dancers in the process of transformation. They are about to change from working-class women into something more ethereal, if artificial ("All wigs and paint"). Symons's poem focuses on working-class women who are transfigured into classical bodies in the space of the halls.

In a fashion characteristic of decadent verse meditation on music hall, Theodore Wratislaw's "At the Empire" (1896) conflates the "calm and brilliant Circes" in the promenade with the spectacular women performers on stage. Every woman the poet encounters in the music hall provokes only additional ennui in an already terminally lethargic spectator:

Ah! what are these, the perfume and the glow,
The ballet that coruscates down below,

Figure 6. The cultured male gaze. "Behind the Scenes at the 'Empire.'" From *Sketch*, March 21, 1894, 389. (By permission of the British Library)

> *The glittering songstress and the comic stars,*
> *Ah! what are these, although we sit withdrawn*
> *Above our sparkling tumblers and cigars,*
> *To us so like to perish with a yawn?* [86]

Here the spectacle of the halls, with strong images of achieved abundance, underwrites the fashionable tedium experienced by the weary aesthete. Wratislaw's poem indicates how thoroughly literary intellectuals promulgated variety theater spectacle and its commodified vision of ornamental display. His ennui is less aesthetic malady than the complaint of a jaded consumer.

Such verse suggests the debt of decadent poetry to the "spectacular" visions promoted by variety theaters such as the Palace. W. B. Yeats's account of the fin-de-siècle cult of the halls characterizes the work of poets including Symons, Wratislaw, and Selwyn Image as representative of "the cultivated man" in "a somewhat hectic search for the common pleasures of common men."[87] However, the poetry from the music-hall cult transmits images very far removed from plebeian diversion. In the images of sexual availability they circulate, these poems elaborate on the lessons of conspicuous consumption that performances at the "aristocratic" music hall broadcast. Symons's and Wratislaw's poems offer their middle-class readership images of the spectacular consumption exemplified by tableaux vivants and music-hall ballet.

The success of spectacular entertainment in the nineteenth century was remarkable and remarkably sustained; still, other responses to this extravagant spectacle were available to music-hall patrons. Throughout the spring of 1894, the *Pall Mall Gazette* remained ambivalent about the spread of Living Pictures. However, the complaints reviewers lodged against tableaux vivants partook of the logic of spectacle in their demand for continual novelty. One reviewer protested: "It is always annoying to find managers weakening their companies on the strength of Tableaux Vivants. We cannot help looking at these when they come, but we had much rather they stayed away."[88] Yet, if writers such as Arthur Symons were often content with insisting on the erotic unity of the spectacle, at least for the masculinist spectator, others drew attention to what the ideal vision of spectacle excluded. It is an achievement of the purity movement that its members were capable of moving from the *Pall Mall Gazette*'s vague boredom or passivity to a realized critique.

Somerset's Protest

The connections that Palace tableaux forged between scopic pleasure and cultural capital were symbolically powerful, yet still open to dispute. Lady Henry Somerset, leader of the Woman's Christian Temperance Union, turned the organization newspaper, the *Woman's Signal*, into a platform against the tableaux in general and the Palace in particular. Somerset filed a complaint against the Palace's liquor license on behalf of the National Vigilance Association largely based on the Living Pictures. Her *Woman's Signal,* an appeal "to the women of England," resisted the links tableaux drew between cultural capital and the bodies of working women. She troubled the entertainment's claims to be art: "Go to the South Kensington Museum and look at Mr. Watts' 'Psyche,' and then go to the 'Palace' and wait for the 'Moorish Bath.' The one is a glorification of womanly form; genius and reverence are confessed in every touch. The mind would have to be diseased indeed to which that picture could suggest unruly thoughts. But the other—!"[89] Somerset's own aesthetic shares common ground with the aesthetic extolled by men of rank and prestige, including a professional class of journalists. The "genius" of the individual artist elevates genuine art above the libidinal response to female display evidenced by the untrained observer. Reverence for the female form is a keynote of "genius" in Somerset's own aesthetic economy—the truly aesthetic is always the fully sublimated.

Somerset, however, differs from the pictures' defenders in her insistence that the new tableaux vivants fail to transform the forms they evoke: "These 'tableaux' violate every artistic canon," she writes, because what they present "is sham nudity, not spiritualized and made ideal by the hallowed creating hand of genius, but palpably gross and disgusting in its suggestive flesh-coloured tights." Somerset's response to the performance suggests that the elaborate technology Kilyani and Dando designed to breach the gulf between the coarse bodies of poses plastiques and the classical body privileged by high artistic taste was not always successful; it could be seen through. For Lady Somerset, the bodies of the Living Pictures could not be worked over aesthetically; models were fated to bear the markings of their class.

Somerset's colleague W. A. Coote offers a similar objection in a *Daily Chronicle* interview republished in the *Woman's Signal.* When asked how tableaux vivants could prove more indecent than the original paintings they reproduced, Coote elaborated on the "marked difference between the two": "The great difference is just that which makes the one true art and deprives the others of any semblance of it. In the picture you have the artist's soul and ideal beautifying the subject, and sometimes making even the nude an inspiration for good. In the other, you have apparently the full personality of the flesh and blood of the individual."[90] In the tableaux vivants, the "full personality" of the performer, tainted by social and economic standing, remains too readily apparent. It is the "full personality" of these lower-class women that suggests to Coote that they require safeguarding.

The style in which Coote and Somerset argue against living statuary serves to draw further attention to the working-class women who labored as models on the music-hall stage. Somerset makes the models the explicit subject in her appeal, directed to other women of England: "It is the performers who call for our intervention; and I make this appeal to the English public as accomplices in the ruin and degradation of these girls. . . . I am speaking . . . of young women whose modesty and purity is of just as much account in the sight of God as the virtue of the highest in the land, whose dishonour is just as much a blot and infamy on the community as would be publicly tolerated insult or outrage on the most royal of princesses."[91] The attack on the spectacle of the tableaux vivants generates, in Somerset's hands, a counterspectacle: a potential media scandal focused on pure but beleaguered working women. Of course, Somerset's counterspectacle is indebted to previous media provocations launched by social purity workers, especially the controversial Maiden Tribute dispute. As with W. T. Stead's popular image of working-class girls threatened by aristocratic rakes, Somerset's "appeal to the women of England" provokes others to defend against threats to female honor. She represents the Palace as a site where unscrupulous men threaten working-class women unable to defend themselves.

Somerset's construction of the tableaux vivants models as women in distress created a media sensation; nearly twenty papers are quoted two weeks later in the *Woman's Signal* in explicit response to Somerset's public appeal. Images of victimized performers stirred male and female readers; a correspondent to the *Signal* expresses horror that

> men can sit and gaze at the presentment in the nude of the beautiful form of woman—the form of poetry, beauty, nobleness, and purity and not remember that they are men, the descendants of men who worshipped and carried their veneration for women almost to a religion, and not ask their memories to travel so far back. How can they forget that the form held up to the gaze and mockery of the idle crowd is the form they venerated and loved in their mothers and their sisters and love and worship in their wives?[92]

Within the social purity imaginary, the sanctity of English women remains tied to the stability and persistence of imperial power. The letter closes with the ominous warning that "the surest sign of a great empire's ruin is the want of veneration for noble womanhood." In connecting victimized womanhood with endangered nationhood, this correspondent only elaborated Somerset's own suggestions in her initial protest against the Palace Living Pictures. In Somerset's words, "No one who sees but must agree here is the gravest insult and dishonour that has been put upon woman in our time; for at last we have, in letting women make public merchandise of the beauty of their bodies, surpassed even the Oriental standard of female degradation."[93] That tableaux vivants perform for pay links their exhibition with another illicit form of commerce with the female body, prostitution. Somerset's Orient stands in typical fashion as antithesis to the West, and Oriental spectacle imperils national integrity. Her rhetoric collapses the distinction between English values and Eastern mores.[94]

In key areas, Somerset's rhetorical appeal demands respect for its daring. She enlists working-class women within the cause of social purity and takes a clear stand against male hegemony by assailing the Victorian sexual double standard. However, the models that she speaks for can stand beside "the women of England" only if they consent to Somerset's management; worse, the models must relinquish the ability to define the parameters of their work and assent to the argument that they are simply victimized by their work. Somerset insists that the place of the model within English and feminine protocols is fully conditional.

Annie Holdsworth, coeditor of the *Woman's Signal,* followed Somerset's strategy and cast the Living Pictures models as victims in need of public intervention. Her short story "Footlights: The Story of a Living Picture" suggests the pathos of this strategy and its ability to dramatize oppression; the fiction also demonstrates the limitations that appeals to "save" working-class women placed on feminine agency.

The story begins with Cecil Rhys, a New Woman journalist, entering into a discussion about the Living Pictures at the Progressive Club. Cecil, a devotee of the pictures, declares that it is "the people of narrow views that are the real enemies of purity."[95] Her feminism is at odds with the stated policies of social purity workers: "'Women are ruining their own cause by all this pother,' she went on, talking rapidly to cover the confusion. 'I would not in the least mind being a Living Picture. I see no harm whatever in it. I would just as soon earn my bread that way myself.'"[96] Geraldine Staunton, a woman artist and Progressive Club member, informs Cecil that one of her Living Pictures models, Grace Fleming, needs a substitute so she can visit her ailing mother. Geraldine asks Cecil to take Grace's place and perform that night at the Folly music hall. In a mood of daring, Cecil takes the challenge as a journalistic opportunity: "Why should she not do it? In her profession she had already assumed many nondescript *roles*. She had been barmaid, milliner, organ-grinder. What she had attempted for journalism might well be done for a dying woman. Besides, it would be good copy, and she would prove her case." The manager of the Folly meets Cecil; he is eager to take her up on her offer to replace Grace. Holdsworth uses the exchange to dramatize the disposability of models. The reader is privy to the manager's internal musing regarding Cecil's benefits over Grace for the job: "Grace had been posing for the Venus Aphrodite, but Grace had gone off lately. She had looked peaked and haggard, and here was a Venus that would make the success of any picture."

When Cecil replaces Grace as a "nude" Venus, Holdsworth's story demonstrates how, in Cecil's own words, "a world of difference lay between the picture before the footlights and the picture behind them." The narrative emphasizes the degrading labor behind the spectacle of living statuary. As Cecil begins to lose her nerve, a model tells her what keeps the Living Pictures models at work: "Take a drop of brandy before you go on. We all have to the first time, just to keep us up. Bless you, not one of us would go through it if Collins didn't make us half-drunk first! But that's only the first few nights!—you soon get hardened."[97] When Cecil goes onstage, the conversation among the men in the audience suggests that the boundaries that separate working as a picture and prostitution are all too permeable:

> "My! ain't she a stunner?"
> "She won't stay here long. She'll soon be down at the other shop."
> "Carriage and pair, you bet."

Cecil doesn't register this conversation: all she can register is "the speech of the eyes looking at her. She felt as if she had stepped into a bath of pollution. Would she ever be clean again as long as she lived?"

Cecil's performance as Venus ends abruptly when she hears the voice of her boyfriend, a self-professed "aesthete," in the Folly audience: her hands reach up to cover her face before the curtain falls. Upon seeing Cecil in distress, Clarke, the boyfriend, renounces his aestheticism in an impassioned speech to his companion Rawson, who had passively enjoyed the diversion: "You brute! Suppose it was your sister standing there! It's a vile shame to allow it!" In an interesting reversal of the male gaze, Clarke becomes humiliated by Cecil's eyes, which "[meet] his in a despairing appeal for Pity" as the curtain rises again: "It was his turn then to grow pale, his turn to cover his face with his hands. But he could not shut out the sight of the humiliation of the girl he loved. He was powerless to silence the coarse remarks that pointed the ringing applause of the audience." Holdsworth represents the effects of public display on women performers as irrevocable. The performance ruins Cecil's relationship with Clarke: at the close of the performance she realizes that "the footlights, like a flaming wall, would stand between them for ever."

Holdsworth's story supplements Somerset's own account of Living Pictures model psychology: passive, maltreated women, prone to abuse by rogue male audiences and unscrupulous managers. The strength of such rhetoric to elicit media reaction had a clear precedent; the Maiden Tribute controversy had demonstrated that such rhetorical appeals might challenge the natural status of male sexual prerogative. However, the essentialist notions of femininity that Holdsworth relies on—the denial of sexual agency to working-class women, the presentation of performance as an agent of contamination—would be interrogated as the controversy over the Living Pictures raged on. The dispute over the Living Pictures was primarily fought on the discursive terrain of legitimate female performance.

For some, the dispute over the pictures needed to be engaged on the same terms as the struggle against Chant's simultaneous suit against the Empire. Journalists protested against the unqualified "amateur" who meddled in matters of decorum over which gentlemen could peacefully disagree. The *St. James Gazette* refused to take seriously Lady Somerset's argument that Living Pictures models were contaminated by public performance: "Is it really true that they degrade themselves more than Gaiety chorus girls, or serpentine skirt-dancers?" The *Gazette* suggests instead that all such disputes were, finally, matters of taste: "If Lady Henry Somerset had attacked the tableaux because they are stupid and ugly, we could understand her better."[98] The *Gazette* speaks here for the collective cultured subject, the imperial "we" who passes over those hapless enough to confuse disagreements about taste with ethical problems. *Fun,* a journal chronicling the political scene and theatrical entertainment, attacked Lady Henry Somerset's defense of the "Newer Drama" in what it described as her "new womanly journal," the *Woman's Signal,* even more pointedly than her protest against tableaux vivants. Somerset's defense of the "problem play" (1894 was also the year of Sydney Grundy's *The New Woman,* H. A. Jones's controversial *The Case of Rebellious Susan,* and Henrik Ibsen's *An Enemy of the People* in London) drew this disdainful response: "No, my dear Lady Henry, return to your attacks on the publicans—it amuses you and it doesn't hurt them. But for Heaven's sake, leave the theatres alone. You know nothing about them, and it is silly to display your ignorance."[99] Such disputes over taste suggested it was important to settle who possessed the proper credentials to arbitrate aesthetic questions. The diatribes of *Fun* and the *St. James Gazette* against Lady Somerset's comments on theater and music-hall performance suggest that a proper resolution of aesthetic disputes was a matter of moment in the fin-de-siècle public sphere.

George Bernard Shaw's defense of tableaux vivants in response to W. A. Coote's complaint against the Palace, filed on behalf of the National Vigilance Association (NVA), demonstrates a similar optimistic progressivism. Coote's testimony on behalf of Lady Somerset and the NVA receives a sharp rebuke from Shaw, focusing on the matter of Coote's credentials to settle artistic disputes: "As a critic, I at once perceived that Mr. Coote had placed before the public an issue of considerable moment: namely, whether Mr. Coote's opinion is worth anything or not. For Mr. Coote is a person of real importance, active, useful, convinced, thoroughly respectable, able to point to achievements which we must all admit honourable to him. . . . But all this is quite compatible with Mr. Coote being in artistic matters a most intensely stupid man."[100] Shaw's review stages the struggle over the Palace as a drama of competing authorities, a clash between activism and journalism, which Shaw declares he wishes to fight fairly: "I do not want to take an unfair advantage of the fact that in writing about art I am a trained expert and Mr. Coote a novice."[101]

Shaw's defense of the Palace Living Pictures favors the transfiguring effects of spectacle; he believes in the transformation of the model in the pictures, at least with the right technology. He also lauds the hygienic qualities of the display, qualities he hopes might have a direct effect on the audience for the exhibition: "It was only too obvious to a practiced art critic's eye that what was presented as flesh was really spun silk. But the illusion produced on the ordinary music-hall frequenter was that of the undraped human figure, exquisitely clean, graceful, and, in striking contrast to many of the completely and elaborately dressed ladies who were looking at them, completely modest." The special effect that witnessing "clean, graceful" bodies might exert on working-class women in attendance is the crucial point in Shaw's favoring the pictures: "Many of the younger and poorer girls in the audience must have gone away with a greater respect for their own persons, a greater regard for the virtues of the bath, and a quickened sense of the repulsiveness of that personal slovenliness and gluttony which are the real indecencies of popular life." Shaw's concern with the response that the pictures might elicit in spectators is evident. The performance, he suggests, might indoctrinate "classical" decorum in women with working-class manners—"slovenliness," "gluttony." For this reason Shaw extols the pictures as "not only works of art" but "excellent practical sermons," and he can "urge every father of a family who cannot afford to send his daughters the round of the picture galleries in the Haymarket and Bond Street, to take them all (with their brothers) to the Palace Theatre."[102] Despite the hyperbole, Shaw's aims in this review are clear: the tableaux vivants are necessary since they circulate classical culture by other means, and at other sites than the public art gallery.

Since Shaw bases his claims for the artistic merit of the pictures on their ability to promote social hygiene, he confidently proceeds to refute Coote's claim, similar to Lady Somerset's own argument, that there remains a "marked difference between the canvas or marble and the living picture, much to the disadvantage of the latter." In contrast with the purity reformers, Shaw insists on the power of the technology of the pictures to transform bodies. The models hired to play Living Pictures become artistic entities through detailed work of stage design and lighting, controlled by skilled impresarios. Shaw also defends the rights of artistic experts against amateur "critics" like Coote:

> Let Mr. Morton, the manager of the Palace, request Mr. Dando, the arranger of the pictures to stand aside and entrust his functions for one night . . . to Mr. William Alexander Coote. Let the entire resources of the establishment be placed absolutely under his direction; and let us then see whether he can take advantage of their being "no art in it" to produce a single tableau that will not be ludicrously and outrageously deficient in the artistic qualities without which Mr. Dando's compositions would be hooted off the stage.

Like other managerial intellectuals, Shaw has faith that change can emanate from a central source of authority, through the progressive use of technology. Shaw also implies that all managerial types are equal; however, Coote's inability to produce correct aesthetic judgment compels Shaw to distinguish his own reformist vision from Coote's. The Shavian expert is aligned with the interests of the people, who, like Shaw, know art when they see it and who can learn more about proper aesthetic protocols from the entertainment. Working-class audiences are believed capable of recognizing and esteeming the classical form in a manner that Coote, the mere bourgeois, cannot. In Shaw's estimation, Coote represents a particularly intransigent portion of the untrained public.

Frederick Wedmore defended the tableaux against purity workers on similar grounds, relying on the public's ability to discern that the "nude in a tableau vivant" was obviously not an unclothed model:

> Before the interventions of the Puritan became necessary, the public itself would have interfered. But in the matter of the tableau vivant, the public rightly recognized what the Puritan ignored—that the nude in a tableau vivant, with its accessories, with all its associations, is no longer an undressed woman, but the nude in art—the nude to be seen, therefore, with something, at least, of artistic appreciation of refined colour and of ordered and intricate line.[103]

Like Shaw, Wedmore regards it as self-evident that the tableau vivant represents civilized values because it represents the classic human form. This argument in favor of the intuitive artistic sense of popular audiences centers around the transformed Living Pictures models as much as it relies on the public's aesthetic sense. Even when the models in the pictures were evaluated in Wedmore's formalist terms of "refined colour" and "ordered" lines, the controversy over the pictures rarely moved too far from the real women who performed in the entertainment.

The heightened interest in the models in the pictures sometimes allowed explicit class concerns to be aired. The public protest of Reverend Wilson Carlile against the Palace, stirred by Lady Henry Somerset's complaints, elicited this response from Palace manager Charles Morton:

> Mr. Carlile had a short conversation with Mr. Morton as to the dangers incurred by the young woman who plays "The Polar Star," and is exposed for several seconds every night to the unfeeling public's gaze. Mr. Morton assured him that the young woman was in no danger of being contaminated on his stage, and he thought that their [sic] chances of remaining an ornament to her sex while she was receiving 5 pounds a week were far greater than they would be if she was receiving smaller

enumeration for the more arduous task she might be obliged to perform
had she a less exquisite shape.[104]

The exchange between Carlile and Morton suggests that Carlile shared Annie
Holdsworth's fears that performers might be contaminated by means of the
audience's gaze. It is hard to imagine how Morton's defense of the pictures as
better than minimum wage labor pacified Carlile, since Morton assumes the
proximity between models and prostitutes that alarmed purity workers.[105]
The encounter between minister and manager, with its acknowledgment of
labor and class determinants, is an exception in media coverage of the pictures. More typical were human interest stories such as the one the *Standard*
ran on tableaux vivants, in which a young woman is portrayed in a series of
pictures being "transformed" from a model artist into a "classical" Living Picture. Picture number six of the story bears a caption noting that the complete
transformation of the model must be postponed. The manager is shown in-
forming the model that "he will have omit her 'turn' this evening, as Lady
Henry Somerset's watchers are in the theatre."[106] In this photo exposé, Lady
Somerset's "watchers" impede the magic technology of the Living Pictures
and the possibilities they offer to refigure the female body.

The *Standard* story also indicates that the purity workers who instigated
the controversy quickly lost control of how their protests and the pictures
themselves would be represented in the press. If Lady Somerset and other female philanthropists cast the Living Pictures as victims, competing images
of the performers in the press worked against the notion of the models as
passive quarry for men. Besides the argument for the "transfigured" body in
Shaw, Wedmore, and the *Standard,* the discourse of professionalism complicated public notions regarding the Living Pictures model.

Even before the purity worker attack on the Living Pictures, the rhetoric
of professionalism was invoked in order to legitimate the exhibition. The
Sketch, for example, praises W. P. Dando's version of the Living Pictures at
the Palace early on as "simply exquisite" with "absolutely nothing about
them to offend even the most sensitive or modest temperament"[107] Still, the
Sketch concedes that "even to the hardened artistic nerve, to find oneself in
the midst of a group of beautiful girls attired in the very scantiest of raiment
was a position, to say the least of it, of some delicacy." To allow spectators to
overcome this embarrassment, the *Sketch* provides a symbolic solution: the
notion of the Living Pictures model as dance professional. "As, however,
most of the ladies taking part in the representations are models well known

in the artistic world, they probably felt far less embarrassment than the ordinary onlooker. To them it is part of their ordinary day's work, whether they are posing before a Palace Theatre public or in the privacy of an artist's studio, for habit is second nature." When the *New Review* published a public forum on the Living Pictures in November 1894, Arthur Symons, fittingly, further elaborated the notion of the models' professional ethos. Symons suggests that what might normally corrupt other women was not an issue where experts were concerned. He especially finds fault with Lady Somerset's suggestion that models required others to defend them from vice:

> I believe that Lady Henry Somerset grounded her objection on
> the presumable "moral ruin and degradation" which the wearing of
> tights and the removal of corsets would cause to a girl who took part
> in such a performance. If anyone really believes that, I can only say
> that such a person must be very ingenuous and very ill-informed.
> A girl who is accustomed to the stage thinks no more about the eyes
> of the audience and the cut of her costume than you or I, when we are
> walking along the street, think about the swift, imperceptible criticism
> of the indistinguishable crowd. Or if she thinks of the matter at all,
> it is as a friend of mine thought when she said to me, only the other
> day: "I sometimes wish I had a better figure; I never think about any-
> thing else."[108]

Symons utilizes his insider knowledge of models to counter what he takes as Lady Somerset's misreading of the psychology of artistic professionals. He represents the Living Pictures model as aloof, professional, self-obsessed, but not easily victimized.

Lady Somerset conceived the Living Pictures model as a figure too fragile to avoid the dangers associated in the Victorian mind with public display. Her representation of the passive model was actively countered in the press during her speaking engagement in New York at the height of the pictures model controversy. While in New York in August 1894, Somerset voiced concern regarding Kilyani's Living Pictures in New York, then appearing in the Proctor variety theater. As in London, some public responses countered Lady Somerset's campaign with defenses of the high standards of the profession. The manager of the Koster and Bial music hall appealed to the "peculiarly modest and respectable" nature of professional models:

> It seems to have been imagined by the public that the young woman
> who could pose in a living picture . . . must be bereft of all modesty, and
> Lady Somerset and her co-laborers seem to have conceived the idea that
> they ought to reform these young women, whom they imagine are de-
> praved. Now it is well known among artists and professional people, and
> fairly understood among intelligent people, that artists' models are a pe-
> culiarly modest and respectable type. Any artist will tell you that the
> young woman who will pose has a certain confidence in herself . . . while
> a woman who is at all lacking in self-respect, you understand, cannot be
> hired to pose for any price.[109]

The virtues of expert models are represented, predictably, as standing above
the lure of mere commerce. The description separates professional virtues
from commercial value; the "true" model displays a "natural" confidence
that, of course, has little to do with nature and everything to do with culture
and social status.

One of the major exhibitors of Living Pictures in New York, music-hall
manager Suzie Kirwin, tested Somerset's rhetoric of besieged womanhood.
Kirwin's public rebuke of Somerset in the New York daily press brought the
matter of class to bear on the protest in unexpected ways. In response to
Lady Somerset's comment to the *New York Times* that "the models pose for
dollars, for bread and butter, not to educate the public taste for art," Kirwin
responds:

> The "clear cut commercial situation," so pointedly referred to by Lady
> Somerset, presents itself to most of us born without titles and estates.
> No doubt, some of the young women in living pictures would gladly ex-
> hibit themselves solely for love of art if worldly circumstances would
> permit. Young women and matrons of fair repute have freely displayed
> such charms of feature and form as Heaven has favored them with in
> the cause of charity. The professional model, whether of the studio or
> the living picture cabinet, is less fortunate in worldly endowment.[110]

Kirwin endeavors to claim the Living Pictures controversy as a struggle over
access; at issue is the possibility of unskilled labor gaining entrée in the job
market: "The honorable avenues of employment open to women are none
too many. Lady Somerset, as a philanthropist, must know this. Why seek to
close any of them?" Like the manager of the Koster and Bial, Kirwin stresses

the professional attributes of the working-class women who model: "I have found them clear headed, modest, well behaved young women—self-reliant and courageous enough to fight the never ceasing battle for support— women who prefer honest toil to vice. They and other women of this type, no matter what vocation in life, in my humble opinion, lend to the glorification, not to the degradation of their sex."[111]

The notion of Living Pictures model as hapless victim of commodified sexuality was further complicated when the models themselves contested this image in the New York daily press. In the *New York Tribune,* the women in Kilyani's troupe spoke for themselves. Esther Gaab, a renowned German model, takes up Suzie Kirwin's argument in favor of employment opportunities that the pictures offered women: "Wouldn't it be better if (Somerset) fed the hungry and clothed the naked (sic), than if she shut off another avenue of honest employment? Surely, there are few enough open to women."[112] Another model in the troupe, Miss Eggert, expresses her belief in the autonomy of art: "On what grounds, . . . does this English lady charge the Living Pictures with immorality? If it is because men come to see us with impure thoughts, are we to blame? When a masterpiece is painted who can object to it? Only those who are not pure in mind. And we are like the beautiful models who rejoice every painter's heart." The language of high art, so often used to denigrate the women who portrayed living statuary, here is deployed to legitimate a woman's professional identity. Eggert goes on to make claims about artistic sovereignty that would fit comfortably alongside the contemporary claims of the aesthete for the autonomy of artistic values: "I do not want blame or pity or condonement for my art. It is art and needs no excusing." In the same *New York Tribune* article, an anonymous model cleverly suggests her disregard for the responses the pictures might elicit from audiences: "As for the effect on the young men, I do not know that we are accountable for that. It isn't half so bad for them to look at the living pictures than at some of the dead ones they have in their rooms."[113]

Somerset's protest over the Living Pictures not only incited literary intellectuals to intervene, but also provoked performing women to speak as authorities on their own work in a manner few contemporaries might have anticipated. Female philanthropists clearly set the terms of the debate, claiming the Living Pictures model as an embodiment of gender inequity. No doubt this appeal for women to act on behalf of "womanhood" resulted in the explicit curiosity about the models themselves that increasingly preoccupied journalistic coverage of these women. Some of the claims maintained by the performers—regarding the autonomy of art, the importance of experts in an increasingly professionalized field—may surprise even contemporary readers. Suzie Kirwin's argument for the pictures appealed to something that Somerset's concern with "true womanhood" allowed her to overlook: the material conditions of working women. What Somerset and the NVA failed to anticipate was the popular discontent with their tutelary efforts to speak for other women. The protest over tableaux vivants—perhaps against Somerset's intention, which appears to have been to speak for women unable to articulate their own concerns—established these women as speaking subjects in a public sphere.[114]

The women of the tableaux seem to have rejected an old, male-defined discourse that interpreted female display associated with "common" bodies as vulgar and unrefined. They seem to have freed themselves as well from male-defined prejudices against feminine display and the notion of art as exclusively male property. The tableaux vivants workers asserted themselves against a male-based spectator practice and social prejudice that equated nudity with working-class identity or with the abject. They met these objections using more than the alibi of art; they also invoked their vocation and common enterprise, their aesthetic professionalism. The recourse to a notion of dignified labor demystifies the middle-class Victorian spectacle of female nudity fostered by the old penny gaff display or the high-toned Palace Theatre spectacle. The discourse of these women workers even tugs at the ethereal notions of art and artistic autonomy. Yet their media pronouncements do not establish that they imagined their work as a fully collaborative endeavor, or a step beyond standard middle-class notions of self-fashioning or self-promotion. The archive of recorded comments from these workers offers little to suggest the tableaux women believed their labor was a social expression, reflecting common interests or collective practice: although it must be remembered that the racy New York Police Gazette had another ideological agenda for female spectacle, and tended to interpret the work of female performers in a limited ideological fashion.

Still, Lady Somerset's social critique, subsuming economic factors under moral imperatives, led her to neglect a crucial aspect of the Living Pictures phenomena—the inclusive character of consumer spectacle. She underestimated the dynamic force of market culture, as professionals are wont to do. From the outset, the pictures were nothing if not inclusive, provided one could pay to view. With this proviso, scopic pleasure was not an exclusively male, heterosexual business.[115] The success of the Palace tableaux encouraged Eugene Sandow, advertised as "The Modern Hercules and the Perfect Man," to tour as a tableau vivant (he debuted as a tableau vivant at the Palace Theatre six months before Kilyani's troupe).[116] After the notoriety of Kilyani's troupe, Sandow's performances regularly included exhibitions of the strong man in tight silk shorts and laurel crown, covered only by bronze makeup, in classical poses as Apollo or Hercules. During a tour of San Francisco, women especially were encouraged to attend Sandow's matinee performances. In London, the *Music Hall and Theatre Review* reprinted a comic squib by a Californian poet on Sandow's tour. The poem considers what other cultural arbiters repressed: the basis of the entertainment's commercial success in vulgarity. Of course, a difference between visual pleasure provided for men and that provided for women was that the latter could readily be denigrated as sexualized display, and arguments for its aesthetic integrity were more vulnerable to demystification:

> *Oh, dear, how the ladies did hustle to see*
> *The perfect man pose at his great matinee; . . .*
> *The ladies from most of our Art Schools were there,*
> *The "old" and "homely," the young and the fair . . .*
> *For nearly one hour they sat and they gazed*
> *At Sandow's nude figure and gushingly praised*
> *His form and his muscles, his curls and his face,*
> *His curves and his outlines, his ease and his grace,*
> *And vowed it was, oh! such an artistic sight,*
> *They could linger with pleasure there night after night,*
> *And so when the "horrid old curtain" came down*
> *Each lady declared with a very deep frown*
> *She thought the performances was really too short*
> *They did not see half the "art pictures" they ought.*[117]

The doggerel verse enforces a double standard for scopic pleasure, patronizing women in search of visual enjoyment. However, Sandow's popularity highlights what Lady Somerset's protest overlooked in the spectacle of the Living Pictures. The success of Sandow "The Modern Hercules" demonstrates the difficulty purity workers encountered when they claimed that, in a world of commodified entertainment, collective resistance to vulgar pleasure might define womanhood. Somerset's appeal to the women of England underestimated the appeal of a nascent image of womanhood—as empowered consumer, and as a demographic.[118]

La Milo's Ride

The controversy over the Palace Living Pictures resulted in few substantial changes in the pictures themselves aside from the withdrawal of "The Moorish Bath." Despite W. A. Coote's testimony before the LCC Theatres and Music Halls Committee about the indecencies of tableaux vivants—what another National Vigilance campaigner called the exhibition's "mere nudities"—the committee decided that spectators had to adjust their own perspective rather than the Palace change its entertainment. If the Palace presented "works of art," the committee decided, spectators needed to remind themselves that the bodies they watched were, in fact, covered by tights.[119] The burden of aesthetic consciousness was thrust back on the spectator/consumer.

The Palace, throughout its existence as a music hall, until it became a cinema, maintained its reputation as one of London's primary sources for feminine spectacle.[120] The Palace increasingly diversified its exhibits to serve its patrons with greater efficiency. If the primary result of the public debate over Living Pictures was heightened publicity for those who performed in them, spectacular entertainment was able to accommodate this curiosity toward working women. Tableaux vivants soon centered on individual stars and their star images rather than collective troupes overseen by solitary impresarios like Kilyani or Dando.[121]

The tableaux vivants were defended against moral protest by declarations of their aesthetic merit; living statuary faced the burden of maintaining this justification into the next century. When another London licensing dispute over tableaux vivants flared up in 1906, the *Music Hall and Theatre Review* defended the exhibitions on the grounds that "there are degrees" of living statuary. Yet the paper went on to complain that the abundance of tableaux on the music-hall stage had started "competition[s] in daring": "We began with the perfect woman, modestly clad. We proceeded to the partly perfect woman, not so carefully guarded against the weather. We advanced to mis-shapen creatures who had not even beauty or symmetry to excuse their indecency."[122] The editorial expresses the fear that the logic of the marketplace can transform "proper" tableaux into demeaning spectacle; at any moment, the grotesque, "mis-shapen" body so inimical to artistic taste can blight the halls.

One of the most celebrated exceptions to the fears expressed by the *Music Hall and Theatre Review* was believed to reside in the Living Pictures' Pansy Montague, an Australian model who performed under the name of "La Milo." Her career in the Edwardian age represents a culmination of sorts for living statuary performance in the nineteenth century. La Milo's initial success occurred when she imitated Velasquez's Rokesby Venus, capitalizing on the acquisition of the painting by the National Portrait Gallery.[123] This performance had a long and successful run at the London Pavilion in 1906, during which the *Sunday Chronicle* asserted, "[H]er chaste and beautiful suggestions of marble statuary, have revived a fashion."[124] However, for a picture performer to maintain success amid the competition it was necessary—if increasingly difficult—to cordon off authentic performance from debased imitation. Advertising was one means of establishing faith in the unique prestige of a tableaux star, but even ad copy faced clear limits. The same ad that boldly asserts in one instance that "there is *only one* 'La Milo'" contains the rueful admission that "[t]o be successful is to court imitation." The advertisement for La Milo appeals to the lay expert to establish the performer's real singularity: potential customers are advised to "Listen to *Critics*—not Mugtown reporters!" The excerpts from reviews that follow typically declare La Milo to be a legitimate artistic event; in the words of one paper, "There are half a dozen poseuses competing for popular favour, but none of them, so far, has so rare a distinction as 'La Milo.'" A review from *Entr'Acte* claims that La Milo's work is "in a class by itself," while the *Daily Express,* giving the game away, declares, "'La Milo' stands for high Art."

The poseuse's success signified the greater tolerance, at least in music-hall London, for working-class women who wished to assume the classical form. No less an authority than W. T. Stead, whose *Pall Mall Gazette* exposés made working-class prostitution a political issue and galvanized reaction against the Contagious Diseases Act with his own brand of media scandal, exempted La Milo from his denigration of music-hall entertainment as "[d]rivel for the dregs." Stead's highly publicized first visit to a music hall in 1907 resulted in a celebrated editorial about the "imbecility" of the halls. However, La Milo's performance stood, in Stead's estimation, as the sole exception to "the depths of the abyss in which these trousered and petticoated savages of civilisation wallow." In his words:

Imagine my surprise and delight to find that the exhibition of La Milo was the only redeeming feature in the long monotonous succession of ugliness and vulgarity. There can be no difference of opinion as to the beauty and ideal loveliness of the pictures to which La Milo formed the centre figure. . . . Those who came to gloat over indecency were pretty considerably sold, but the audience, unintelligent and vulgar though it was, seemed to be thrilled for a moment by the beauty of the spectacle.[125]

In Stead's praise, the turbulent negotiations between class and taste that involved public displays of the classical nude, from poses plastiques to Living Pictures, nearly stabilize. In the applause of the crusading journalist for the classical body represented by La Milo, we have the "apotheosis" of the music-hall body. The body of the working woman becomes authorized to represent artistic canons of taste.

Stead even suggests that the pedagogic effect of La Milo might prove the sole hope of the "dregs" who attend the halls. Until her performance, he claims, "I had regarded them as something like the fishes in the mammoth cave in America, whose optic nerve had perished from long sojourn in the regions of eternal night. They seem to have lost all consciousness either of morality, or beauty, or intelligence. But . . . It was sufficient to display a picture instinct with a soul of beauty to elicit an immediate, although it might be but a transitory response. In that fact lies a great hope." As her advertisements claim, La Milo's value is in her difference from other performers. Stead's appraisal performs the difficult task of preserving the aura of a distinctive work of art from contamination by "drivel."

I have suggested that the professional tableaux vivants did not make a comprehensive break with Victorian patriarchy or with Victorian convention; the individual artists often spoke the language of competitive, assertive individualism that we would expect from the mid-Victorian entrepreneur. The spectacular case of La Milo's horseback ride as Lady Godiva in the 1907 Coventry pageant underscores the failure of the practice to produce new structures of feeling. The tableaux vivants woman worker commanded notoriety rare in the Victorian context. La Milo's ride may have represented a scandal or travesty, but of the sort that accrues individual gains and, as we will see, offers the kinds of display that media apparatus easily turn to spectacle. The Lady Godiva ride represented the kind of subversion that, as Guy Debord might icily observe, ideology exists to neutralize.

Still, La Milo both participated in and to a degree manipulated her own spectacle. On her own initiative, Pansy Montague, an expert horsewoman, took part in the Coventry city pageant, celebrating Lady Godiva's ride for municipal charity. There was controversy over La Milo's attire, particularly fears that she would wear the flesh-colored costume often used in tableaux vivants for the pageant. La Milo's assurances to the planning committee were conciliatory and well publicized: "Let it be distinctly understood that I have no desire to be seen in a costume, or lack of costume, which would give offenses to the most susceptible."[126]

La Milo's ride, replete with body-length wig, proved a media extravaganza. The *Sketch* supplement photographed La Milo's ride through Coventry, flanked by a reproduction of an old Coventry coin remodeled to depict La Milo ringed by the caption *Pro Bono Publico*. Such public display typified an age of "invented traditions"[127] when new state ritual and civic pageantry proliferated. La Milo's ride carefully made use of civic ritual—and a national symbol—in order to bestow more legitimacy on her profession. Against those who might dub her ride mere prurient display, Montague was vocal in her defenses of the "womanly" reasons she had for riding. She requested, against those who protested, that the celebration be supported by all "liberty-loving men and women . . . [who wish to] help in the triple cause of charity, chastity, and chivalry."[128] For a performer linked to poses plastiques to plausibly represent a national heroine, and to appeal to "charity" and "chastity," illustrates a new veneration for the music-hall body, so often denied access to high artistic values before the Palace statuary.

It is probably going too far to regard La Milo's ride in Coventry as resembling contemporary performance art in its desire to have practical, social consequences: yet her performance shares the same impatience with traditional aesthetic criteria. The record of the event that we have figures some of the perceptible limits faced by Montague's endeavor to escape gender bias. Along with the photographic depiction of the ride in a full two-page supplement, the *Sketch* ran a small picture of the original "Peeping Tom" as surrounding border. The caption for the photo observes that the picture was "taken specially for us from the King's Head Hotel" where the original "Peeping Tom" spied on Godiva's ride. The photo of La Milo's ride contained by its own Peeping Tom suggests the event retained a sensational aspect despite Montague's serious public pronouncements. However, Pansy Montague's attempt to control the reception to her public display anticipates the efforts that experimental dancer Maud Allan exerted to manage audience response to her performance as Salome at the Palace music hall a year later. Allan's ability to legitimate her physical display and taunt her critics through the same print media used by her detractors seems anticipated by Montague's example.[129]

An attempt to intervene in powerful images of traditional femininity for her purposes, La Milo's ride at Coventry reveals an inchoate politics. Yet her part in the procession is a colorful example of female agency and of how the desire to pose could be put to one's own purposes. Before the pageant ride, the *Era* reported with surprise La Milo's trial run. "Seized with a desire to emulate Lady Godiva," she rode through Coventry in the same attire in which she performed, only under the gaze of her manager and dresser.[130] This solitary ride suggests the ludic appeal of posing, and its potential for empowerment. On a whim, La Milo took the stage to the streets. The Coventry pageant utilized the conservative imagery of national instruction, but it also framed La Milo's self-display as consumer spectacle. The ride was likely more provocation than politics; yet, having taken place in a culture in which literary intellectuals and journalists largely worked to enforce class-based distinctions in mass culture, La Milo's ride deserves reconsideration.

The controversy over tableaux vivants had, throughout the 1890s and beyond, uneven results. Initially the dispute over the Palace Living Pictures empowered middle-class women to assume a custodial role over women performers from primarily working-class backgrounds. However, as the controversy over tableaux vivants was played out in the press, performers themselves gained a degree of power as self-proclaimed aesthetic professionals whose work exempted them from the temptations faced by mere stage amateurs. The controversy over the Palace in 1894 suggested that autonomy might be gained through publicity, a possibility that individual performers such as La Milo would attempt to enact during their music-hall careers.

The ability to manipulate one's self-display was overlooked or condemned out of hand by the female philanthropists who protested the Living Pictures. The class gulf between models and purity workers resulted in an unwillingness to allow performers the opportunity to speak about their work on their terms. The social purity movement, adept at marshaling the media to defend women against rapacious male sexuality, had difficulty in imagining how women performers could be the agents rather than the subjects of their publicity. Performers were instead categorized as inclined to "fall." In this instance, purity workers, like male professionals in journalism, claimed to speak as authorities, without considering the material conditions of theatrical labor and the gendered division of labor in Victorian society. The dispute over tableaux, however, suggests that, to a degree, aesthetic values might have some collective ownership. Standards for evaluation were the lingua franca for all participants in the debate, and the aesthetic ideal the court of appeals recognized by most of the disputants in the controversy.

In my conclusion, I contend that the potentially exclusive categories of professional culture could nonetheless provide some common ground between amateurs and experts divided by class and gender. The music hall was the premiere nineteenth-century example of a marginal culture practice that conquered the mainstream. In so doing, performance in the halls increasingly catered to the tastes of its growing middle-class audience. The bourgeois takeover of the music hall expanded and thereby transformed the values of the new class that appropriated the entertainment. I suggest that expert discourse on the music hall could destabilize a too-rigid separation between amateurs and professionals.

Conclusion

CYRENE AT THE ALHAMBRA

At the turn of the last century, London music hall crossed class lines, drawing a substantial middle- and upper-class patronage along with its core working-class audience. When culture forms cross over in this way, they acquire a spate of interpreters, with a range of interpretations, for crossover elicits interpretive diversity, and the social work of interpretation further enhances cultural mobility. Observers disagreed over the significance of music hall's popular success; public debate exposed some core late-Victorian beliefs regarding class and gender identity. The movement of the music hall into the dominant culture unsettled the confidence of some middle-class observers that taste and class could serve as a natural divide between social groups.

188

It also enabled a new group of observers to speak on behalf of a different England.

The greater diffusion of music-hall culture raised significant questions about the secure fit between class and taste. In his magisterial work *Distinction*, Pierre Bourdieu provides powerful evidence that taste claims are the indirect but inevitable expression of class status, and thus sustain class difference and hierarchy. Bourdieu provides a synchronic view of the relations between social rank and taste preferences that verges on positing direct causal links between an individual's taste and affect and his or her status. He describes the *habitus* of culture as "a structuring structure" and "also a structured structure"—forceful efforts to overleap structure by compounding what structure means, and to consider the relation between taste and status as a process.[1] Nevertheless, these compound terms inevitably leave us with a stable notion of taste as it relates to class hierarchy: and when culture forms break out to larger audiences, the connections between taste claims and various forms of belonging, whether racial, classed, or gendered, shift in unpredictable ways. Like any elite, intellectuals can and do work to naturalize their class position through taste statements; they can also serve as sensitive registers of changing relations between cultural preferences and social position.

We can better map social relations between class and taste if we treat taste making as a dialogic process, diachronically as well as synchronically. In tracing the changes that late-Victorian music hall made to the dominant culture, I join a conversation in cultural studies with, among others, Stuart Hall, Andrew Ross, and Janice Radway. These scholars attend to the many ways in which the circulation of culture forms expands the very categories that enable cultural flow, so that, for example, Janice Radway, in *A Feeling for Books: The Book-of-the-Month Club, Literary Taste, and Middle-Class Desire*, draws attention to how the production of the middlebrow unsettles the divide tastemakers established between high- and low-culture product. Andrew Ross, in *No Respect*, details how the reception of discourses like erotica or bebop depends on the mutual labor of both culture producers from various class strata and aspiring intellectual, predominantly bourgeois, tastemakers. Stuart Hall, in "Notes on Deconstructing the Popular," forcefully argues that scholarly attempts to recover the popular as pure vernacular expression obscure the very processes by which the popular is constructed. The historicist attempt to recover the real vernacular, like the purist search for culture as authentic product, cannot register the subtle but pervasive changes that occur in producers, audiences, and conceptual categories when cultural forms travel.

My claim that fin-de-siècle language of the popular should be read as a professional discourse builds on Hall's argument. For example, in the process of packaging proletarian comedy and dance to middle-class spectators, music-hall theater owners and promoters often watered down the variety fare they packaged. This compromise, however, was not well received by some of music hall's middle-class critics. These bourgeois observers sometimes interpreted the conscious effort to sanitize the music hall as an attempt to neutralize it, an appropriative gesture that revealed the greed and sterility—the worst qualities—of the culture of their class. These critics were angry that music hall's success situated it in the cultural middle; they were also upset with the apparent satisfaction of bourgeois audiences with this state of affairs. The middle-class patron of the halls insufficiently esteemed the low, according to critics like Max Beerbohm, a feature of whose "highbrow" taste discourse was hatred of the middle. The move of music-hall entertainment toward the middle of the road caused Max Beerbohm to treat conventional tastes more skeptically, rather than relinquish his positive response to the earlier, déclassé music hall. The inevitability of the bourgeois co-optation of vernacular culture spurred Beerbohm to imagine music hall as the culture of the opposition, even if that opposition included only himself and an elite corps of observers.

The transformation of the music hall into middle-class culture had myriad consequences. For example, the diffusion of the form made it more difficult for middle-class observers to distinguish their own culture from that of the working class. The ambiguity of the music hall, the puzzling nature of its hold on a broad English public, made it an ideal talking point for intellectuals seeking to flex their muscles as culture definers and interpreters. In the process of becoming dominant, a subaltern culture form clarified the practice of its "other": a professional cultural criticism that often used music-hall analysis to address broader national and cultural concerns.

This new professional critic no longer worked according to the assumption of the critic's exclusive, privileged relation to culture. The very success of the music hall had made apparent the double-voiced, composite nature of English culture, and the stance of the aficionado shared this synergy. In this fashion, the accounts of the middle-class observer of the halls mirrored the form of the late-Victorian halls, which mingled bourgeois and working-class modes of thinking in an effort to hail the broadest possible audience.

When late-Victorian intellectuals assumed the mantle of culture legislators, articulating the music hall as the popular, they often produced a trope

that alienated the people from the popular. But the growing social prominence of the music hall also provoked professional middle-class observers to
assume complex spectator positions, like Arthur Symons's pose of the aficionado. He assumed a shifting, hybrid perspective on the entertainment that
melded the disinterested view of the trained culture critic with the view of
the passionate advocate.

There is an egalitarian arc evident in Symons's writing on music hall: the
critic's respect for professional conduct comes to include the labor of music-
hall performers, and this respect comes to mitigate his sexism. Symons's essay
"At the Alhambra" taps into a storehouse of images received from Symons's
many viewings of music-hall ballet at this upscale London hall. At first,
Symons's essay suggests that the writer appreciates only the hidden drama
offstage and the coded mating rituals of the dancers and their often upper-
class admirers in the hall's front seats (where, Symons proudly iterates, he
always seats himself at the Alhambra). The initial result is a sexualized portrait of the dancers that blurs distinctions between them and the prostitutes
who also worked the halls of luxurious London variety theater.

However, Symons expands his canvas to include views of the training,
preparation, and dogged labor of the chorister, a disciplined and gravity-
defying worker: Symons produces an admiring sketch of the dancers as notable cultural hybrids. He appreciates that their work involves extremes that
the dancers nevertheless appear to balance or harmonize. Despite the essay's
fragmented form—its apparently haphazard assemblage of various impressions of music-hall ballet—the conclusion of the essay suggests the progress
of the writer to more enlightened views. In "At the Alhambra," Symons travels from a fetishized view of dancers to a conscious awareness of the complex experience of the dancers and their various labors.

The essay provides elegant testimony for the case that London music hall
produced performative occasions that blurred boundaries between participants and observers in a manner that produced, at least for a moment, new
relations between different classes and genders. We have some record of
these cross-class exchanges; they suggest that the popularity of music hall
occasioned carnival-like role reversals and inversions, allowing experts a
chance to imagine an escape from bourgeois respectability and socially marginal performers an opportunity to assert their central importance within
the culture. In these special cases, we can use the word "fan" and "expert" in-
terchangeably, since both terms are enhanced to include a desire to study, respect, represent, and specialize.

Arthur Symons's 1893 interview with Cyrene, a celebrated American skirt dancer, provides a moment of cross-class encounter, destabilizing and transformative, that can suitably end my story. Symons covered "the celebrated dancing phenomenon," in his words, for the *Sketch.* He interviewed Cyrene before she performed, and the exchange is marked by an intimate, personal, familiar tone. Of course, Symons constructs the personal with an eye toward its public consumption. Yet another kind of exchange, besides the commodified personal, is figured in this account. Symons uses the interview to authorize both Cyrene and himself as credible culture critics, and validates her testimony based on the comparative value of dance and dancers on the English scene.

The piece is structured around an idiosyncratic fantasy that Symons often repeated elsewhere: the "penetration" into the interior area of the music-hall backstage. As such, the interview might seem to be of a piece with the fetish images of dancers memorialized in Symons's poem "Behind the Scenes at the Empire," or the more lurid backroom stories of offstage flirtation that Symons narrated to friends like fellow music-hall enthusiast Herbert Horne. I would argue, however, that the interview with Cyrene follows a trajectory much closer to the scrupulous arrangement of music-hall experience that Symons would later elaborate in "At the Alhambra," in which he admires the dancers' ability to balance conflicting aims and ideals through their very labor.

The interview closes with a review of Cyrene's latest performance, framed in the traditional language of aesthetic response. Here Symons responds to what he perceives as the decorous nature of the dance and lauds the escape it promises from the degrading everyday. He notes of Cyrene's dance that "the extravagance of the thing was never Vulgar, its intricate agility was never incorrect; there was genuine grace in the wildest moment of caprice, there was real science in the pointing of the foot in its most fantastic flights above the head."[2] The account stresses Cyrene's avoidance of "vulgarity" and the "science" of her dance. It is a rhetorical construction of Cyrene as a professional in the most traditional sense of the term: a worker who has brought her labor under rational control, a trained subject whose display, though sensational, follows strict protocols.

Tellingly, Symons also suggests that his enlightened view results from an educational process. Symons admits that both he and Adolph Birkenruth, the *Sketch* artist who accompanies him, approach the meeting confident that Cyrene is merely an object for the cultured gaze. For Bikenruth and Symons, Cyrene is but "a possible subject for a drawing [and] a possible subject for a *chronique.*" However, once the two men are backstage, Symons and Cyrene enter into a long discussion of dance and its history; the conversation ends with Cyrene demonstrating a high kick.

The exchange moves the account into an altogether different register. Symons concludes:

> We drew back as close as we could against the wall, the little smiling maid who waited on her retreated into another corner, and, with a sudden kick, done with the greatest ease in the world, Cyrene tapped the palm of her hand, held just above her head, with instep. The fantastic foot flew into the air, descended, almost before one had time to realize it. "Never did La Goulue, never did Nini Patte-en-l'Air, do a kick like that," I assured her; and we talked of the French high-kickers of the Parisian public balls.

The backstage scene, replete with shoptalk, is no longer a mere account but a performative occasion in its own right, with participant and observer shifting roles. Cyrene and Symons at first disclose their shared interests: they converse on Parisian balls they have witnessed and what they have learned about dance from the occasions; they discourse as well on their favorite dancers. Cyrene is suggested to have her own cultish passions—"we spoke of Nellie Nevette, and it was with some anxiousness that she named that brilliant dancer." She speaks with interest on her peers and competition.

The account attempts to subsume classed and gendered difference into the category of shared acumen. The common interests and affection of the two for the "French high-kickers" of the Parisian ball suggest the discovery of a common ground achieved in the face of difference. This commonality is signified by the exchange of observation and inside knowledge; the two professionals meet and trade inside secrets and details meaningful to those in the know.

The interview form is designed to produce accessible versions of celebrities. Accordingly, the format should offer Symons many opportunities to exaggerate the differences between stars and private people. Instead, he crafts the encounter as a moment when one professional hails another. His and Cyrene's recognition of each other's expertise has the effect of leveling the cultural playing field. Symons's desired recognition as an insider in music-hall culture is publicized; simultaneously, Cyrene displays her knowledge of her work as craft and art. No longer a mere reflection of the cultured gaze, she is represented as a cultured subject in her own right.

She is so much a cultured subject, in fact, that Symons increasingly merges his own affective investment in the dance with Cyrene's own passion for her trade. His sympathy with Cyrene translates into shared agitation; as he observes, "As No. 11, her turn, came near, we began to feel quite nervous ourselves, such much did Cyrene seem to us, by that time, like an old friend, so anxious did we feel that she should succeed." The twinned emotional responses—Cyrene's anxiety to perform well and Symons's anxiousness that Cyrene's dance live up to both their expectations—also trouble the professional/amateur binary: for Symons's anxiety stirs from his desire to be recognized as a fan, the passionate amateur as well as the seasoned expert. Cyrene emerges as a critic as well, versed in the lore of her profession. And both performer and critic disclose their identity as fans; they emerge, in fact, as fans of their own fandom.

I have characterized the encounter between Symons and Cyrene as an exchange, but what goods are proffered or transacted in the meeting? Clearly, Cyrene gains some cultural capital among middle-class readers from having elicited the interest of a "serious" poet and critic. Yet the Cyrene of Symons's portrait does not seem to desire either his patronage or the investment of the critic's capital. The demonstration of her own various dance literacies demonstrates that, like Symons, she can assume various relations to her vocation. Cyrene does not require any tutelage on how to gain distance from her experience or her labor. The dynamic encounter of Symons and Cyrene suggests that fin-de-siècle dance permitted both the literary intellectual and the performer various opportunities to display distinct, but overlapping, cultural literacies.

The Symons/Cyrene meeting suggests the complex nature of late-Victorian demotic literacy. Symons's account of Cyrene's performance avoids what had become, for Symons, the standard English response to the skirt dance as "the mad Bacchic dance of modern Paris." Cyrene's performance takes up little space in Symons's review; it is left to Birkenruth, Symons's companion, to visualize the dancer's performance. Even here, Birkenruth's static images deny sensationalism, representing Cyrene in a formal pose. Symons's account avoids a description of Cyrene's dance, instead further crafting his image of the achieved intimacy, the peer camaraderie, linking Birkenruth, Cyrene, and Symons. The conversation among the three is described as continuing long after another journalist has left Cyrene in privacy. His departure leaves the three cognoscenti to "fall to chatting about trifles and matters of moment."

In this instance, professional discourse here allows the critic and the dancer to discover their common ground. The recognition between Symons and Cyrene is based on common categories like training, education, and achievement. The use of these categories does not mean the encounter escapes the larger cultural category of gender difference: Symons still appears to move in a world of male critics and female performers. Still, his account demonstrates how capacious the category of critic can be. He suggests the unity of critic and performer, noting how each state modulates into its "other"; the result expands the common understanding of the professional domain and breaches the supposedly huge gulf separating professionals and amateurs.

The exchange, I believe, suggests much about the practice of culture mingling brought on by the serious scrutiny of late-Victorian music hall by middle-class observers. This meeting between professional dancer and professional critic exceeds mere middle-class surveillance of now increasingly visible and culturally prominent working-class bodies. If the 1890s initiated the rise of professional society, as Harold Perkin and others maintain, the rise of this class should not be confused with its hegemony.[3] As the Cyrene/ Symons encounter reminds us, extending hegemony necessarily entails changing the terms of rule. If Symons broadens the reach of the bourgeois in hailing Cyrene as a professional, the result both extends the categories of middle-class culture and exerts a powerful, revisionist pressure on them. To claim that the exchange merely neutralizes social inequality by subsuming difference under culture neglects the subtle shifts in role-playing, the energetic mix and match of poses that both Cyrene and Symons perform. Symons's account, finally, might be said to provide the symbolic resolution of difference that serves as the blueprint for later, material change in the structures of economic and social injustice.

Symons's confidence that aesthetic professionalism encompasses both the reporter or critic and the celebrity indicates a shift away from the mid-Victorian social order to modernity as I have attempted to describe it. The account contains in miniature the broad-scale social transformations from individualist to corporate consciousness detailed in this study. The occupation of everyday life by experts, a new professional class, requires and produces a shift in consciousness from the solitary ego to something more social, more dynamic and dispersed. This is the struggle Harold Perkin traces in mid-Victorian society, which was caught between the entrepreneurial ideal with its faith in market-created social equity and harmony—as well as in the absolute value of the aggressive and resourceful businessman—and the complex, highly mediated, professional ethos.[4] Symons's brief treatment of Cyrene leaps beyond a purely individual point of reference, implying that aesthetic consciousness can foster a more collective spirit. His slant on the encounter with another art worker implies a new division of labor that produces experts confident that they are not a class set apart, due to their links with a larger public.

The *Sketch* interview suggests the existence of something like a collective effort across the class divide to partake in discourses of middle-class taste and expertise. Symons and Cyrene bond on the subject of taste, and the result suggests a reality more complex than the closed world between taste and class that designates Bourdieu's *habitus*. The account should prompt us to suspect those modes of contemporary cultural studies that bracket off the notion of aesthetic value or blunt it by collapsing the problem into the larger network of class difference.[5] The Cyrene/Symons encounter reveals the potential for evaluative practice to produce commonality. To dismiss the incident too quickly leaves us with the untenable option of a classist popular and the ultimately demeaning assumption that popular audiences are only authentic provided they refuse the exercise of aesthetic judgment or expertise.

Without claiming essential, transhistorical similarities between early and late forms of popular culture, the complex responses to a mainstream music hall raise issues relevant to thoughtful producers and consumers of popular culture today. Music hall was a vernacular form with a celebrated impact as mass culture, a cultural technology that recast the relation between the popular and the people, and a pedagogical tool of the professional middle classes eager to school others in Englishness. However, its very success suggests that cultural syncretism could provoke more material expressions of social integration. Then as now, the popular constitutes a foundation for cultural authority, but what kind of authority it founds remains open for challenge whenever the rules of expertise shift to accommodate new practices.

Notes

Introduction

1. For more on the development of music hall, as well as on issues of audience and class, see Penelope Summerfield, "The Effingham Arms and the Empire: Deliberate Selection in the Evolution of Music-Hall in London," in *Popular Culture and Class Conflict, 1590–1914,* edited by Eileen and Stephen Yeo (Sussex, UK: Harvester Press, 1981), 209–40; and Peter Bailey, "Custom, Capital and Culture in the Victorian Music Hall," in *Popular Culture and Custom in Nineteenth-Century England,* edited by Robert Storch (New York: St. Martin's Press, 1982). The scholarly essays collected in Peter Bailey, ed., *Music Hall: The Business of Pleasure* (Milton Keynes, UK: Open University Press, 1986); and J. S. Bratton, ed., *Music Hall: Performance and Style* (Milton Keynes, UK: Open University Press, 1986), are essential reading. For specific studies of music-hall song and lyrics, see Martha Vicinus, *The Industrial Muse: A Study of Nineteenth Century Working-Class Literature* (New York: Barnes and Noble, 1974); Peter Davison, *Songs of the British Music Hall* (New York: Oak, 1971); J. S. Bratton, *The Victorian Popular Ballad* (Totowa, NJ: Rowman and Littlefield, 1975); and Lawrence Senelick, "Politics as Entertainment: Victorian Music-Hall Songs," *Victorian Studies* 19 (1975–76): 149–60. Peter Bailey's *Popular Culture and Performance in the Victorian City* (Cambridge: Cambridge University Press, 1998) is a sustained effort to bring cultural studies perspectives to the phenomena of music hall. Dagmar Kift's *The Victorian Music Hall: Culture, Class and Conflict* (Cambridge: Cambridge University Press, 1996) provides a thorough account of the marketing and commercial history of the music hall throughout the century; it details shifts in the composition of the music-hall audience. Kift also gives necessary attention to provincial music halls. For a comprehensive bibliography of the music hall, see Lawrence Senelick, David Cheshire, and Ulrich Schneider, editors, *British Music-Hall, 1840–1923* (London: Hamden Press, 1981).

2. Eric Lott observes that the multiple entertainments combined in the minstrel show are still familiar to anyone "who has seen American television's 'Hee Haw'" in his book *Love and Theft: Blackface Minstrelsy and the American Working*

Class (New York: Oxford University Press, 1993), 5. The capsule summary of the form that Lott provides here also describes British music-hall entertainment. Readers who recall American TV's long-running Ed Sullivan show also have a ready analogue to variety theater.

3. There is another justification for my focus on the London halls. The nation's major metropolis was and remains a synecdoche for the nation. Interpreters of the London music hall often overlook the local nature of the entertainment in order to highlight its universal—i.e., national—meaning. See my reading of Percy Fitzgerald's *Music-Hall Land* below and of Henry Nevinson's short tale "Little Scotty" in chapter 4.

4. Like Lawrence Grossberg, I understand cultural studies as constituting a body of work that originated in debates within British Marxism; cultural studies insists, in Grossberg's words, that "much of what one requires to study culture is not cultural"; see Grossberg's *We Gotta Get Out of This Place* (New York: Routledge, 1991), 21. Cultural studies work attempts to provide a social context for artistic practice, without indulging in the illusion that context makes for absolute knowledge. The practice of cultural studies accepts the impure, uneven working conditions that impact the production of art and scholarship. Grossberg again: "[Cultural studies] does [not] attempt to smooth over the complexities and tensions; it chooses instead to live with, to see any historical struggle as neither pure resistance nor pure domination but, rather, as caught between containment and possibility" (21–22). My understanding of cultural studies also draws on the rich, contextual work of Raymond Williams, including *The Long Revolution* (New York: Columbia University Press, 1961), *The Country and the City* (New York: Oxford University Press, 1973), and *Marxism and Literature* (London: Oxford University Press, 1977). I owe a considerable debt to the work of Stuart Hall as well, especially his generous and insightful accounts of debates within cultural studies. Such work includes "Cultural Studies and the Centre: Some Problematics and Problems," in *Culture, Media, Language: Working Papers in Cultural Studies, 1972–79*, edited by Stuart Hall et al. (London: Hutchinson, 1980), 115–47, and "Cultural Studies and Its Legacies," in *Cultural Studies*, edited by Nelson Grossberg et al. (New York: Routledge, 1991). In a manner suggestive of the syncretism of cultural studies, Hall includes debates within cultural studies as constitutive of the field.

5. Hall argues against interpretive modes that essentialize popular culture and substantiates his case by specific recourse to British culture in the years between 1880 and 1920, in a landmark essay, "Notes on Deconstructing the Popular," in *People's History and Socialist Theory*, edited by Raphael Samuel (London: Routledge and Kegan Paul, 1981), 227–40. Morag Shiach's *Discourse on Popular Culture* (Stanford, CA: Stanford University Press, 1989) also underscores the fabricated character of the popular. Shiach details how rhetoric of the popular, developed in state discourse and later applied to the notion of the culture, distinguished the interests of the nation or state from the specific interests of working-class people. Discourse on popular culture fostered tension between the construct of the popular and the working class. Professional discourse, too, evidences a similar, rhetorically productive tension between its categories of the public and the expert. As with the discourse on the popular, professional discourse is subject to various formulations and can express a range of political positions. The rhetoric that governs relations between professionals and their public can variously emphasize differences between groups or emphasize commonality.

6. See Paul Gilroy, *The Black Atlantic* (Cambridge, MA: Harvard University Press, 1993), 72–111. Simon Frith offers similar objections to the fetish of authenticity in popular music. In his review of Bruce Springsteen's *Live—1975–85*, Frith argues that authenticity claims are built on a shaky foundation of binaries: "Firstly, authenticity must be defined against

artifice: the terms only make sense in opposition to each other" (*Music for Pleasure* [New York: Routledge, 1989], 98).

7. Peter Bailey's *Popular Culture and Performance in the Victorian City* constitutes a sustained attempt to bring cultural studies perspectives to the British music hall, and evinces a canny suspicion of essentialist class analysis. I am greatly indebted to his judicious reading of music-hall cultural practice and his effort to sound out signifying practices in music hall that exceed the "culture of consolation" label Gareth Stedman Jones pins on the halls. See also Jones, "Working-Class Culture and Working-Class Politics in London, 1870–1900: Notes on the Remaking of a Working Class," *Languages of Class: Studies in English Working-Class History, 1832–1982* (Cambridge: Cambridge University Press, 1983), 179–239. Bailey also presents a strong argument against evaluating the representation of working-class culture within the music hall solely by contemporary standards of political correctness; see *Popular Culture,* 130.

8. Typically, the relation between the professional and various publics gets cast in the starkest terms of class hegemony and expropriation. The notion that the rise of the professional changes some protocols of capitalist culture, or that professional protocols might be revised in the face of public demand, often gets overlooked. Barbara and John Ehrenreich, for example, conclude that the managerial class functionally commits "overt and sometimes violent expropriation" of knowledge and skills that originate among the working class; see "The Professional-Managerial Class," in *Between Labor and Capital,* edited by Pat Barker (Boston: South End Press, 1979), 5–45.

9. Harold Perkin, *The Rise of Professional Society: England since 1880* (New York: Routledge, 1989), and Burton Bledstein, *The Culture of Professionalism* (New York: Norton, 1976) remain classic studies of the rise of modern professions. I claim that "the professional ideal, based in trained and certified expertise" (4) that Perkin details inflected status and prestige claims made in the cultural realm. For recent studies of the links between professional culture and domestic ideology, see Monica Cohen's *Professional Domesticity in the Victorian Novel* (Cambridge: Cambridge University Press, 1998). I discuss the rise of the professions and some of their contemporary critics in regard to Arthur Symons and the problem of cultural expertise in chapter 2.

10. See W. Macqueen-Pope's *The Melodies Linger On: The Story of Music Hall* (London: Allen, [1950]) for more on the rise of the commercial music hall and successful Victorian/Edwardian music-hall managers like John Hollingshead or Oswald Stoll, who helped make music hall respectable enough to attract polite and prosperous crowds. Writing on late-Victorian painter Byam Shaw's sketches of the Coliseum, a variety theater managed by Sir Oswald Stoll, Tim Barringer details Stoll's ambitions as music-hall owner to draw to the hall "a mass audience with a range of socially improving theatrical entertainments" and transform music hall into "a highly capitalized and sanitized middlebrow forum"; see "'Not a "Modern" as the Word Is Now Understood'? Byam Shaw, Imperialism and the Poetics of Professional Society," in *English Art, 1860–1914,* edited by David Peters Corbett and Lara Perry (New Brunswick, NJ: Rutgers University Press, 2001), 76. In "The Creation of the Avant-Garde: F. T. Marinetti and Ezra Pound," Lawrence Rainey also invokes the Coliseum as representative middlebrow entertainment; see *Modernism/Modernity,* 1.3 (1994): 195–220. In Rainey's words, the Edwardian music hall "was already a corpse that was experiencing a brief but spurious afterlife through its incorporation into the 'Palace of Variety,' the new institution of an advancing consumer society" (209). Interestingly, the commercial music hall still elicits Rainey's most scathing rhetoric, suggesting a personal disappointment that exceeds the bounds of historical overview.

11. Clark, *Farewell to an Idea: Episodes from a History of Modernism* (New Haven: Yale University Press, 1999), 7.

12. My book expands on many incidents and music-hall partisans touched on in John Stokes's discussion of the social history of music hall, *In the Nineties* (Chicago: University of Chicago Press, 1989). Like Stokes, I argue that music-hall performance challenged traditional aesthetic categories of high culture; we both read Arthur Symons for a glimpse at how a representative literary intellectual negotiated the challenge to elite aesthetic values. I have a broader interest in how music hall fostered a Victorian discourse of expertise, a topic necessarily subordinated in Stokes's more compact account of the music hall.

13. Eric Lott could claim with some justice that the study of American minstrelsy (also a part of the English music-hall tradition) unduly emphasized "the printed record (songsters, playlets and so on) of what was in fact a negotiated and rowdy spectacle of performer and audience"; see *Love and Theft,* 9. Such a charge has less purchase on music-hall scholarship, in which song sheets have not been a sole focus of scholarly work for many years now. Convincing efforts to historicize music hall have been made by social historians such as Gareth Stedman Jones (1974) and Penelope Summerfield (1981). John Stokes (1989) situates fin-de-siècle halls within English literary and cultural history, and Peter Bailey's *Popular Performance in the Victorian City* (1998) focuses on performance/audience dynamics in late-Victorian theater and music hall, analyzed from cultural studies perspectives.

14. Elizabeth Robins Pennell, "The Pedigree of the Music Hall," *Contemporary Review* 63 (April 1893): 583.

15. M. L. Larson, *The Rise of Professionalism* (Berkeley and Los Angeles: University of California Press, 1977), 24.

16. See Geoffrey Russell Searle, *Morality and the Market in Victorian Britain* (Oxford: Clarendon Press, 1998) for a study of public resistance to Victorian professionals. Searle contends that the medical profession at least largely succeeded in convincing the public that uniform standards of training and licensing were not special privileges or exemptions but necessary for the commonweal as well as for the practitioner, and that doctors legitimately required protection from competition in the marketplace (85).

17. Henry Mayhew, *London Labour and the London Poor* (New York: Penguin, 1989), 37. Subsequent references to this edition of Mayhew will be noted parenthetically.

18. For a useful account of Mayhew's ambivalence to bourgeois norms as well as vernacular culture, see Andrew Tolson's essay "Social Surveillance and Subjectification: The Emergence of Subculture in the Work of Henry Mayhew," in *The Subcultures Reader,* edited by Ken Gelder and Sarah Thornton (New York: Routledge, 1998), 302–15.

19. Common anxiousness is evident in James Grant's penny gaff tale in *Sketches of London* (London: Saunders and Otley, 1839) and in Mayhew's later chronicle. Grant's concerns about the potential for social unrest in working-class group assemblies suffuse his account of the entertainment. It is worth noting that such fears are less prominent in Mayhew's study, perhaps allowing him a clearer view of the autonomous and competitive nature of the gaff's information culture.

20. Wayne Koestenbaum, *The Queen's Throat* (New York: Norton, 1989), 114.

21. Bailey's essay begins with Mayhew's brief reconstruction of penny gaff song as evidence of music hall's productive function in broadcasting the experience and significance of city life to the urban poor; see *Popular Culture,* 139.

22. Keith Wilson, "Music-Hall London: The Topography of Class Sentiment," *Victorian Literature and Culture* 23 (1996): 23–35.

23. See Wilson, "Music-Hall London," 57.

24. I owe the analogy between cultural knowingness and hazing to W. T. Lhamon.

25. The odd copyright disclaimer contributes to the surreal effect of Fitzgerald's text, in which he transcribes song lyrics and details audience reaction to songs, then observes that "the songs in this little book have not yet been sung in Music-hall Land, but they are at the service of its 'sweet singers,'" thus placing in question the documentary status of his book. I am indebted to Scott Banville for this and other observations on *Music-Hall Land*.

26. Percy Fitzgerald, *Music-Hall Land* (London: Ward and Downey, 1890), 2. Subsequent references to this edition will be made parenthetically.

27. T. S. Eliot, "Marie Lloyd," in *Selected Prose of T. S. Eliot*, edited by Frank Kermode (New York: Farrar, Straus and Giroux, 1975), 172–75.

28. Walter Frith, "The Music-Hall," *Cornhill* 60 (July 1889): 68.

29. Ibid., 79.

30. Eric Lott makes a similar point in relation to the American mass culture entertainment of blackface minstrelsy. While conceding that popular culture sometimes enables social control, he desires (as do I) to maintain a cautious optimism about the relative autonomy of pop culture forms. This is his measured assessment of the politics of the minstrel show "popular": "Because the popular is always produced, capitalized, it is hardly some unfettered time-out from political pressures, a space of mere 'leisure.' . . . But as Stuart Hall has insisted, neither does it passively mirror political domination taking place in other parts of the social formation, as though it were only epiphenomenal . . . or, in the Frankfurt School scenario, wholly administered and determined"; see Lott, *Love and Theft*, 17.

31. As Harold Perkin observes, "[A] professional society is not merely the old class society fitted out with a new ruling class. It is a society structured around a different principle," namely the "competition for public resources"; see *Rise of Professional Society*, 9. Accordingly, an imagined public is articulated and hailed in middle-class music-hall accounts. The public central to these proclamations of professional identity is variously cajoled, criticized, and counseled. By turns, the public is to be feared and persuaded: yet it remains a constant imaginative presence for the serious music-hall interpreter.

Chapter 1

1. T. S. Eliot, "Marie Lloyd," in *Selected Prose of T. S. Eliot*, edited by Frank Kermode (New York: Farrar, Straus and Giroux, 1975), 172. All subsequent references are to this edition.

2. George Orwell, "The Art of Donald McGill," in *The Collected Essays, Journalism and Letters of George Orwell* (New York: Harcourt Brace Jovanovich, 1968) 2:162.

3. Colin MacInnes's *Sweet Saturday Night* resurrects the world of music-hall song in response to the first stirrings of an English popular song industry, modeled on the marketing of rock to teenagers in America. The Beatles resurrect music-hall styles on both *Sergeant Pepper's Lonely Hearts Club Band* (Capital, 1967) and *The Beatles* (Capital, 1968); these songs serve as homage to the English musical past and as marks of the band's ironic distance from these traditions. They provide a sense of the band's regional identity that might be gainsaid by their global success. Similarly, the Kinks' *The Village Green Preservation Society* (Pye, 1968) yokes rock with Englishness by name checking the music hall and taking many of the old musical arrangements into the new setting of the four-piece beat group. These efforts to knit English rock to English identity react against the emergent narrative of a global (i.e., Americanized) pop music.

4. Linda Dowling emphasizes the collective character of the intellectual predilection for music hall; see *Language and Decadence in the Victorian Fin de Siècle* (Princeton, NJ: Princeton University Press, 1986), 238. Max Beerbohm's essay "The Blight on the Music Halls" (1899) suggests music-hall partisanship followed a group dynamic: "Everyone had seen Mr. Sickert's paintings. Soon other painters began to frequent the Halls. Mr. Arthur Symons cut in, and secured the Laureateship. Mr. Anstey wrote satires. Mr. Frederic Wedmore began to join in the choruses with genteel gusto"; see "The Blight on the Music Halls," in *Works and More* (London: Bodley Head, 1952), 201. Interestingly, Dowling neglects the purposive cast of the assembly, reading their fandom as a cult of the irrational, while Beerbohm credits the music-hall cognoscenti with too little, while blaming them for too much. "The Blight on the Music Halls" insinuates that music-hall partisans were largely unthinking advocates of the form, and hints that their enthusiasm only hastened the halls' assimilation into genteel culture.

5. Beerbohm, "Blight," 201.

6. I take the debate over the music hall as a controversy between, first and foremost, members of a privileged class of culture makers. My account follows a trajectory similar to that of Joel Pfister, who reads the cultural prominence attained by Eugene O'Neill's drama as a reflection of the desire of the burgeoning professional-managerial elite for artistic work that privileges depth models of subjectivity compatible with their self-image. See *Staging Depth* (Chapel Hill: University of North Carolina Press, 1995), especially chapter 2.

7. See Andrew Ross, *No Respect* (New York: Routledge, 1989).

8. Convinced that the consensus as to what constitutes true culture had been lost, Archer often discoursed at length on the different values manifest in cultural objects; he surely must have realized that such elaborate discussions troubled his argument for universal cultural standards. In "The Indictment of the Music-Hall" (*Living Age* 292 [Fall 1917]: 313–16), he asks, "By what principle can we allow ourselves to laugh at Rabelais or Sterne and refuse to laugh at Mr. George Robey and Miss Marie Lloyd? Is the physical basis of life a fit subject for laughter? If it is, where are we going to draw the line?" (316). Archer must be aware of the concession he offers his opposition simply by framing the comparison; the distinction between Sterne and Lloyd is best preserved by avoiding the analogy. Raising the issue compels Archer to provide his readers reasons for his selections, turning the assured statement of taste into special pleading. Reflecting on cultural distinctions may not overturn them, but it inevitably makes matters of taste seem less matter of fact, less natural. See Barbara Herrnstein Smith, *Contingencies of Value* (Cambridge, MA: Harvard University Press, 1991) for an account of the contradictions that arise when Enlightenment intellectuals like Hume and Kant elevate taste preferences into philosophic axioms.

9. William Archer, "Theatre and Music-Hall," in *The Theatrical World of 1895* (London: Walter Scott, 1896), 96–97. All subsequent references are to this edition.

10. Archer's argument that music hall encouraged its middle-class patrons to abandon their critical reserve is not groundless; music-hall song, early and late, broadcast the message to its mass audience that it was good to stop thinking, to relax, and to loosen up. The popular song "It's Nice to Be Common Sometimes," sung by Daisy Hill (1935), itemizes the virtues of living at a remove from middle-class formalities and constricted behavioral codes. See Peter Gammond, *Best Music-Hall and Variety Songs* (Boston: Plays, Inc., 1975), 410–11.

It is worth noting that some music-hall acolytes suggested that the appreciation of the form demanded a new kind of attention on the part of its truly discerning spectators. To the casual observer, variety theater may have seemed chaotic or fragmented; yet Arthur

Symons asserted, "[You] will find a queer kind of unity in the midst of all this seemingly casual variety, and in time—if you think it worth the time—you will come to understand the personality of the music-halls"; see Symons to the *Star,* June 18, 1982, in *Arthur Symons: Selected Letters, 1880–1935* (Basingstoke, UK: Macmillan, 1988), 85–86. His statement is tentative, and hesitating, and demands to be read with the same sly attention it advocates. Symons hints that he has developed a heightened form of attention that can extract sense from distraction. When the National Vigilance Association attacked the Empire music hall, and temporarily closed the promenade on grounds of solicitation, Symons wrote on behalf of the Empire. He retained the aficionado's confidence that the distractions of the promenade would not prevent the true devotee from realizing the real reason for the Empire's success: "the excellence of its entertainment"; see *Selected Letters,* October 15, 1894, 108. Archer suggests that music-hall patrons were stupefied by the entertainment; in contrast, Symons intimates that the form elicited a heightened concentration of cognitive faculties.

In chapter 4, I touch on other reasons for Symons's public defense of the Empire— namely, the respect of an aspiring cultural expert for a well-regulated urban space. The entrepreneur and the aesthete find common ground in their desire for a properly managed music hall. Countering the charges made against solicitation in the halls, Symons asserts, "Vice, unfortunately, cannot be suppressed; it can only be regulated"; see *Selected Letters,* 108. Lurking in this laconic claim is the admiration of the aficionado for public spaces managed by professionals.

11. Ross, *No Respect,* 101.

12. In *Secular Vocations: Intellectuals, Professionalism, Culture* (New York: Verso, 1993), Bruce Robbins provides an exceptionally supple account of professional gestures; he conceptualizes professional ideology dialectically. I return to Robbins's account of professional decorum in the following chapter.

13. Krishan Kumar, "'Englishness' and English National Identity," in *British Cultural Studies,* edited by David Morley and Kevin Robins (Oxford: Oxford University Press, 2001), 51.

14. Philip Dodd, "Englishness and the National Culture," in *Englishness: Politics and Culture, 1880–1920,* edited by Robert Colls and Philip Dodd (London: Croom Helm, 1986), 10–11.

15. Archer's 1895 essay "The County Council and the Music Halls" cites Pennell as proof that the music hall is not new, but timeless. "In one sense," Archer writes, "it has been always with us; in another it is a creation of yesterday" (317). "Broadly speaking," he continues, "the art of the music hall is simply art of vulgarity." His own version of the historicist apology for music hall shifts from an apology, however, to a final verdict on the real value of the contemporary music hall. Archer writes, "Is it not an appalling thought that, while thousands of songs are written every year for the music halls, and have been for the last half-century or so, not one song of them . . . has passed into literature?"; see "The County Council and the Music Hall," *The Contemporary Review* 67 (March 1895): 326. For Archer, the value of popular culture resides solely in its ability to hatch more complex culture forms worth esteeming.

16. Archer fends off the argument that music hall "reflects the life of the lower middle-classes" by denying the main tenet of the partisan faith: namely, that music hall stood in authentic relation to its audience. In "The County Council and the Music Halls," Archer contends that the music hall has been irredeemably vulgarized by commerce, and that consequently it is more debased than its audiences. Appropriated by business interests, the

form no longer represents its working-class and lower-middle-class patrons, or does so partly and therefore misleadingly. The music hall, Archer writes, "reflects" its audiences "affectations, their snobberies; their superficialities—in brief, their vulgarities; but of the serious side of lower middle-class life, its real joys and sorrows and crimes and heroisms, it conveys scarcely a hint" (327).

17. Elizabeth R. Pennell, "The Pedigree of the Music Hall," *The Contemporary Review* 63 (April 1893): 575.

18. Ibid., 576.

19. Terry Eagleton, *Heathcliff and the Great Hunger* (London: Verso, 1996), 3.

20. Ibid., 4.

21. Before "Demos' Mirror," Max Beerbohm relied on similar analogies in the review/essay "In a Music Hall": "[T]he entertainments in Music-halls are the exact and joyous result of the public's own taste. . . . There is no compromise, no friction, between the form and the audience. The audience is the maker of the form, the form is the symbol of the audience"; see "In a Music Hall," in *More Theatres* (1899; reprint, New York: Taplinger, 1969), 397. All subsequent references are to this edition.

22. Beerbohm, "Demos' Mirror," 273.

23. Beerbohm's essay "The Blight on the Music Halls," included in *More Theatres,* also tries to make sense of such a perceived change.

24. Beerbohm, "The Older and Better Music Hall," in *Around Theatres* (New York: Alfred A. Knopf, 1930), 384, 382.

25. As the title of "The Blight on the Music Halls" suggests, the earlier essay already sounds the note of cultural pessimism that resonates through the later essay, "The Older and Better Music Hall." Both essays produce an authentic culture/commercial culture binary that relies on essentialized notions of "the people." As Beerbohm puts it, "In its early stage, the Music Hall was a very curious and interesting phenomenon, a popular art"; he also claims that "vulgarity is an implicit element of the true Music Hall" (203). The essay is full of contradictions on the working of cultural co-optation. At one point, the critic complains that he, and his middle-class readers, were directly to blame and, like "fools," drove "[vulgarity] from its most convenient haunt" (203). Yet Beerbohm initially suggests that the appropriation of music hall was an inevitable, if apparently unplanned, result of commercial enterprise: "One must not marvel that those days are over. With sumptuous palaces erected in the heart of London, and with the patronage of fashion, new modes were bound to come in, sooner or later" (200).

26. Beerbohm, "Older and Better," 383.

27. Ibid., 383–84.

28. Pennell, "Pedigree," 383.

29. John Stokes, *In the Nineties* (Chicago: University of Chicago Press, 1989), 61.

30. Arthur Symons, letter to the *Star,* June 18, 1897. Cited in *Selected Letters,* 87.

31. It is my claim that Symons achieved a more exemplary self-consciousness in his essay on the famous Leicester Square music hall, the Alhambra; see chapter 2.

32. Pierre Bourdieu, *An Invitation to Reflexive Sociology* (Chicago: University of Chicago Press, 1992), 84.

33. See Dick Hebdige, "In Poor Taste: Notes on Pop," in *Hiding in the Light* (New York: Routledge, 1988), 116–43, for a similar reading of the unsettling strategies of pop art intellectuals. Hebdige reads pop "as an inspired move in the culture game, the object of which is to fix the shifting line between . . . 'low' and 'high,' 'art' and 'non-art'" (120).

34. For an argument about the resistant potential that can accompany the assiduous observance of established rules, see Homi Bhabha, "Of Mimicry and Man: The Ambivalence of Colonial Discourse," *October* 28 (Spring 1983): 124–33.

35. Archer, "Theatre and Music-Hall," 96–97, 100.

36. Ibid., 98–99.

37. Ibid., 102.

38. Ibid., 103.

39. William Archer, "The Music Hall, Past and Future," *Living Age,* 8th ser., 4 (Fall 1916): 102.

40. Archer's "The Indictment of the Music-Hall," published in 1917, voices a similar distaste for, and impatience with, popular "vulgarity."

41. Archer, "The Music Hall," 104.

42. G. H. Mair, "The Music Hall," *English Review* 9 (August–November 1911): 124.

43. Christopher Ricks's notes in his edition of early and unpublished poetry of Eliot, *Inventions of the March Hare* (New York: Harcourt, Brace, 1996), suggests that Eliot knew much of Symons's poetry and even criticism by heart.

44. Colleen Lamos, *Deviant Modernism: Sexual and Textual Errancy in T. S. Eliot, James Joyce, and Marcel Proust* (Cambridge: Cambridge University Press, 1998), 24.

45. David Chinitz, "Reading Marie Lloyd" (unpublished manuscript, 1998).

46. Ibid., 22.

47. Eliot, "Marie Lloyd," 173.

48. Ibid., 174.

49. Ibid., 173.

50. Or, as Alan Marshall suggests, Eliot may be thinking of Eastern religion; the language of sympathy and understanding, of course, suffuses the end of *The Waste Land.* See Marshall, "England or Nowhere," in *The Cambridge Companion to T. S. Eliot,* edited by David Moody (Cambridge: Cambridge University Press, 1994), 104.

51. I claim Arthur Symons gains a quite different insight in his visit to the Alcazar, a Spanish music hall: that neither performer nor music-hall patron is in thrall to difference, or fully determined by class status. See chapter 2.

52. Eliot, "Marie Lloyd," 174.

53. Ibid., 175.

Chapter 2

1. Arthur Symons, "A Spanish Music-Hall," in *Cities and Sea-Coasts and Islands* (New York: Brentano's, 1919), 145.

2. For a provocative and wide-ranging study of the rise of the expert in England, see Harold Perkin, *The Rise of Professional Society: England since 1880* (London: Routledge, 1989).

3. Symons, "A Spanish Music-Hall," 146.

4. Pierre Bourdieu and Terry Eagleton, "In Conversation: Doxa and Common Life," *New Left Review* 191 (January/February 1992): 111–21.

5. Bruce Robbins levels this charge of reductionism against Bourdieu in Robbins's *Secular Vocations: Intellectuals, Professionalism, Culture* (New York: Verso, 1993), 208.

6. John Stokes examines Symons's relation to music-hall culture, recognizing that music hall revised Symons's attitudes to culture and aesthetics; see Stokes, *In the Nineties* (Chicago: University of Chicago Press, 1989), 53–95. Stokes also realizes that Symons's pose as aficionado or self-styled amateur assumes a complex relation to cultural values, although

he does not place Symons's stance within the broader framework of professionalism. Peter Bailey's fine essay "Conspiracies of Meaning" connects music-hall fandom to camp; his emphasis on working-class communities at the music hall leads him to pass over the singular case of Symons. See Bailey, "Conspiracies of Meaning," *Past and Present* 144 (1994): 138–70.

7. Susan Sontag, "Notes on Camp," in *Against Interpretation* (New York: Dell, 1966), 275. There is much to learn about camp from Wayne Koestenbaum's *The Diva's Mouth* (New York: Penguin, 1989): for example, Koestenbaum's awareness that camp transforms both the camp spectator and the character of the object of affection. A narrative digression on camp in Christopher Isherwood's *The World in the Evening* (New York: Ballantyne, 1967) is also wonderfully suggestive. Isherwood sees camp as both double consciousness and catalyst: something that liquefies conceptual categories—or, more precisely, dialecticizes them. Isherwood's mouthpiece, Stephen Monk, proclaims: "You can't camp about something you don't take seriously. You're not making fun of it; you're making fun out of it. You're expressing what's basically serious to you in terms of fun and artifice and elegance" (106).

8. Symons, "A Spanish Music-Hall," 145.

9. Andrew Ross, *No Respect* (New York: Routledge, 1989), 146.

10. Raymond Williams, *Marxism and Literature* (Oxford: Oxford University Press, 1977), 123.

11. Mark Booth, *Camp* (New York: Quartet Press, 1983), 183.

12. In *Secular Vocations,* Robbins elaborates on Pierre Bourdieu's contradictory assessment of intellectuals (208). As an example: in *An Invitation to Reflexive Sociology* (Chicago: University of Chicago Press, 1992), Bourdieu argues that intellectual populism amounts to little without a prior or ongoing redistribution of social and cultural capital: "We must—I have never stopped repeating it—work to universalize in reality the conditions of access to the sensibility and subjectivity present in the faux universal of the aesthetic experience" (84–85). Bourdieu leaves unanswered how this universalized culture is to come into being without experts, institutions, and even the "slumming" intellectuals whom he mistrusts.

13. I am arguing that Symons attains reflective distance from his spectator practice; like Roland Barthes, I equate achieved reflection with theoretical stances. Barthes extols "an attitude of reflexivity (we were speaking just now of *theory,* to me it's the same thing)," and suggests the stance has a "real effect on culture," since it facilitates "the extremely vigilant perception of one's own position in language." See Roland Barthes, *The Grain of the Voice: Interviews, 1962–1980,* translated by Linda Coverdale (New York: Hill and Wang, 1984), 154.

14. Robbins, *Secular Vocations,* 34. Robbins stresses that professionalism carries a theoretical component with it that can potentially curb the elitism of experts. It is the possession of theory that simultaneously distinguishes the professional and produces the possibility for ethical practice. "Theory" enables a reflection on aims and ends, in which the public emerges as a felt pressure within the expert's otherwise private deliberations; it can also ensure, ideally, that the public is never fully marginalized by expert deliberation. In Robbins's words, "The original sense of profession was a declaration of belief made upon entry into holy orders; to enter into membership was to announce a shared theory. If what discriminates professions from other crafts and occupations is the necessary possession of theory, associated with a potential (even if unrealized) for the overcoming of self-interest . . . then a door opens in professionalism for a scrutiny of values and ends"; see *Secular Vocations,* 34.

15. Symons, "A Spanish Music-Hall," 146.

16. Ibid., 146–47.

17. Ibid., 148.

18. Ibid., 151.

19. Ibid., 152.

20. Examples include Oscar Wilde's *Salome*, Jack Smith's *Flaming Creatures*, even Elizabeth Taylor's Cleopatra as camp cult figure. I owe the suggestion to Stephen Shapiro's unpublished work on Gramsci and *Paris Is Burning*, "Social Historians Study the Vagaries of Women's Fashions: Gramsci, Drag, and the Wars of (Subject) Position."

21. Symons, "A Spanish Music-Hall," 153.

22. Ibid., 154–55.

23. Roland Barthes, *Image, Music, and Text* (New York: Hill and Wang, 1977), 182.

24. Ibid., 181.

25. See W. T. Lhamon, *Raising Cain* (Cambridge, MA: Harvard University Press, 1998), esp. chap. 1. Lhamon's analysis of New York circa 1830 stresses that modern concepts of rootlessness, cosmopolitanism, and alienation had their vernacular expression prior to its formalization at the hands of the educated but deracinated artist. Different idioms developed to express the same affective intensities: of alienation, fury, love, and displacement. Symons and Villaclara speak fundamentally the same language.

26. I may seem to be doing handsprings to establish that Symons's treatment of Villaclara is somehow egalitarian. Like many others, I am largely persuaded by T. J. Clark's masterful *The Painting of Modern Life: Paris in the Art of Manet and His Followers* (1984; rev. ed., Princeton, NJ: Princeton University Press, 1999), which emphasizes the darker consequences of bourgeois fascination with the lower middle class they encountered in urban leisure spaces. Clark suggests that the bohemian artist found in petit-bourgeois entertainers "alter egos of the avant-garde," but adds that the avant-garde inserted these liminal figures back into a class hierarchy through their own representations of performers (142). In Clark's words, a painting of the petit-bourgeois, Manet's *Olympia* for example, "in some sense described these people's belonging to the class system." Clark adds the disclaimer that the painter's heightened class consciousness "only happened occasionally"; one further assumes that such higher consciousness was not shared by the subjects of these paintings.

My quarrel with Clark lies in my different understanding of the consequences of bourgeois representations of the subaltern. For while I agree with Clark's argument that representations of the petit-bourgeois stirred middle-class artists into recognizing their difference from members of the lower middle class, I do not believe this was the only consequence of these productions. Such representations are built on interclass encounters and reallocated cultural capital, albeit in partial, incomplete ways. The Symons/Villaclara exchange discloses how representations might change how relations between spectators and performers are framed.

Representations inevitably function as transactions. Symons recognizes Villaclara and isolates in her performance and stance certain skills that suggest the observer and observed perform similar labor in different venues. Both strive to manage the attention of others, albeit in different mediums. The encounter entails the recognition of shared labor and the assignation of surplus value: preconditions for the redistribution of cultural and other forms of capital. The recognition of labor enhances the value ascribed to both labor and laborers.

27. Symons, "A Spanish Music-Hall," 155.

28. Bailey, "Conspiracies of Meaning," 150.

29. Ibid., 169.

30. Wayne Koestenbaum, *The Diva's Mouth* (New York: Penguin, 1989), 81.

31. Symons to Herbert Horne, c. March 1893, in *Arthur Symons: Selected Letters, 1880–1935,* edited by John Munro and Karl Beckson (Iowa City: University of Iowa Press, 1989), 101.

32. Symons, "At the Alhambra," *Savoy* 5 (September 1896): 81.

33. Ibid.

34. A description of *Aladdin* is provided in Ivor Guest's book on Alhambra ballet. It was staged with the most elaborate light show possible, with, in Guest's words, "a delicate curtain of 'crystal lacework' made of 75,000 glass facets that were held together by twenty-four miles of wire and illuminated by lights of many different colours"; see *Ballet in Leicester Square: The Alhambra and the Empire* (London: Dance Books, 1992), 47. Guest quotes the *Era,* which adds that "streams of silver 'rain' . . . fringed the curtain above, and the view through its network, of a beautiful central figure, with a branch of electric lights on each side of it" closed the show. While Mlle. Marie played Aladdin, actor/dancer Fred Storey is recalled as moving the house with the "splendid looseness of his trips and flings." All told, *Aladdin* seems to have put its various means to a particular end: to free bodies from their moorings in gender.

35. Symons, "At the Alhambra," 83.

36. Ibid., 82.

37. In other words, Symons relies on parataxis to narrate the ballet; "the Princess enters" is a cue, "and then" something else happens. We are told "there is another transformation" followed by a series of "enchantments": then abruptly, "there is another transformation" (ibid.).

38. Ibid., 75.

39. Ibid.

40. Ibid., 78.

41. Ibid., 79.

42. Ibid.

43. Ibid., 77.

44. I take heart, though, from Steven Connor, whose brand of cultural phenomenology parallels Symons's approach to the ballet so neatly I must remind myself that Symons never in fact read it (although Symons did read an early version of a similar stance in that celebrated paean to luminous surfaces, Walter Pater's conclusion to his *Studies in the Renaissance*). The phenomenologist, Connor observes, works to attain a sense of how observers "always already" inhere within a given scene. Symons's relations to music hall and the ballet assume his location within a specific place and situation. See Connor's provocative online manifesto, "CP, or a Few Don'ts by a Cultural Phenomenologist," November 7, 1998 (www.hbk.ac.uk/Departments/English/skc/Cp/notman.htm).

45. Symons, "Alhambra," 73.

46. Ibid., 80.

47. Ibid., 83.

Chapter 3

1. Jeffrey Weeks, *Sexuality* (London: Routledge, 1990), 35. He also observes that female prostitution was less a constant object of state regulation at the turn of the century than

"subject to a peculiar 'compromise' that sought neither outright repression nor formal state regulation"; see "Inverts, Perverts, and Mary-Janes: Male Prostitution and the Regulation of Homosexuality in England in the Nineteenth Century," in *Hidden from History*, edited by Martin Duberman, Martha Vicinus, and George Chauncey Jr. (New York: Meridian, 1990), 200. Weeks offers the straightforward view that "advocates of social purity did reach toward straightforward repression." I challenge the claim that Chant, and purity workers in general, exerted a single-minded disciplinary power over the urban poor.

2. Peter Stallybrass and Allon White, *The Politics and Poetics of Transgression* (Ithaca, NY: Cornell University Press, 1986), 134.

3. Judith Walkowitz, *Prostitution and Victorian Society* (Cambridge: Cambridge University Press, 1980), 245.

4. Judith Walkowitz complicates this judgment of purity reformers in *The City of Dreadful Delight* (Chicago: University of Chicago Press, 1992). Having criticized the social purity legacy "for reinforcing women's subordination and sexual fear," she now recognizes that "these campaigns also opened up new heterosexual expectations for middle-class women, even as they set into motion repressive public policies, mostly directed against working-class women on the streets" (7).

5. Karl Beckson's account of "Prostitutes on the Promenade" in *London in the 1890s: A Cultural History* (New York: Norton, 1993) notes that the hostile reaction to Chant challenges stereotypes about puritanical Victorians: "[T]he reaction to the campaign against the Empire reveals the ferocity with which the presumably staid Victorians often resisted the attempts of the anti-vice reformers to regulate places of public amusement" (118). This chapter suggests some reasons why a purity reformer's protest over public sexuality failed to gain hegemonic status in the culture, despite repressive tendencies at large in the culture.

6. Detailed information on Chant outside of the controversy over the promenade is relatively sparse; there does not yet exist a full-length study of Chant's long history of work as a reformer, lecturer, and woman of letters (she wrote a novel entitled *Sellcuts' Manager* [1899], as well as poetry). Phillipa Levine mentions Chant's activity on the executive committee of the National Society for Woman's Suffrage in passing, but Chant's life and work have been undervalued and neglected by cultural historians; see Levine, *Feminist Lives in Victorian England: Private Roles and Public Commitments* (Cambridge, MA: Basil Blackwell, 1990), 93. Edward J. Bristow's *Vice and Vigilance: Purity Movements in Boston since 1700* (Totowa, NJ: Rowman and Littlefield, 1977) details the work of the "prudes" in the historical context of purity movements, but from a liberal perspective that denies complex motives to antilibertarians. E. S. Turner's *Roads to Ruin: The Shocking History of Social Reform* (London: M. Joseph, 1950) devotes an entire chapter to the Empire controversy; I follow Turner in paying careful attention to newspaper accounts in the disputes. In *Madonnas and Magdalens* (New York: Holmes and Meier, 1976), Eric Trugdill mentions Chant's encounter with the Empire in passing (192–93); Tracy Davis mentions it in passing in *Actresses as Working Women: Their Social Identity in Victorian Culture* (New York: Routledge, 1991), 154–57. More recently, Judith Walkowitz discusses Chant's polemics in the *Pall Mall Gazette* in defense of women's unhampered access to leisure and labor in urban spaces; see "Going Public: Shopping, Street Harassments, and Streetwalking in Late Victorian London," *Representations* 62 (1998): 1–30.

A crucial step toward Chant's "canonization" was taken when Karl Beckson gave the controversy over the Empire a full narrative account in his chronicle *London in the 1890s: A Cultural History.* John Stokes's account of the Empire controversy is concise, useful, and balanced. It stands, I believe, as the very first fully judicious treatment of Chant's protest in literary critical or belles-lettristic accounts of music hall; see *In the Nineties* (Chicago: University of Chicago Press, 1989).

7. See Dellamora, *Masculine Desire: The Sexual Politics of Victorian Aestheticism* (Chapel Hill: University of North Carolina Press, 1990), 193–218, for a fuller discussion of how late-Victorian sexual scandal established social consensus.

8. George Bernard Shaw complained in the *Pall Mall Gazette* about Chant's recklessness in making information she obtained about the earnings of prostitutes public; the *Daily Telegraph*'s drama critic, Clement Scott, attacked the reformers harshly as "a lot of ignorant busybodies, unwomanly women and unmanly men, prudes and prowlers, citizens and citizenesses with morbid consciences, vigilants and purists sworn not to correct pleasure but to put down all pleasure whatsoever, as their forefathers did of old" (*Era*, October 27, 1894, 3). For Scott, the general progress and refinement of the music halls, largely the work of sturdy entrepreneurs, was endangered by meddlers and androgynes. Arthur Symons argued that the women who spoke against the halls lacked the expertise to recognize the importance of the Empire promenade's aesthetic qualities: "By closing the promenade, you take from the Empire . . . its privileges as a music-hall, and reduce it to the level of constraint and discomfort of an ordinary theatre" (*Pall Mall Gazette,* October 25, 1894, 3). I discuss Symons's responses at greater length in this chapter. For more on Churchill and the Empire, see Churchill's *My Early Life* (London: Reprint Society, 1944), 60–68.

9. *Sketch,* "The Empire," October 31, 1894.

10. See Walkowitz, *City,* 187–89, on the highly aestheticized nature of male professionalism. Professional behavior was defined in ways contrary to the norms of the marketplace; public service and disinterested behavior were valorized in professionals. Again, see Harold Perkin's *The Rise of Professional Society: England since 1880* (Routledge: New York, 1989) for a helpful overview.

11. Chris Waters, "Progressives, Puritans, and the Cultural Politics of the Council, 1894–1934," in *Politics and the People of London: The London County Council, 1889–1965* (London: Hambledon Press, 1989), 61.

12. Cited in Waters, "Progressives," 62.

13. Ibid.

14. Joseph Donoghue, "The Empire Theatre of Varieties Licensing Controversy of 1894: Testimony of Laura Ormiston Chant before the Theatres and Musical Hall Licensing Committee," *Nineteenth Century Theatre* 15 (Summer 1987): 50–59.

15. Information on the Empire and a transcript of Chant's own testimony are both available in Joseph Donoghue's helpful account of the licensing controversy, "Empire Theatre."

16. *Times* (London), "Music, Dancing and Theatre Licensing," October 11, 1894, 7.

17. In *Actresses as Working Women,* Tracy Davis draws attention to the testimony of D. Wilton Collin before the London County Council's Theatres and Music Halls Licensing Committee. Collin witnessed the same prostitutes at St. James Restaurant in Piccadilly Circus and in attendance at the Alhambra and the Empire music halls on the same evening (145).

18. Qtd. in E. S. Turner, *Roads to Ruin: The Shocking History of Social Reform* (London: Michael Joseph, 1950), 210.

19. Many such testimonies are provided in E. S. Turner's account of the Empire controversy. Music-hall historian Archibald Haddon labeled the Empire's promenade "vicious"; qtd. in Turner, *Roads to Ruin,* 1. Seymour Hicks called the Empire "the annexe of London's smartest clubs" with a "scented-sachet demi-[mondain]" who were "ladies of

distinction in their unfortunate profession"; see Seymour Hicks, *The Vintage Years* (London: Cassell, 1943), 152. Cf. James Agate on "The Passing of the Empire" in *My Theatre Talks* (London: Arthur Barker, 1933) for more gilded accounts of prostitution in the hall. (Agate, however, met and admired Chant herself.)

20. *To-Day,* "Letters of a Candid Playgoer," November 17, 1894, 337.

21. *Sketch,* "Notes from the Theatres," November 7, 1894, 3.

22. See Symons, *Pall Mall Gazette,* October 25, 1894, 3. As John Stokes writes, "Symons knew full well that the halls were the scene of sexual encounters, a secret he kept badly by endlessly celebrating his own assignations in poems and essays"; see *In the Nineties,* 60. See Beckson, *London in the 1890s,* for a reading of Symon's "Maquillage" (1891), a poem that celebrates the upscale glamour of the "representative" Empire prostitute (113–14).

23. Donoghue, "Empire Theatre," 54.

24. *Music Hall and Theatre Review,* "Babble," October 12, 1894, 4.

25. Cited in Turner, *Roads to Ruin,* 211. Seymour Hicks's description of the Empire also marks it as a masculine enclave, an "annexe of London's smartest clubs, frequented by the best-known Men about Town, who scanned strange faces somewhat critically"; see *The Vintage Years,* 152. According to Hicks, "the Empire Lounge was known throughout Britain and her Dominions as a place where soldiers and sailors back from foreign service, or travellers who had not been in England for many a year, could make almost certain of meeting someone with whom they had been acquainted in the old days, and in this they were seldom disappointed" (153).

26. Qtd. in Turner, *Roads to Ruin,* 211.

27. See "Meeting of Protest," *Daily Telegraph,* October 22, 1894, 3, for a sense of the popular outcry against Chant.

28. Davis notes that the prices of West End theaters and halls favored the middle class; see *Actresses as Working Women,* 142. In "Empire Theatre" Donoghue gives the Empire's prices for admission as 1–3 guineas for private boxes; 7s. 6d. for box stalls; 1s. for the pit; 6d. for the gallery (55).

29. W. Macqueen-Pope, *Twenty Shillings in the Pound* (New York: Hutchinson, 1951), 275.

30. Martha Vicinus, *The Industrial Muse: A Study of Nineteenth Century British Working-Class Literature* (New York: Barnes and Noble, 1974), 250.

31. W. Macqueen-Pope, *The Melodies Linger On: The Story of Music Hall* (London: Allen, [1950]), 233.

32. The Empire also boasted a fairly wealthy clientele; H. G. Hibbert notes it was the first music hall Prince Edward attended casually; see *Fifty Years of a Londoner's Life* (New York: Dodd and Mead, 1916), 88.

33. Stokes, *In the Nineties,* 59.

34. For the definitive reading of Victorian collectivist politics, see Stuart Hall and Bill Schwarz's "State and Society, 1880–1930," in *The Hard Road to Renewal: Thatcherism and the Crisis of the Left,* by Stuart Hall (New York: Verso, 1988), 95–123. The account stresses the Foucauldian aspects of this statist turn, as bureaucrats took up "the positive role of producing and accumulating new knowledge about the specific subjects and categories which came under their disciplinary regimes" (108).

35. Donoghue, "Empire Theatre," 55.

36. Ibid., 56.

37. See also *Times* (London), October 11, 1894, 3.

38. Judith Walkowitz notes how crucial interviews with the urban poor were for female philanthropists. Charity workers often relied less on statistical knowledge and

more on informal discussion, and Walkowitz labels these accounts as "incipient urban ethnography"; see *City,* 56.

39. Donoghue, "Empire Theatre," 57.

40. For more information on Chant's methods, see L. N. Sawyer, "Mrs. Laura Ormiston Chant and the Empire Theatre," *Lend a Hand* 14 (1896).

41. Walkowitz, *City,* 55.

42. Martha Vicinus, *Independent Women: Work and Community for Single Women, 1850–1920* (Chicago: University of Chicago Press, 1985), 320.

43. Cited in Sawyer, "Laura Ormiston Chant," 338.

44. Elizabeth Langland, "Nobody's Angels: Domestic Ideology and Middle-Class Women in the Victorian Novel," *PMLA* 107 (March 1992): 294.

45. For Chant, the streets allowed for dramatic encounters with dangerous men. In the *Pall Mall Gazette,* July 19, 1887, Chant relates chasing "a well dressed man of middle age" away from a girl of twelve, and asserts the rights of womanhood to London's streets and public places (3).

46. The phrase is Chant's; see Donoghue, "Empire Theatre," 59.

47. *Times* (London), "Promenade to Be Closed," November 2, 1894.

48. Chant's class antagonism and solicitude for women working the promenade are more fully expressed in her interview in the *Westminster Gazette,* October 15, 1894, 3; her statements complicate John Fiske's generalizations about music-hall spectatorship, offered in *Understanding Popular Culture* (Cambridge, MA: Unwin Hyman, 1989). Observing that "middle- and upper-class men visited some of the more respectable halls in order to meet working-class women," Fiske concludes that "it is not surprising . . . that when such activities attracted social discipline it was directed toward the work of the women rather than the leisure of the men" (77). Chant's critique of male privilege was clearly understood by the angry men who responded to the protest in the *Daily Telegraph.*

49. *Music Hall and Theatre Review,* October 12, 1894, 4.

50. Walkowitz observes that most journalism agitating against the "traffic in women" gravitates toward melodrama; W. T. Stead's "Maiden Tribute of Modern Babylon" in the *Pall Mall Gazette* is the *locus classicus* of these cultural uses of melodrama (July 1885). Stead's account of the Maiden Tribute, in Walkowitz's words, circulated one of the most "popular themes of nineteenth-century melodrama, street literature, and women's penny magazines": "the seduction of poor girls by vicious aristocrats"; see Walkowitz, "Male Vice and Feminist Virtue: Feminism and the Politics of Prostitution in Nineteenth Century Britain," *History Workshop* 13 (Spring 1982): 83. Melodramatic values also inflect Chant's interpretation of events at the Empire.

51. *Our Day,* "A Noted English Reformer: Mrs. Laura Ormiston Chant; An Interview," 16 (1896): 431.

52. *Pall Mall Gazette,* "Aim of the Purity Crusaders," October 23, 1894, 7.

53. Davis defends Chant's complaint that ballet costumes provoked desire; however, Davis's assertion that "the contiguity of behavior in the promenades to the performance on stage . . . preoccupied the witnesses" requires a slight qualification in Chant's case (156). Chant seemed unwilling to conclude that onstage performance was responsible for the corruption of women in the promenade; rather, it was the presence and visible success of solicitation that might dispirit women and seduce them to a life of vice. In the *Westminster Gazette,* Chant contrasts crowd reaction to the Living Pictures portrayal of "The Lost Chord" and the excitement of the crowd with "an indecent remark, in a strident voice, from a painted woman behind me." "The enthusiasm of the house and the conduct of this

woman in the promenade are a significant object lesson," Chant concludes, thereby contrasting a proper mode of spectatorship with improper kinds of response. This defense of music-hall performance, it should be noted, is one of the few occasions in the controversy in which Chant is on record as blaming women for the plight of women, rather than the upscale men of the lounge.

54. The letter and editorial pages of the *Daily Telegraph* served as a fractious public sphere for a month; the *Telegraph*'s letter column and editorials previously had allowed two months of response to Mona Caird's attack on marriage in the August 1888 *Westminster Gazette*, the skirmish producing twenty-seven thousand letters; see Trugdill, *Madonnas and Magdalens*, 241.

55. H. A. Bulley, *Pall Mall Gazette*, October 18, 1894, 3.

56. Freedom, *Times* (London), October 19, 1894, 2

57. *Pall Mall Gazette*, October 26, 1894, 3.

58. Arthur Symons, "The Case of the Empire," *Saturday Review*, November 10, 1894, 501–2.

59. Since the 1850s, expert accounts of prostitution considered it an inescapable fact of urban life. W. R. Greg called it "a constant fact—a social datum which we have to deal with—an evil inseparable from the agglomeration of large numbers in one locality"; cited in Lynda Nead, *Myths of Sexuality* (Oxford: Basil Blackwell, 1988), 117. William Acton suggested that prostitution was, as Steven Marcus puts it, "an inevitable, almost an organic, part of society"; see Marcus, *The Other Victorians* (New York: Basic Books, 1964), 4. Acton's solution to the social evil was "the intervention of government in a regulatory but minimal capacity" while preserving "personal liberty and laissez-faire." Of course, Chant disrupted the consensus of medical experts like Acton on these points regarding prostitution.

60. "A. B.," *Daily Telegraph*, October 16, 1894, 2.

61. T. Werle, *Daily Telegraph*, October 19, 1894, 2.

62. *Daily Telegraph*, October 27, 1894, 2.

63. *Daily Telegraph*, October 19, 1894, 2.

64. The *Sketch* claimed that the last word on the entire debate belonged to Raven Hill's sketchbook, *The Promenaders*, with its twenty-two full-page drawings concerning the dispute. "Of the great fight over the Promenade," the *Sketch* concludes, "perhaps the only relic which will be left of it is Mr. Raven Hill's album." Such a statement indicates that a professional aestheticism provided the last word on a debate that, for some, simply concerned matters of amusement.

65. *Punch* 107 (October 1894): 194–95.

66. See Lisa Tickner, *The Spectacle of Women* (Chicago: University of Chicago Press, 1988), for analysis of the many caricatures of the feminist prevalent in the late-Victorian and Edwardian eras, 160–70.

67. Terry Eagleton, *The Ideology of the Aesthetic* (Oxford: Basil Blackwell, 1990), 20.

68. *Punch*, 107 (October 1894): 195.

69. "Another Englishman," *Daily Telegraph*, October 16, 1894, 3.

70. *Daily Telegraph*, editorial, October 15, 1894, 3.

71. *Daily Telegraph*, editorial, October 18, 1894, 3.

72. *Music Hall and Theatre Review*, October 12, 1894, 3.

73. Michel Foucault, *Discipline and Punish* (New York: Vintage Books, 1979), 200.

74. *Daily Telegraph*, editorial, October 18, 1894, 2.

75. *Sketch*, October 31, 1894, 4.

76. Qtd. in *Daily Telegraph*, October 18, 1894, 3.

77. "A Londoner," *Daily Telegraph,* October 18, 1894, 2.

78. "Persecuted," *Daily Telegraph,* October 21, 1894, 2.

79. Burton Bledstein, *The Culture of Professionalism: The Middle Class and the Development of Higher Education in America* (New York: Norton, 1976), 89.

80. Jerome K. Jerome, editorial, *To-Day,* October 20, 1894, 337.

81. The phrase is from Beatrice Webb; it is her description of female charity workers in the 1880s, cited in Walkowitz, *City,* 57.

82. "A. B.," *Daily Telegraph,* October 16, 1894, 2.

83. *Daily Telegraph,* "Meeting of Protest," October 22, 1894, 2.

84. *Sketch,* "The Empire: The Decline and Fall," October 31, 1894, 3.

85. Stokes, *In the Nineties,* 9.

86. Jerome, *To-Day,* October 27, 1894, 369.

87. Walkowitz emphasizes the pleasures of fulfilled power indulged in by some middle-class women in charity work; the belief that philanthropists enjoyed their labor made their labor doubly suspicious to some, and these doubts were exposed in the correspondence elicited by the Empire controversy; see *City,* 57.

88. Waters, "Progressives," 70.

89. Turner, *Roads to Ruin,* 221.

90. *Pall Mall Gazette,* "Aim of the Purity Crusaders," October 19, 1894, 7.

91. Levine, *Feminist Lives,* 13.

92. Judith Walkowitz also provides a fascinating account of the Men and Women's Club, formed in 1885, that demonstrates the attraction that positivism and secularism had for trained, intelligent men and women with managerial aspirations; see *City,* 135–69. Chant's millennial expectation of the full redemption of working-class streetwalkers was keyed into religious traditions that no longer exclusively motivated those born into the trained, professional classes. Still, there remained viable, and vital, links between progressive feminism and millenialist religion in this period. At the World's Congress of Representative Women, which Chant attended in Chicago the year before the Empire controversy, African American intellectual Francis Harper, the author of *Iola Leroy,* addressed the power of reforming women with chiliastic fervor. Harper assured her audience that they were "on the threshold of woman's era," when "Eden would spring up in our path, and Paradise be around our way"; see Harper, "Women's Political Future," in *World's Congress of Representative Women,* edited by Mary Wright Sewall (Chicago: Rand McNally, 1894), 433 and 437. Harper also spoke of the special role that women would play in ameliorating the "social evil" of prostitution (436). For more on Harper and the persistence of residual Judeo-Christian ideology among progressive African American women, and for a useful supplement for understanding Chant's own intellectual background, see Hazel Carby, "'On the Threshold of Woman's Era': Lynching, Empire and Sexuality in Black Feminist Theory," *Critical Inquiry* 12 (Autumn 1985): 262–77.

93. Beverly Skeggs, *Formations of Class and Gender: Becoming Respectable* (London: Sage, 1997), 8.

94. *Pall Mall Gazette,* "Concerning a Council of Morality," October 19, 1894, 4.

95. Waters, "Progressives," 70.

96. The coincident rise of professionalism and consumerism is detailed by Richard Wightman Fox and T. J. Jackson Lears in *The Culture of Consumption: Critical Essays in American History, 1880–1980* (New York: Pantheon, 1983). Bruce Robbins challenges the argument that these emergent forces entail the necessary demise of humane and democratic possibilities in *Secular Vocations: Intellectuals, Professionalism, Culture* (New York: Verso, 1993), 51.

97. Robbins, *Secular Vocations,* 52.

98. I discuss some reasons to reconsider and embrace our professional identity at length in the chapter on Symons (who is portrayed negatively in this chapter, since he un-characteristically insisted on his music-hall expertise as a mode of privilege during the Empire controversy).

99. The promenade of the Empire was eventually closed, but not until World War I hysteria mounted over the spread of syphilis; see Beckson, *London in the 1890s,* 127. For an example of how Chant's allegedly power-mad personality was read into the historical record, see Colin MacInnes's otherwise essential reconstruction of music hall, *Sweet Saturday Night* (London: MacGibbon and Kee, 1967). In most respects, MacInnes's probing eye for the social circumstances behind popular forms makes his book a precursor to the best work of the Birmingham Centre for the Study of Contemporary Culture. However, MacInnes's analytical skills falter in the case of the Chant controversy. He (inaccurately) blames Chant for closing the promenade (for more than a brief time), insinuating that she "killed" the hall as a going concern and lively social venue. The charm of imagining oneself as a flaneur on the promenade is real enough seventy years on to entice MacInnes to provide a loving evocation of the space and issue a spirited tirade against Chant the meddler. In his imaginative recasting, the "Empire was famous for its Promenade, from which you could see the show and, from closer to, courtesans who spent the evening there waiting for you to offer them a b. and s. or some bubbly" (142). The passage invites the reader to join the author in the role of aspiring dandy. He adds with some indignation that this "delightful and harmless place came to be thought by moralists . . . scandalous," a state of affairs for which he fully blames "the indefatigable machinations of one Mrs. Ormiston Chant."

100. *Music Hall and Theatre Review,* October 19, 1894, 3.

101. Tony Bennett's study *The Birth of the Museum* (New York: Routledge, 1995) indicates how rare Chant's attitudes were among individuals with a managerial inclination. While many within the professional classes were optimistic that public spaces accommodating art, museums, and art galleries could play a role in tutoring and transforming working-class patrons, most intellectuals refused to believe that mass culture arenas might serve a pedagogic function; see Bennett, *Birth of the Museum,* 66. Newspaper editorials that touched on this issue during the Empire controversy voiced their concern over the pernicious effects of the music-hall "vulgarity" that Chant countenanced, even appeared to embrace, in her press comments on the entertainment. The *Western Daily Press* shared some of Chant's open-minded tolerance toward patrons who chose to spend time and money on London music halls rather than frequent the city's opera or museums, but also displayed a significant condescension toward them. One editorial states, "[T]he young man who returns to lonely lodgings after a heavy and, perhaps, a disappointing day's work, is not necessarily badly disposed because if, as a choice of entertainments, he is offered a lecture on Moabite inscriptions or a seat in a music-hall, he prefers the latter. Nor need he be absolutely brainless if there are times when he would rather sit in a music-hall, and listen to songs with a swinging refrain and see graceful dancing, and have a quiet smoke and think of nothing in particular, than follow with intellectual strain a Lyceum performance of *Lear,* or a Haymarket version of *Hamlet*"; qtd. in *Why We Attacked the Empire* (London: Horace Marshall and Son, 1895), 31–32. This is certainly a timid defense. The *Echo* also tolerated, and patronized, the "men and women of all classes, . . . whose mental calibre is such that . . . 'Knock 'em in the Old Kent Road,' appeals far more pleasantly than one of Bach's fugues, and the rhyme of 'Daisy and Bicycle Made for Two' is infinitely more fascinating than the immortal story of Dante and his sweet Lady Beatrix"; qtd. in *Why We Attacked,* 26–27.

102. *Era,* October 27, 1894, 1.

103. Arthur Symons, "Imperium Et Licentia," *Pall Mall Gazette,* October 25, 1894, 3.

104. Ibid.

105. Bledstein, *Culture of Professionalism,* 90.

106. See Pierre Bourdieu, *Distinction* (Cambridge, MA: Harvard University Press, 1984), 28–30.

107. *The Sketch,* October 31, 1894, 4.

108. Grant Richards, *Memoirs of a Misspent Youth* (London: Heinemann, 1932), 324.

109. Ibid., 326.

110. Roland Barthes, *Mythologies* (New York: Hill and Wang, 1957), 11.

111. Bledstein, *Culture of Professionalism,* 90.

112. Ibid., 92.

Chapter 4

1. The end of this hegemony is amply demonstrated in the comprehensive case studies that comprise Judith Walkowitz's *The City of Dreadful Delight* (Chicago: University of Chicago Press, 1992). See especially chapter 2, "Contested Terrain: New Social Actors," 41–81.

2. For a helpful discussion of gender and performance at the halls, see Jane Traies, "Jones and the Working Girl: Class Marginality in Music Hall Song, 1860–1900," in *Music Hall: Performance and Style,* edited by J. S. Bratton (Milton Keynes, UK: Open University Press, 1986). For a provocative analysis of the metaphors that gendered mass culture upon its emergence in the nineteenth century, see Andreas Huyssen's "Mass Culture as Woman: Modernism's Other," in *After the Great Divide* (Bloomington: Indiana University Press, 1986), 44–65. Huyssen argues that working-class culture, unlike mass culture forms such as popular magazines, best-sellers, and serial novels, was never stigmatized as "seductive" spectacle by critical observers within the middle class. This argument would appear to exclude the music hall from being conceptualized as seductive, since the halls were, for most of the nineteenth century, a metonym for working-class culture and conviviality. Nonetheless, the gender categories that Huyssen suggests were mobilized in debates over cultural value and hierarchy touched the debate over the halls themselves. For example, gender categories allowed observers to periodize the form, and abetted in the creation of middle-class patrons who could imagine themselves true curators of the entertainment. The 1880s and 1890s witnessed the rise of large-scale variety theaters that, as Gareth Stedman Jones observes, attracted "a new audience" to the form, including "sporting aristocrats . . . military and civil officials on leave from imperial outposts, clerks and white-collar workers, . . . university, law and medical students"; see Gareth Stedman Jones, "Working-Class Culture and Working-Class Politics in London, 1870–1900: Notes on the Remaking of a Working Class," in *Languages of Class: Studies in English Working Class History, 1832–1982* (Cambridge: Cambridge University Press, 1983), 194. The variety theater became, in the eyes of some, the home of class interlopers, who can be imagined and marginalized as undesirables. Jones characterizes the variety theater as "a natural focus of jingoism, upper-class rowdyism and high-class prostitution." Henry Nevinson's depiction of the music hall presents the "old," downscale, East End music hall as the repository of healthy culture, in comparison with its tradition of robust homosociality.

3. The "discovery" of East London by middle-class chroniclers and journalists is detailed in Peter Keating's *The Working Classes in English Fiction* (London: Routledge and

Kegan Paul, 1971). Walkowitz speaks of the convergence of "high and low literary forms, from Charles Booth's survey of London poverty, to the fictional stories of Stevenson, Gissing, and James, to the sensational newspaper stories of W.T. Stead and G.R. Sims," in encouraging a "geographic division of London into a hierarchical separation, organized around the opposition of East and West"; see *City*, 17. The inherent difficulties faced by middle-class representations of the working class also organize Regenia Gagnier's careful study of the many Victorian discourses of self-writing and self-disclosure, *Subjectivities* (Oxford: Oxford University Press, 1991).

4. Walkowitz, *City*, 60.

5. Walter Besant's most notorious text in this regard is *The Revolt of Men* (London: W. Blackwood and Sons, 1882), which imagines women taking over all of professional society.

6. Walter Besant, *Dorothy Wallis: An Autobiography* (London: Longman's, Green, 1892), 67.

7. The "domestication" of London theater dominated the 1890s, Mary Jean Corbett argues in *Representing Femininity*, yet the possibility of theater becoming an exclusively feminine space troubled the male intelligentsia well into the twentieth century. In 1933, Irish playwright St. John Ervine sounded the alarm that "[t]wo dangers at present threaten the theatre. . . . One that it may become womanized; the other that it may become a machine for party propaganda. . . . The first [danger] is graver than the second. The man's Theatre became the recreation of the community; the woman's Theatre is likely to be the recreation of a single sex, and *that* will kill it"; see Ervine, *The Theatre of My Time* (London: Rich and Cowan, 1933), 136.

8. Besant, *Dorothy Wallis*, v.

9. Ibid., ix.

10. Ibid., 53.

11. W. R. Greg, "Why Are Women Redundant," in *Literary and Social Judgments* (Boston: James Osgood, 1873), 306.

12. Actress and suffragette Cicely Hamilton claimed a Besant heroine served as her role model and her introduction to the difficulties faced by women in a male-dominated workplace. Hamilton recalled how she was moved by the "unsophisticated maiden" in Besant and James Rice's *The Golden Butterfly*, who visited London's business district and "[gazed] round with eyes of wonder," asking, "Where are all the women?. . . . Why is there nothing but men in this part of London?" See Cicely Hamilton, "The Working Women," in *Wonderful London*, edited by Almey St. John Adcock (London: Fleetway House, 1935), 190.

13. Besant, *Dorothy Wallis*, 311.

14. Ibid., viii.

15. Besant recalls in his autobiography founding a Woman's Bureau of Work, an endeavor that tied philanthropic impulse to a desire for controlled surveillance of working-class women. In Besant's words, the bureau offered "offices all over the country and in the colonies, where women who want work, and places which want women workers, might be registered, classified, and made known"; see *The Autobiography of Walter Besant* (New York: Dodd, Mead, 1902), 93. The impulse to empower women and discipline them is casually intertwined in Besant's scheme.

16. See Mary Jean Corbett's careful reading of Irene Vanbrugh's autobiography in *Representing Femininity* (Oxford: Oxford University Press, 1992), 145–46.

17. Besant, *Dorothy Wallis*, vi.

18. Madge Kendal, *Dramatic Opinions* (Boston: Little, Brown, 1890), 196.

19. Dorothy's cousin Daniel is an avid patron of the Empire music hall, and even considers taking to the stage himself. When Dorothy, Rachel, and Oney subsequently tour with

a theatrical troupe, Oney wonders aloud if an absent Daniel "went on the music-hall stage" instead (188). Even as variety theaters gained the patronage of working-class audiences, both Besant's fiction and his more sociological chronicles of city life suggest how difficult it was to extricate the music hall from working-class culture—and criminality. In Besant's chronicle of *East London* (London: Chatto and Windus, 1901), the writer details the habits of East End hooligans, stressing that they inhabit East End halls but routinely go "farther afield, and may be found in the galleries of even West End music-halls to see a popular turn" (181).

20. Besant, *Dorothy Wallis*, 62.

21. Ibid., 63.

22. Ibid., 68.

23. Ibid., 69.

24. Ibid., 230.

25. Ibid., 109.

26. Ibid., 281.

27. Ibid., 77.

28. Ibid., 282.

29. Ibid., 283.

30. Kendal, *Dramatic Opinions*, 80.

31. Ibid., 82.

32. Besant, *Dorothy Wallis*, 307.

33. Ibid., 306.

34. Besant, *East London*, 65.

35. Martha Banta stresses the contradictory advice offered to women such as Dorothy and an American contemporary, Theodore Dreiser's Carrie Meeber, in current periodicals. In Ruth Batchelder's "The Country Girl Who Is Coming to the City," young women are advised not to leave home for a job. In contrast, in James Montgomery Flagg's *Adventures of Kitty Cobb* (both were published in the *Delineator*, edited by Dreiser from 1906 until 1910), the heroine marries the right man, just as Besant suggests Dorothy will eventually, and attains lifelong happiness after her initial struggle. As Banta remarks, "if young women followed Flagg's version of 'The Country Girl' they would hasten to the city as quickly as possible"; see Banta, *Imaging American Women* (New York: Columbia University Press, 1986), 781. These conflicting narratives of Batchelder and Flagg lie cheek by jowl in the run of the same literary magazine. Besant's novel expresses both ideologies: the promise of success for ambitious women and the likely consequences of compromised femininity and lost respectability.

36. Besant, *Dorothy Wallis*, 172.

37. John Stokes provides a fine discussion of the new journalism and the then-novel interview, which fostered belief that public events might be explained through the analysis (and representation) of individual motives. The interview bolstered late-Victorian concepts of individual agency; see *In the Nineties*, 19–21.

38. Besant, *Dorothy Wallis*, 202.

39. The *Bookman* speculated that "so capable a person will not always wait for her sluggish and dilatory lover," and suspected that Dorothy's career would resume; see A. C. Deane, *Bookman* 2 (1892): 121. The *Dial* meanwhile criticized the absent Alec for his near-criminal neglect of Dorothy and for his delay in placing Dorothy under his husbandly care: "[W]e suppose he will provide for her eventually . . . but we cannot forgive [him] for per-

mitting her to lead for so long a life of so great privation and suffering" (309). Of course, Dorothy's misfortunes prove not only her virtue, but also her innate professionalism as Besant sees it.

40. Deane, 121.

41. Besant, *Dorothy Wallis,* 202.

42. Ibid., 9–10.

43. Walter Besant, "At the Music Hall," *Longman's Magazine* 22 (June 1893): 163.

44. Ibid., 164.

45. Ibid., 165.

46. Besant, *Dorothy Wallis,* 191.

47. Ibid., 168.

48. Ibid., 169.

49. Hall Caine, *The Christian* (New York: D. Appleton, 1899), 75.

50. Judith Walkowitz's account of the "Maiden Tribute" controversy in *City* details how the various narratives surrounding Victorian sexual scandal circulated by the Victorian press could be mobilized in favor of "the people" and against the rakish aristocrat. In Walkowitz's words, these narratives established and activated "political potentialities for action for men and women" (120).

51. Walkowitz, *City,* 57.

52. Ibid., 59.

53. Caine, *Christian,* 280.

54. Ibid., 320.

55. Ibid., 539.

56. Beerbohm's comment on Caine's novel comes from his review of the stage adaptation; see Beerbohm, "Greeba in London," *Saturday Review,* October 21, 1899, 515.

57. Caine, *Christian,* 228.

58. Caine's portrayal of music-hall performers provoked indignant responses from those in the profession. T. Brock-Richards worries that "Mr. Hall Caine's book will be read by thousands who are entirely ignorant of the profession, and who will therefore get an altogether wrong idea of those within its circle . . . you will not find a class of people more hardworking, taking them en masse, or more worthy of our admiration"; see *Era,* September 4, 1897, 19.

59. Caine, *Christian,* 184.

60. Ibid., 232.

61. Ibid., 283.

62. Ibid., 284.

63. Ibid., 323.

64. *Idler,* "Two at the Play," 16 (August–January 1899): 629.

65. The *Era's* reviewer was clearly interpellated by the scene in which Glory nearly becomes a fatal victim of Storm's righteous anger. The struggle between male rectitude and a feminized weakness and vice was clearly integral to the popular success of both the novel and play; see *Era,* February 17, 1907, 23.

66. Caine, *Christian,* 535.

67. Keating, *Working Classes,* 198–99.

68. Margaret Nevinson, *Life's Fitful Fever* (London: A. and C. Black, 1926), 80.

69. Martha Vicinus provides a useful history of the forces that led to the founding of Toynbee Hall and the attempts of settlers to "civilize" Whitechapel; see Vicinus, *Independent*

Woman: Work and Community for Single Women, 1850–1920 (Chicago: University of Chicago Press, 1985), 211–46. An example: for Canon Barnett, the working class constituted a "dull undifferentiated mass, devoid of culture," that nonetheless might benefit from the trickle down of culture (215). To this end, Barnett brought young students at Oxford and "the finest in contemporary culture" to an impoverished area. The characters in "Little Scotty" demonstrate a thorough mistrust of philanthropists who impose moral codes and culture from on high. Many male settlers at Toynbee Hall shared Nevinson's apparent misgivings. By century's end, most of the men at Toynbee Hall had moved on to professional occupations, leaving women to supervise slum work.

Judith Walkowitz argues that the desire of men to renounce charity work in favor of professional opportunities masked their envy of the success that women charity workers had, comparative to men, with reaching working-class women. The philanthropy subplot of Caine's novel bears out this charge of *ressentiment* aimed at successful women philanthropists; see Walkowitz, *City*, 60.

70. Keating, *Working Classes*, 201.
71. Regenia Gagnier, *Subjectivities* (Oxford: Oxford University Press, 1991), 127.
72. Henry Nevinson, "Little Scotty," in *Neighbours of Ours* (New York: H. Holt, 1895), 126.
73. Ibid., 120.
74. Ibid., 124.
75. Ibid., 125.
76. Ibid., 129.
77. Ibid., 126.
78. Walkowitz, *City*, 26.
79. J. A. Hobson's *The Psychology of Jingoism* (London: Grant Richards, 1901) codifies such charges, accusing music hall of fostering a dangerous, excessive nationalist fervor.
80. Nevinson, "Little Scotty," 134.
81. Patrick Joyce, *Visions of the People* (Cambridge: Cambridge University Press, 1991), 326.
82. Roger Henkle, "Morrison, Gissing and the Stark Reality," *Novel* 11 (Spring 1992): 312.
83. Walkowitz, *City*, 44.
84. Nevinson, "Little Scotty," 134.
85. Ibid.
86. Ibid., 136.
87. Ibid., 138.
88. Ibid., 141.
89. Ibid., 142.
90. See Dagmar Hoher's "The Composition of Music-Hall Audiences, 1850–1900," in *Music Hall: The Business of Pleasure,* edited by Peter Bailey (Milton Keynes, UK: Open University Press, 1986), 73–93; and more generally Dagmar Kift's book *The Victorian Music Hall: Culture, Class and Conflict,* translated by Roy Kift (Cambridge: Cambridge University Press, 1996).
91. Walkowitz, *City*, 45.
92. Ibid., 47.
93. Jones, "Working-Class Culture," 232.
94. Huyssen, "Mass Culture," 9.
95. Rachel Bowlby, *Just Looking* (New York: Methuen, 1985), 65.
96. Banta, *Imaging American Women*, 654.
97. Ibid., 641.

Chapter 5

1. Susan Pennybacker, "The London County Council and the Music Halls," in *Music Hall: The Business of Pleasure*, edited by Peter Bailey (Milton Keynes, UK: Open University Press, 1986), 120–41.

2. Ibid., 130.

3. Ibid.

4. See Judith Walkowitz's discussion of the 1885 Maiden Tribute and its various "cultural consequences" in *The City of Dreadful Delight* (Chicago: University of Chicago Press, 1992), 121–35.

5. Susan Pennybacker's essay "London County Council" indicates how difficult it was to draw lines of propriety either in the content of songs or with the tableaux vivants. Tableaux vivants were in effect halted by the LCC in 1907, when the Bishop of London acted in concert with the National Vigilance Association to stop London exhibitions; see *Times* (London), August 7, 1907 12.

6. From Theatres and Music Halls Committee, Presented Papers, Palace Theatre of Varieties (August 23, 1894), unsigned letter from MP; cited in Pennybacker, "London County Council," 130.

7. Pennybacker, "London County Council," 130.

8. John Stokes, *In the Nineties* (Chicago: University of Chicago Press, 1989), 77.

9. Andrew Ross, *No Respect* (New York: Routledge, 1989), 5.

10. Laura Mulvey, "Visual Pleasure and Narrative Cinema," in *Feminism and Film Theory*, edited by Constance Penley (New York: Routledge, 1988), 57–62; 67.

11. My reading of tableaux vivants is influenced by Joy S. Kasson's analysis of the complicated reaction Hiram Powers's *The Greek Slave* elicited among nineteenth-century American viewers in the 1840s and 1850s. Kasson details how Powers worked to make the depiction of a nude young Greek girl in chains acceptable by providing not only visual cues but a written narrative commentary that tried to foreclose erotic readings of the statue. The complex response to Powers's statue—which sometimes incited political meditation, at other times sexual reverie—illustrates how disorderly the presentation and reception of the female nude could be in the nineteenth century; see Kasson, "Narratives of the Female Body: The Greek Slave," in *Marble Queens and Captives* (New Haven, CT: Yale University Press, 1990), 46–73.

Likewise, Robert C. Allen's study of American burlesque explores Linda Williams's suggestion that female display before the cinema needed to be situated in various contexts, to be narrativized; see Allen, *Horrible Prettiness* (Chapel Hill: University of North Carolina Press, 1991). See for example Allen's reading of stereographic renderings (in which two photos set side by side and seen through a special camera produced a 3-D composite image) of burlesque jokes (259–62). Allen finds the tendency to narrative Williams locates in Muybridge already evident in the spectacular dramas of captive sexuality staged by the celebrated burlesque performer Mazeppa (263).

12. Mulvey, "Visual Pleasure," 62. Mulvey's picture of male-dominated cinema in her 1975 essay is monolithic enough to ensure that, in Tania Modleski's words, "feminists were stymied"; see *The Women Who Knew Too Much: Hitchcock and Feminist Theory* (New York: Methuen, 1988), 9: Janet Bergstrom, Gaylyn Studler, Teresa de Lauretis, Linda Williams, Tania Modleski, and Mulvey herself (in 1981's "Afterthoughts on 'Visual Pleasure and Narrative Cinema'") have all endeavored to think about male and female spectatorship more

tolerantly than Mulvey's initial foray into the matter permitted. This revisionary thinking about spectatorship is collected in Constance Penley, ed., *Feminism and Film Theory* (New York: Routledge, 1988). However, as Modleski observes in *The Women Who Knew Too Much,* many of Mulvey's critics follow her in speaking of a distanciated response to cinema as the proper one; in so doing, they replicate Mulvey's initial dichotomy between critical viewers and passive spectators (9).

13. Simon Frith and Howard Horne, *Art into Pop* (New York: Methuen, 1987), 12.

14. Laura Kipnis argues that bringing class into debates of pornography breaks down "the theoretical monolith of misogyny" that dominates feminist analysis of libidinal entertainments; see "(Male) Desire and (Female) Disgust: Reading *Hustler,*" in *Cultural Studies,* edited by Nelson Grossberg et al. (New York: Routledge, 1992), 374.

15. Here I rely on Jody Berland's inventory of changes in the halls taken from her essay "Angels Dancing: Cultural Technologies and the Production of Space," in Grossberg and Treichler, *Cultural Studies,* 42. But see also Martha Vicinus's *The Industrial Muse: A Study of Nineteenth Century Working-Class Literature* (New York: Barnes and Noble, 1974) or Bailey's *Music Hall* for more on capitalist development of the halls during the 1890s.

16. Guy Debord, *Society of the Spectacle* (Detroit: Black and Red, 1977).

17. For prudent criticism of Debord's tendency to totalize, see Thomas Richards's introduction to his *The Commodity Culture of Victorian England* (Stanford, CA: Stanford University Press, 1990), especially 15–17.

18. Martha Banta, *Imaging American Women: Ideas and Ideals in Cultural History* (New York: Columbia University Press, 1986), 659.

19. In *The Painting of Modern Life: Paris in the Art of Manet and His Followers* (Princeton, NJ: Princeton University Press, 1984), T. J. Clark famously argues that the female nude of Manet's *Olympia* signified class difference to male bourgeois spectators of the work. Manet's female nude is no longer the classless courtesan existing outside of time and place, but a figure who fits comfortably in modern Parisian society. The representation of the modern prostitute broke with traditional ways of framing the female nude, made classic and standardized by earlier portraits such as Titian's *Venus of Urbino.* The painting shattered the myth of the classless courtesan while breathing life into a new urban myth of the city's takeover by women workers like the prostitute. In the Paris of 1865, Clark asserts, all this added up to "unpopular art" (100). Clark's reading of Manet's painting suggests links between female nudity and the otherwise-invisible working class; it also provides a more sophisticated account of the shock value associated with tableaux vivants than recourse to the cliché of Victorian propriety offers.

I argue that, in a fashion similar to Manet's *Olympia,* London tableaux vivants "altered and played with identities the culture wished to keep still": the nude, the bodies of working-class women, the prostitute, and the notion of high art. That in midcentury Paris, *Olympia* represented unpopular art to the middle class, while in 1894 London, the tableaux vivants performance represented edgy mass culture itself suggests the growth of a professional criticism capable of absorbing cognitive shock and cultural transgression.

20. Jack McCullough, *Living Pictures on the New York Stage* (Ann Arbor, MI: UMI Research Press, 1981), 7.

21. Johann Goethe, *Italian Journey: 1786–1788,* translated by W. H. Auden and Elizabeth Mayer (New York: Schocken, 1958), 340.

22. Banta, *Imaging American Women,* 661.

23. See McCullough, *Living Pictures,* 6.

24. Martin Meisel, *Realizations* (Princeton, NJ: Princeton University Press, 1983), 340.

25. Peter Stallybrass and Allon White, *The Politics and Poetics of Transgression* (Ithaca, NY: Cornell University Press, 1986), 193.

26. Kipnis, "(Male) Desire," 373–92.

27. Ibid., 377.

28. Advertisements for Madame Pauline's performance at the Coal Hole promised that her troupe would faithfully reproduce "gems of art" from the "pictures from the Manchester Art Treasures"; see McCullough, *Living Pictures*, 39.

29. George Augustus Sala, *Gaslight and Daylight* (London: Chapman and Hall, 1859).

30. Ibid., 178.

31. See Thomas Richards on the "spectacular" nature of commodity display in the Crystal Palace and similar exhibits.

32. Sala, *Gaslight and Daylight*, 177.

33. Ibid., 177–78.

34. Harold Scott, *The Early Doors* (London: Nicholson and Watson, 1946), 42.

35. James Greenwood, *The Wilds of London* (London: Chatto and Windus, 1874), 100.

36. Ibid.

37. Ibid., 163.

38. Ibid., 164. In *Distinction*, Pierre Bourdieu speaks for Greenwood's brand of cultural criticism when Bourdieu remarks on the crucial role visceral disgust can play in aesthetic evaluation: "In matters of taste, more than anywhere else, all determination is negation; and tastes are perhaps first and foremost distastes, disgust provoked by horror or visceral intolerance . . . of the tastes of others. . . . Aesthetic intolerance can be terribly violent. Aversion to different life-styles is perhaps one of the strongest barriers between the classes" (56).

39. Greenwood, 243.

40. Ibid., 106.

41. In *Innocent Flowers: Women in the Edwardian Theatre* (London: Virago, 1981), Julie Holledge observes that the 1870s marked the return of the middle class to the London theater (4).

42. *Saturday Review* 38 (December 5, 1874): 726.

43. Ibid.

44. See Peter Fryer, *Mrs. Grundy: Studies in English Prudery* (London: Dennis Dobson, 1963), 219.

45. Stallybrass and White, *Politics and Poetics*, 191.

46. McCullough, *Living Pictures*, 104.

47. Jean-Louis Comolli, "Machines of the Visible," in *The Cinematic Apparatus*, edited by Teresa de Lauretis and Stephen Heath (New York: St. Martin's Press, 1980), 121–22.

48. McCullough, *Living Pictures*, 116.

49. Linda Williams, *Hardcore* (Berkeley and Los Angeles: University of California Press, 1989), 41.

50. The belief that Kilyani's Living Pictures offered a technological improvement on previous tableaux was widespread; typical is this reaction from the New York tabloid *Police Gazette* when Kilyani's troupe reached New York halls: "[A]ll attempts [that] have been made hitherto to produce the living pictures" were "flat, tawdry and uninviting." Until Kilyani, "the electric light had not reached its present stage of perfection." As a result such displays had been previously only "the vehicle for suggestiveness that approached the border line of indecency" (September 15, 1894, 7). Readers of Linda Williams's *Hardcore* will recognize much of

what I say about the impact of ideology on the formation of cinema. In *Horrible Prettiness* Robert Allen uses Williams's account of film's prehistory to contextualize fin-de-siècle burlesque.

51. Encomiums such as this one from the *Era* were typical: "In tableaux vivants the smallest discord is sufficient to spoil the effect. Every hue and every contour must follow correctly the scheme of the original pictures, so that the harmony already secured by the artist may be attained. Canvas, costumes and the human form divine should be all in accord, and the trouble necessary to attain such a result must be enormous" (February 24, 1894).

52. Toward a genealogy of MTV: the rapid changes between Kilyani's individual tableaux obviously anticipate the quick cuts gained in film montage. The aims of Kilyani's tableaux were fulfilled by the apparatus of cinema. W. Macqueen-Pope saw the pictures as an obvious precursor to cinema; he notes that the successor to the Living Pictures was a "new sensation, pictures of another kind, pictures that moved . . . called The American Bioscope, or Biograph"; see *The Melodies Linger On: The Story of Music Hall* (London: Allen, [1950]), 196. H. G. Hibbert suggests the biograph was the real successor to the Living Pictures at the Palace: "It was many months ere the living pictures lost their attractiveness, if they ever did. And, so far as the Palace was concerned, another attraction was immediately forthcoming—cinematograph pictures of curious excellence." The Palace introduced animated pictures in March 1897; they immediately became a continuous feature of this variety theater. The *Music Hall and Theatre Review* observed in 1901 that "so far from [the Biograph's] popularity being exhausted, it is a greater attraction than ever, and Papa Morton's patrons would kick up a rare hullabaloo if the pictures were ever absent from the bill" (August 23, 1901). And it is no wonder: a Palace patron at this point was prepared to expect new feminine spectacle provided by novel technologies.

53. Michel Foucault, *The History of Sexuality* (New York: Pantheon Books, 1978), 56.

54. Ronald Pearsall, *The Worm in the Bud* (Toronto: Macmillan, 1969), 102.

55. Ibid., 103.

56. *Stage* 26 (October 1893): 13.

57. *Music Hall and Theatre Review*, March 13, 1894.

58. W. Macqueen-Pope, *The Melodies Linger On: The Story of Music Hall* (London: Allen, [1950]), 202.

59. *Music Hall and Theatre Review*, March 2, 1894.

60. *Music Hall and Theatre Review*, March 13, 1894.

61. *Music Hall and Theatre Review*, March 18, 1894, 34.

62. *Music Hall and Theatre Review*, June 29, 1894.

63. H. G. Hibbert, *Fifty Years of a Londoner's Life* (New York: Dodd and Mead, 1916), 165.

64. *Music Hall and Theatre Review*, August 17, 1894.

65. *Music Hall and Theatre Review*, March 11, 1894.

66. See Michael Booth, *Victorian Spectacular Theatre, 1850–1910* (London: Routledge and Kegan Paul, 1981).

67. Richards, *Commodity Culture*.

68. Frederick Wedmore, "The Music-Halls," *Nineteenth Century* 40 (July 1896): 128–36, 131.

69. Ibid., 130.

70. Debord, *Society of the Spectacle*, 4.

71. Richards, *Commodity Culture*, 56.

72. *Era*, December 16, 1893.

73. Macqueen-Pope, *Melodies*, 201.

74. Ibid., 221.

75. *Music Hall and Theatre Review,* August 24, 1894.

76. Debord, *Society of the Spectacle,* 24.

77. *Times* (London), June 26, 1907.

78. *Music Hall and Theatre Review,* July 6, 1906.

79. Peter Bailey, "Custom, Capital, and Culture," in *Popular Culture and Custom in Nineteenth-Century England,* edited by R. Storch (New York: St. Martin's Press, 1982), 180–208, 198.

80. Ibid., 199.

81. Stokes, *In the Nineties,* 62.

82. Ibid., 85.

83. Bourdieu, *Distinction,* 34.

84. Arthur Symons, "To a Dancer," in *London Nights* (London: Leonard Smithers, 1897).

85. Arthur Symons, "Behind the Scenes at the 'Empire,'" *Sketch* 12 (March 1894): 389.

86. Theodore Wratislaw, "At the Empire," in *Orchids* (London: Leonard Smithers, 1896).

87. W. B. Yeats, *The Autobiography of W. B. Yeats* (New York: Anchor, 1958), 146.

88. *Pall Mall Gazette* 13 (September 1894).

89. Lady Henry Somerset, "The Living Pictures: To the Women of England," *Woman's Signal,* August 2, 1894, 1.

90. Qtd. in *Woman's Signal,* August 7, 1894.

91. Somerset, "Living Pictures."

92. *Woman's Signal,* August 14, 1894.

93. Somerset, "Living Pictures."

94. Reverend Carlile of Eastcheap sermonized on the pictures, complaining that the exhibition would have repercussions overseas: "It was time for the country, and especially for the County Council, to awake to the danger. Soon it would be too late. The grit and fibre of our English character will gone, our Colonies would desert us, our forces would be defeated by water and by land . . . then the name of London would be added to the long and mournful roll of Pompeii and Herculaneum, Babylon and Nineveh, Sodom and Gomorrah"; see *Westminster Gazette,* September 10, 1894.

95. Holdsworth, "Footlights," *Woman's Signal,* December 20, 1894.

96. Ibid., 39.

97. Ibid., 40.

98. Qtd. in *Woman's Signal,* August 16, 1894.

99. Gossamer, "Waftings from the Wings," *Fun,* August 21, 1894, 34.

100. George Bernard Shaw, "Pictures at the Palace," *Saturday Review,* April 1894, 442–44, 443.

101. Ibid., 444.

102. Ibid.

103. Wedmore, "The Music-Halls," 130.

104. *Westminster Gazette,* August 27, 1894.

105. Ronald Pearsall observes that "by and large the profession of model was an unholy one" for Victorians, even when they were Royal Academy models; see *Worm,* 107. However, George Du Maurier's *Trilby,* published the same year the controversy over the Palace raged, endeavors to rehabilitate the profession.

106. Qtd. in McCullough, *Living Pictures,* 135.

107. *Sketch,* March 28, 1894.

108. Symons, *New Review* 11 (November 1894): 461–70, 465.

109. Qtd. in *New York Police Gazette,* January 12, 1895.

110. *New York Herald,* August 19, 1894.

111. Ibid., 3.

112. *New York Tribune,* August 29, 1894.

113. As this performer playfully hints, conservative critics of the tableaux vivants feared the pictures were ideal masturbation fodder. Reverend Carlile of Eastcheap, for example, expressed the fear that "thousands of young men and boys, too, who formed the chief worshippers in this idolatry of the 'Living Nude' were being directly led on to that silent sin which usually ended either in open debauchery or in the fearful scourge of suicide"; see *Westminster Gazette,* September 8, 1894.

114. This is not to say that more sexualized images of these models no longer were available: only that they were occasionally complicated by competing images, such as that of the professional worker. The Living Pictures appear, as Robert Allen notes in *Horrible Prettiness,* in the stag Mutoscope films often shown in penny arcades at the turn of the century. (Mutoscope shorts were distributed by the Biograph Company to music halls and vaudeville theaters, with more risqué shorts sent to saloons, penny arcades, and amusement parks [266].) Allen describes one short, discovered in the Library of Congress copyright deposit building in the late 1960s, entitled "The Pouting Model," originally from June 1901. In the film, two woman pull back curtains "to reveal a nude adolescent girl standing with her back to the spectator and posing for a bearded artist seated in the background of the image." In true tableaux vivants style, the artist and the model are static until the film ends with the two women closing the curtain again (267).

115. Although I can fairly claim that Living Pictures were not exclusively a male entertainment, the material I have seen—particularly in the *New York Police Gazette*—allows me to generalize that they primarily were.

116. The *Era* records on March 18, 1893, that Sandow began to add "some novel features" to his performance at the Palace: "Coming on the stage in evening dress he immediately retired behind some plush curtains, which, when drawn aside, disclosed him bared to the waist on a pedestal posing as a statue" (16). Next followed "a display of the biceps, the muscles that cover the ribs, the abdominal muscles, the different muscles of the back." After Kilyani's success, Sandow's forays into tableaux increased, with scenes from the life of Hercules and Apollo added to his act; see McCullough, *Living Pictures,* 126.

117. *Music Hall and Theatre Review,* September 21, 1894.

118. Thomas Richards analyzes the construction of "a specifically female consuming subjectivity" in the 1890s in his chapter on the image of the "seaside girl" that would preoccupy the public imagination of England and America well into the next century; see *Commodity Culture,* 205–9. One can refer to Richards's study of how advertisers "became specialists not only in constituting discourse but in constituting selves—especially female selves—to take up positions within commodity culture" to get an idea of what Somerset's campaign competed against in the public sphere (210).

119. Pennybacker, "London County Council," 125.

120. Theatre historian Ernest Short draws attention to the Palace's role as a primary home for scandalous, modernist dance by women, observing that "Maud Allan, with her Salome dance; the triumphs of Pavlova and Mordkin, particularly in Galzounoff's 'Bacchanale'; and the classic dances of Lady Constance Stewart-Richardson, are Palace memories"; see *Sixty Years of Theatre* (London: Eyre and Spottiswoode, 1951), 226.

121. This tendency toward star turns was in keeping with the stars performers—the Terrys, Irvings, Farrs, Vanbrughs—who dominated English theater in the 1890s. It is interesting to note that the publicity surrounding the Living Pictures in New York led to a celebration

of the individual performers in the troupes more quickly than in London. The New York *Police Gazette,* one of the nation's first tabloids, was obsessed with certain individual stars in the pictures; the paper's in-depth story on Esther Gaab, the "German Venus," is one of many stories on individual picture models during this time (January 5, 1895, 6).

122. *Music Hall and Theatre Review,* March 12, 1906.

123. See Short, *Sixty Years of Theatre,* 213. Because of copyright laws, newspapers refused to sketch the tableaux vivants, so little visual evidence of how these tableaux were performed remains. It is difficult to imagine, however, how La Milo's performance as "The Rokesby Venus" could have had any but a voyeuristic appeal for the audience at the London Pavilion. In Velasquez's painting a nude woman gazes with her back turned to the audience into a mirror; as Griselda Pollack has described the work, "the mirror is murky, her own face vague, unrecognizable, oblivious to the viewer's voyeurism and imposing no demand for recognition of individual identity" (124). Whether the set design for La Milo interfered with the scenario for scopic pleasure that Velasquez established, I have not been able to discover.

124. *Music Hall and Theatre Review,* July 6, 1906.

125. W. T. Stead, qtd. in *Music Hall and Theatre Review,* September 14, 1906.

126. La Milo (Pansy Montague), qtd. in *Music Hall and Theatre Review,* June 21, 1907.

127. This is E. J. Hobsbawn's ironic term for the proliferation of state and civic pageants in England in the years between the passage of the second Reform Bill and the close of World War I.

128. La Milo (Pansy Montague), qtd. in *Sketch,* August 14, 1907.

129. A contemporary observer, theater historian Ernest Short, believed that Allan's uniqueness resided in her ability to aestheticize her own physical display: "Maud Allan showed how lovely the human body can be in a yard or two of *crepe de Chine,* with bare legs and arms"; see *Sixty Years of Theatre,* 228. Allan's artistic credentials were partially borne on her body: Short stresses Allan's appearance as "a shy, serious-looking young girl."

130. *Era,* February 16, 1907.

Conclusion

1. Pierre Bourdieu, *Distinction* (Cambridge, MA: Harvard University Press, 1984), 170.

2. Arthur Symons, "Cyrene at the Alhambra," *Sketch,* April 5, 1893, 610.

3. Cf. Raymond Williams, who characterizes the 1880s and 1890s as marked by "the integration and consolidation of bourgeois cultural institutions," evident most clearly in the "fully extended bourgeois press"; see Raymond Williams, *Politics and Letters: Interviews with New Left Review* (London: New Left Books, 1979), 261–62. But it is the very reach of bourgeois culture that creates the slippages I adduce between the categories of professional and amateur.

4. Harold Perkin, *The Origins of Modern English Society* (London: Routledge and Kegan Paul, 1969), 270.

5. This approach is typified by John Fiske's *Reading the Popular* (Cambridge, MA: Unwin Hyman, 1989), which characterizes popular culture as essentially oppositional.

Bibliography

Agate, James. *My Theatre Talks.* London: Arthur Barker, 1933.

Allen, Robert C. *Horrible Prettiness.* Chapel Hill: University of North Carolina Press, 1991.

Annan, Noel. "The Intellectual Aristocracy." In *Studies in Social History,* edited by J. H. Plumb. Freeport, NJ: Books for Libraries, 1969.

"Another Englishman." Letter. *Daily Telegraph,* October 18, 1894, 3.

Archer, William. "The County Councils and the Music-Hall." *The Contemporary Review* 67 (March 1895): 317–27.

———. "The Music Hall, Past and Future." *Living Age,* 8th ser., 4 (Fall 1916): 98–105.

———. "Theatre and Music-Hall." In *The Theatrical World of 1895,* 97–103. London: Walter Scott, 1896.

———. "The Theatrical World of 1895." *Living Age,* 8th ser., 5 (Winter 1917): 313–17.

Bailey, Peter. "Conspiracies of Meaning." *Past and Present* 144 (1994): 138–70.

———. "Custom, Capital, and Culture." In *Popular Culture and Custom in Nineteenth-Century England,* edited by Robert Storch, 180–208. New York: St. Martin's Press, 1982.

———. "Introduction: Making Sense of Music Hall." In Bailey, *Music Hall.*

———. *Popular Culture and Performance in the Victorian City.* Cambridge: Cambridge University Press, 1998.

———, ed. *Music-Hall: The Business of Pleasure.* Milton Keynes, UK: Open University Press, 1986.

Banta, Martha. *Imaging American Women.* New York: Columbia University Press, 1986.

Barthes, Roland. *The Grain of the Voice: Interviews, 1962–1980,* translated by Linda Coverdale. New York: Hill and Wang, 1984.

———. *Image, Music, and Text.* New York: Hill and Wang, 1977.

———. *Mythologies.* 1957. Reprint, New York: Noonday Press, 1990.

Beckson, Karl. *Arthur Symons: A Life.* Oxford: Oxford University Press, 1988.

———. "The Blight on the Music Halls." In *Works and More,* 199–205. London: Bodley Head, 1952. Originally published 1899.

———. "Demos' Mirror." In *More Theatres,* 223–27. New York: Taplinger, 1969.

229

———. "Greeba in London." *Saturday Review,* October 21, 1899, 515.

———. "Idolum Aularum." In *Around Theatres,* 2:415–18. New York: Alfred A. Knopf, 1930.

———. "In a Music Hall." In *More Theatres,* 395–98. New York: Taplinger, 1969.

———. *London in the 1890s: A Cultural History.* New York: Norton, 1993.

———. "The Older and Better Music Hall." In *Around Theatres,* 2:381–85. New York: Alfred A. Knopf, 1930.

Bennett, Tony. *The Birth of the Museum.* New York: Routledge, 1995.

Berland, Jody. "Angels Dancing: Cultural Technologies and the Production of Space." In *Cultural Studies,* edited by Nelson Grossberg et al., 51–66. New York: Routledge.

Besant, Walter. "At the Music Hall." *Longmans Magazine,* June 22, 1893, 163–69.

———. *The Autobiography of Walter Besant.* New York: Dodd, Mead, 1902.

———. *Bookman* 2 (1892): 121.

———. *Dorothy Wallis: An Autobiography.* London: Longman's, Green, 1892.

———. *East London.* London: Chatto and Windus, 1901.

Bledstein, Burton J. *The Culture of Professionalism: The Middle Class and the Development of Higher Education in America.* New York: Norton, 1976.

Booth, Michael. *Victorian Spectacular Theatre, 1850–1910.* London: Routledge and Kegan Paul, 1981.

Bourdieu, Pierre. *Distinction.* Cambridge, MA: Harvard University Press, 1984.

———. *An Invitation to Reflexive Sociology.* Chicago: University of Chicago Press, 1992.

Bowlby, Rachel. *Just Looking.* New York: Methuen, 1985.

Brake, Laurel. *Subjugated Knowledges.* New York: New York University Press, 1994.

Bristow, Edward J. *Vice and Vigilance: Purity Movements in Britain since 1700.* Totowa, NJ: Rowman and Littlefield, 1977.

Bulley, H. A. Letter. *Pall Mall Gazette,* October 18, 1894, 3.

Caine, Hall. *The Christian.* New York: D. Appleton, 1899.

Churchill, Winston. *My Early Life.* London: Macmillan, 1944.

Clark, T. J. *Farewell to an Idea: Episodes from a History of Modernism.* New Haven, CT: Yale University Press, 1999.

———. *The Painting of Modern Life: Paris in the Art of Manet and His Followers.* 1984. Rev. ed. Princeton, NJ: Princeton University Press, 1999.

Commoli, Jean-Louis. "Machines of the Visible." In *The Cinematic Apparatus,* edited by Teresa de Lauretis and Stephen Heath, 121–42. New York: St. Martin's Press, 1980.

Corbett, Mary Jean. *Representing Femininity.* Oxford: Oxford University Press, 1992.

Daily Telegraph, Editorial, October 15, 1894, 3.

———. Editorial, October 18, 1894, 3.

———. Editorial, October 27, 1894, 2.

———. "An Ex-Police Inspector," October 19, 1894, 2.

———. "A Londoner," October 18, 1894, 2.

———. "Meeting of Protest," October 22, 1894, 3.

———. "Persecuted," October 21, 1894, 2.

———. "Promenade to Be Closed," October 19, 1894, 3.

————. "Prudes on the Prowl," October 19, 1894, 3.

Davis, Tracy. *Actresses as Working Women: Their Social Identity in Victorian Culture.* New York: Routledge, 1991.

Debord, Guy. *Society of the Spectacle.* Detroit: Black and Red, 1977.

Dellamora, Richard. *Masculine Desire: The Sexual Politics of Victorian Aestheticism.* Chapel Hill: University of North Carolina Press, 1990.

Dodd, Philip. "Englishness and the National Culture." In *Englishness: Politics and Culture, 1880–1920,* edited by Robert Colls and Philip Dodd, 1–29. London: Croom Helm, 1986.

Donoghue, Joseph. "The Empire Theatre of Varieties Licensing Controversy of 1894: Testimony of Laura Ormiston Chant before the Theatres and Musical Halls Licensing Committee." *Nineteenth Century Theatre* 15 (Summer 1987): 50–59.

Dowling, Linda. *Language and Decadence in the Victorian Fin de Siècle.* Princeton, NJ: Princeton University Press, 1986.

Eagleton, Terry. *Heathcliff and the Great Hunger.* London: Verso, 1996.

————. *The Ideology of the Aesthetic.* Oxford: Basil Blackwell, 1990.

Eagleton, Terry, and Pierre Bourdieu. "In Conversation: Doxa and Common Life." *New Left Review* 191 (January/February 1992): 111–21.

Ehrenreich, Barbara, and John Ehrenreich. "The Professional-Managerial Class." In *Between Labor and Capital,* edited by Pat Barker. Boston: South End Press, 1979.

Eliot, T. S. "Marie Lloyd." In *Selected Prose of T. S. Eliot,* edited by Frank Kermode, 173–75. New York: Farrar, Straus, and Giroux, 1975.

Era, December 16, 1893, 7.

Era, "Palace Theatre," March 18, 1893, 16 (on Sandow).

Ervine, St. John. *The Theatre of My Time.* London: Rich and Cowan, 1933.

Fiske, John. *Understanding Popular Culture.* Cambridge, MA: Unwin Hyman, 1989.

Fitzgerald, Percy. *Music-Hall Land.* London: Ward and Downey, 1890.

Foucault, Michel. *Discipline and Punish.* Translated by Alan Sheridan. New York: Vintage Books, 1979.

————. *The History of Sexuality.* New York: Pantheon Books, 1978.

Fox, Richard Wightman, and T. J. Jackson Lears. *The Culture of Consumption: Critical Essays in American History, 1880–1980.* New York: Pantheon, 1983.

Frank, Thomas. *The Conquest of Cool.* Chicago: University of Chicago Press, 1998.

Frith, Simon, and Howard Horne. *Art into Pop.* New York: Methuen, 1987.

Frith, Walter. "The Music-Hall." *Cornhill* 60 (July 1889): 68–79.

Fryer, Peter. *Mrs. Grundy: Studies in English Prudery.* London: Dennis Dobson, 1963.

Gagnier, Regenia. *Subjectivities.* Oxford: Oxford University Press, 1991.

Gilroy, Paul. *The Black Atlantic.* Cambridge, MA: Harvard University Press, 1993.

Glasstone, Victor. *Victorian and Edwardian Theatres.* Cambridge, MA: Harvard University Press, 1975.

Goethe, Johann Wolfgang. *Italian Journey: 1786–1788.* Translated by W. H. Auden and Elizabeth Mayer: Schocken Books, 1958.

Gossamer. "Waftings from the Wings." *Fun,* August 21, 1894, 34.

Greenwood, James. *The Wilds of London.* London: Chatto and Windus, 1874.

Greg, W. R. "Why Are Women Redundant." In *Literary and Social Judgments*, 300–342. Boston: James Osgood, 1873.

Gross, John. *The Rise and Fall of the Man of Letters*. New York: Macmillan, 1969.

Grossberg, Lawrence. *We Gotta Get Out of This Place*. New York: Routledge, 1991.

Guest, Ivor. *Ballet in Leicester Square: The Alhambra and the Empire*. London: Dance Books, 1992.

Hall, Stuart. "Notes on Deconstructing 'the Popular.'" In *People's History and Socialist Theory*, edited by R. Samuel, 227–40. London: Routledge and Kegan Paul, 1981.

Hall, Stuart, and Bill Schwarz. "State and Society, 1880–1930." In *The Hard Road to Renewal: Thatcherism and the Crisis of the Left*, by Stuart Hall. New York: Verso, 1988.

Hamilton, Cicely. "The Working Women." In *Wonderful London*, edited by Almey St. John Adcock, 195–200. London: Fleetway House, 1935.

Harper, Francis. *World's Congress of Representative Women*. Edited by Mary Wright Sewall. Chicago: Rand, McNally, 1894.

Henkle, Roger. "Morrison, Gissing, and the Stark Reality." *Novel* 11 (Spring 1992): 302–19.

Hibbert, H. G. *Fifty Years of a Londoner's Life*. New York: Dodd and Mead, 1916.

Hicks, Seymour. *The Vintage Years*. London: Cassell, 1943.

Hobson, J. A. *The Psychology of Jingoism*. London: Grant Richards, 1901.

Hoher, Dagmar. "The Composition of Music-Hall Audiences, 1850–1900." In Bailey, *Music-Hall*, 73–93.

Holdsworth, Annie. "Footlights: The Story of a Living Picture." *Woman's Signal*, December 20, 1894, 39–42.

Huyssen, Andreas. *After the Great Divide*. Bloomington: Indiana University Press, 1986.

Idler, "Two at the Play," 16 (August–January 1899): 627–31.

Isherwood, Christopher. *The World in the Evening*. New York: Ballantyne, 1967.

Jerome, Jerome K. Editorial. *To-Day* 4 (October 20, 1894): 337.

———. Editorial. *To-Day* 4 (October 27, 1894): 2.

Jones, Gareth Stedman. "Working-Class Culture and Working-Class Politics in London, 1870–1900: Notes on the Remaking of a Working Class." In *Languages of Class: Studies in English Working Class History, 1832–1982*. Cambridge: Cambridge University Press, 1983.

Joyce, Patrick. *Visions of the People*. Cambridge: Cambridge University Press, 1991.

———, ed. *Class: A Reader*. Oxford: Oxford University Press, 1995.

Kasson, Joy S. "Narratives of the Female Body: The Greek Slave." In *Marble Queens and Captives*, 46–73. New Haven, CT: Yale University Press, 1990.

Keating, Peter. *The Working Classes in Victorian Fiction*. London: Routledge and Kegan Paul, 1971.

Kendal, Madge. *Dramatic Opinions*. Boston: Little, Brown, 1890.

Kipnis, Laura. "(Male) Desire and (Female) Disgust: Reading Hustler." In *Cultural Studies*, edited by Nelson Grossberg et al. New York: Routledge, 1992.

Koestenbaum, Wayne. *The Diva's Mouth*. New York: Penguin, 1989.

———. *The Queen's Throat*. New York: Norton, 1989.

Koritz, Amy. "Moving Violations: Dance in the London Music Hall, 1890–1910." *Theatre Journal* 42 (1990): 419–30.

Kumar, Krishan. "'Englishness' and English National Identity." In *British Cultural Studies*, edited by David Morley and Kevin Robins. Oxford: Oxford University Press, 2001.

Lamos, Coleen. *Deviant Modernism*. Cambridge: Cambridge University Press, 1998.

Langland, Elizabeth. "Nobody's Angels: Domestic Ideology and Middle-Class Women in the Victorian Novel." *PMLA* 107 (1992): 290–305.

Larson, M. L. *The Rise of Professionalism*. Berkeley and Los Angeles: University of California Press, 1977.

Levine, Philippa. *Feminist Lives in Victorian England: Private Roles and Public Commitments*. Cambridge, MA: Basil Blackwell, 1990.

Lhamon, W. T. *Raising Cain*. Cambridge, MA: Harvard University Press, 1998.

Lott, Eric. *Love and Theft: Blackface Minstrelsy and the American Working Class*. New York: Oxford University Press, 1993.

MacInnes, Colin. *England, Half-English*. London: MacGibbon and Kee, 1961.

———. *Sweet Saturday Night*. London: MacGibbon and Kee, 1967.

Macqueen-Pope, W. *The Melodies Linger On: The Story of Music-Hall*. London: Allen, [1950].

———. *Twenty Shillings in the Pound*. New York: Hutchinson, 1951.

Mair, G. H. "The Music Hall." *English Review* 9 (August–November 1911): 122–25.

Marcus, Steven. *The Other Victorians*. New York: Basic Books, 1964.

Mayhew, Henry. *London Labour and the London Poor*. New York: Penguin, 1989.

McCullough, Jack. *Living Pictures on the New York Stage*. Ann Arbor, MI: UMI Research Press, 1981.

Meisel, Martin. *Realizations*. Princeton, NJ: Princeton University Press, 1983.

Mulvey, Laura. "Visual Pleasure and Narrative Cinema." In *Feminism and Film Theory*, edited by Constance Penley, 57–62. New York: Routledge, 1988.

Music Hall and Theatre Review, May 11, 1894, 10.

———. August 23, 1895, 11.

———. June 21, 1907, 403 (on La Milo).

———. "Babble," October 27, 1893, n.p. (on Kilyani).

———. "Babble," March 2, 1894, 9.

———. "Babble," June 29, 1894, 10.

———. "Babble," August 17, 1894, 9.

———. "Babble," September 21, 1894 (on Sandow), 10.

———. "Babble," October 12, 1894, 4.

———. "The Biograph: And Its Ally the Mutoscope," August 23, 1901, 10.

———. "La Milo: The Natural Girl," July 6, 1906, 16.

———. "London County Council," October 12, 1894, 13.

———. "The Naughty and the Nice," May 29, 1907, 333.

———. "Seen in the Mirror," February 2, 1894, cover.

———. "Stead Shrieks!" September 14, 1906, 165.

National Police Gazette, "For the Sake of Art," December 22, 1894, 7.

Nead, Lynda. *Myths of Sexuality*. Oxford: Basil Blackwell, 1988.

Nevinson, Henry. *Neighbours of Ours*. New York: H. Holt, 1895.

Nevinson, Margaret. *Life's Fitful Fever*. London: A. C. Black, 1926.

New Review, "The Living Pictures," 11 (November 1894): 461–70.

New York Herald, "Defends Living Pictures: Miss Suzie Kirwin Champions the Cause of Animated Art Exhibitions," August 19, 1894, 7.

———, "They Love Their Art," November 28, 1894, 1.

New York Police Gazette, "Her Figure Her Fortune," January 5, 1895, 5.

———, "Masks and Faces," January 12, 1895, 2.

Our Day, "A Noted English Reformer: Mrs Laura Ormiston Chant; An Interview," 16 (1896): 429–32.

Pall Mall Gazette, "Occasional Notes," October 18, 1894, 3

Parker, Rozsika, and Griselda Pollack. *Old Mistresses: Women, Art, and Ideology.* London: Routledge and Kegan Paul, 1981.

Pearsall, Ronald. *The Worm in the Bud.* Toronto: Macmillan, 1969.

Penley, Constance. *Feminism and Film Theory.* New York: Routledge, 1988.

Pennell, Elizabeth Robins. "The Pedigree of the Music Hall." *Contemporary Review* 63 (April 1893): 575–83.

Pennybacker, Susan. "It Was Not What She Said, but the Way in Which She Said It: The London County Council and the Music Halls." In Bailey, *Music-Hall,* 120–41.

Perkin, Harold. *The Origins of Modern English Society.* London: Routledge and Kegan Paul, 1969.

———. *The Rise of Professional Society: England since 1880.* New York: Routledge, 1989.

Plant, Sadie. *The Most Radical Gesture: The Situationist International in a Postmodern Age.* New York: Routledge, 1992.

Punch, "Mrs. Prowlina Pry," 107 (October 27, 1894): 194–95.

Richards, Grant. *Memoirs of a Misspent Youth.* London: Heinemann, 1932.

Richards, Thomas. *The Commodity Culture of Victorian England.* Stanford, CA: Stanford University Press, 1990.

Robbins, Bruce. *Secular Vocations: Intellectuals, Professionalism, Culture.* New York: Verso, 1993.

Ross, Andrew. *No Respect.* New York: Routledge, 1989.

Sala, G. A. *Gaslight and Daylight.* London: Chapman and Hall, 1859.

Saturday Review, December 5, 1874, 726.

Sawyer, L. N. "Mrs. Laura Ormiston Chant and the Empire Theatre." *Lend a Hand* 14 (1896): 334–41.

Scott, Harold. *The Early Doors.* London: Nicholson and Watson, 1946.

Shaw, George Bernard. "The Empire Promenade." *Pall Mall Gazette,* October 16, 1894, 3.

———. "Pictures at the Palace." *Saturday Review,* April 1894, 442–44.

Shiach, Morag. *Discourse on Popular Culture.* Stanford, CA: Stanford University Press, 1989.

Short, Ernest. *Sixty Years of Theatre.* London: Eyre and Spottiswoode, 1951.

Skeggs, Beverly. *Formations of Class and Gender: Becoming Respectable.* London: Sage, 1997.

Sketch, "Cant and Chant," November 7, 1894, 62.

———. "Clothed on with Wig and Gauze: The New Lady Godiva," supplement, August 14, 1907, 6.

———. "The Empire: The Decline and Fall," October 31, 1894, 8.

———. "Notes from the Theatres," November 7, 1894, 63.

Sontag, Susan. "Notes on Camp." In *Against Interpretation,* 275–92. New York: Dell, 1966.

Stage, October 26, 1893, 13.

Stallybrass, Peter, and Allon White. *The Politics and Poetics of Transgression.* Ithaca, NY: Cornell University Press, 1986.

Stokes, John. *In the Nineties.* Chicago: University of Chicago Press, 1989.

Symons, Arthur. Arthur Symons to Herbert Horne. In *Arthur Symons: Selected Letters, 1880–1935,* edited by John Munro and Karl Beckson. Iowa City: University of Iowa Press, 1989.

———. Arthur Symons to the *Pall Mall Gazette,* October 15, 1894. In *Arthur Symons: Selected Letters.*

———. Arthur Symons to the Star, June 18, 1892. In *Arthur Symons: Selected Letters.*

———. "At the Alhambra." *Savoy* 5 (September 1896): 75–83.

———. "Behind the Scenes at the 'Empire.'" *Sketch,* March 21, 1894, 389.

———. "The Case of the Empire." *Saturday Review,* November 10, 1894, 501–2.

———. "Cyrene at the Alhambra." *Sketch,* April 5, 1893, 610.

———. "Imperium Et Licentia." *Pall Mall Gazette,* October 15, 1894, 3.

———. *Pall Mall Gazette,* October 25, 1894, 3.

———. "A Spanish Music-Hall." In *Cities and Sea-Coasts and Islands.* New York: Brentano's, 1919.

———. "Tableaux Vivants at the Palace Theatre." *Sketch,* March 1894, 482.

———. "To a Dancer." In *London Nights.* London: Leonard Smithers, 1897.

Tickner, Lisa. *The Spectacle of Women.* Chicago: University of Chicago Press, 1988.

Times (London), "London County Council," June 26, 1907, 12–13.

———. "Music, Dancing and Theatre Licensing," October 11, 1894, 7.

To-Day, "Letters of a Candid Playgoer," 5 (November 17, 1894): 53.

Traies, Jane. "Jones and the Working-Class Girl: Class Marginality in Music Hall Song, 1860–1900." In *Music Hall: Performance and Style,* edited by J. S. Bratton. Milton Keynes, UK: Open University Press, 1986

Trugdill, Eric. *Madonnas and Magdalens.* New York: Holmes and Meier, 1976.

Turner, E. S. *Roads to Ruin: The Shocking History of Social Reform.* London: Michael Joseph, 1950.

Vicinus, Martha. *Independent Woman: Work and Community for Single Women, 1850–1920.* Chicago: University of Chicago Press, 1985.

———. *The Industrial Muse: A Study of Nineteenth Century British Working-Class Literature.* New York: Barnes and Noble, 1974.

Walkowitz, Judith. *The City of Dreadful Delight.* Chicago: University of Chicago Press, 1992.

———. "Male Vice and Feminist Virtue: Feminism and the Politics of Prostitution in Nineteenth Century Britain." *History Workshop* 13 (Spring 1982): 72–93.

———. *Prostitution and Victorian Society.* Cambridge: Cambridge University Press, 1980.

Waters, Chris. "Progressives, Puritans, and the Cultural Politics of the Council, 1894–1934." In *Politics and the People of London: The London County Council, 1889–1965.* London: Hambledon Press, 1989.

Wedmore, Frederick. "The Music-Halls." *Nineteenth Century* 40 (July 1896): 128–36.

Weeks, Jeffrey. *Sexuality.* London: Routledge, 1990.

Werle, T. Letter. *Daily Telegraph,* October 19, 1894, 2.

Westminster Gazette, "The 'Living Pictures' Denounced," September 10, 1894, 8.

———. "Mr. Carlile and the Living Pictures," August 29, 1894, 7.

———. "The Real Ormiston Chant," October 18, 1894, 3.

Williams, Linda. *Hardcore.* Berkeley and Los Angeles: University of California Press, 1989.

Williams, Raymond. *Politics and Letters: Interviews with New Left Review.* London: New Left Books, 1979.

Wilson, Keith. "Music-Hall London: The Topography of Class Sentiment." *Victorian Literature and Culture* 23 (1996): 23–35.

Woman's Signal, "Living Pictures," August 9, 1894, 2.

———. "The Living Pictures: To the Women of England," August 2, 1894, 1.

———. "The London County Council and the 'Living Pictures,'" October 11, 1894, 229.

———. "Press Comments on the Appeal to the Women of England," August 18, 1894, 109.

Wratislaw, Theodore. "At the Empire." In *Orchids.* London: Leonard Smithers, 1896.

Yeats, W. B. *The Autobiography of William Butler Yeats.* New York: Anchor Press, 1958.

Index

Lightning Source UK Ltd.
Milton Keynes UK
UKOW04f0850130315

247828UK00001B/29/P